Imperialism and Nationalism
in the Middle East

Imperialism and Nationalism in the Middle East

The Anglo-Egyptian Experience 1882–1982

EDITED BY

KEITH M. WILSON

Mansell Publishing Limited

Mansell Publishing Limited
6 All Saints Street
London N1 9RL, England
First published 1983

83-239411

Distributed in the United States and Canada by
The H. W. Wilson Company, 950 University Avenue, Bronx, New York
10452

British Library Cataloguing in Publication Data

Wilson, Keith M.
    Imperialism and nationalism in the Middle East.
    1. Great Britain—Foreign relations—Egypt
    2. Egypt—Foreign relations—Great Britain
    I. Title
    327.41'062   DA47.9.E/

    ISBN 0-7201-1682-1

Printed and bound in Great Britain by
Butler & Tanner Ltd, Frome and London

For Marie

Contents

Introduction
In Egitto: *Myths and Realities*

On 7 July 1857, Palmerston told the House of Commons that the undertaking for a canal which would link the Mediterranean with the Red Sea was one which 'in point of commercial character, may be deemed to rank amohg the many bubble schemes that from time to time have been palmed upon gullible capitalists'. He advised Members of Parliament not to invest in it. In November 1875 Disraeli informed Queen Victoria that it was vital to Her Majesty's authority and power 'that the Canal should belong to England', and proceeded to purchase the shares of the Khedive of Egypt for the sum of four million pounds sterling.

Late in 1859 the British Ambassador in Constantinople warned his government in London of the consequences of unsuccessful opposition on their part to the construction of such a waterway as both the Egyptians and the French wished to see. Bulwer wrote:

> To be beaten here in any question about this Canal, would be to be beaten in a question of influence, the effects of which would possibly extend throughout the East—even to India as well as Persia, and provoke dangers which are now slumbering, and apparently unconnected with it.

Six months later one member of the Foreign Office included, in a draft memorandum given the title 'Insuperable Objections of H.M.'s Govt. to the Projected Suez Canal', the statement, 'It would in fact be a suicidal act on the part of England to assent to the construction of this Canal':

> A great cut three hundred feet wide and twenty eight feet deep, as this ship canal is meant to be, with fortifications on its bank, and War Steamers properly placed in it, wd effectually stop any Army coming from Syria, and from the day when such a Canal was finished, Egypt might be reckoned a Dependency of France.

The British Government not only continued to oppose the Canal; they gave their official assent to the project in March 1865.

"MOSE IN EGITTO!!!"

Punch 11 December 1875, reproduced by permission

In 1877 *The Nineteenth Century* published two articles, 'Our Route to India' and 'The Future of Egypt', by the editor of the *Observer*, Edward Dicey. Mr Gladstone wrote in reply, 'It seems to be forgotten by many that there is a route to India round the Cape of Good Hope'; the seven-day longer passage, moreover, 'will hardly make the difference to us between life and death in the maintenance of our Indian Empire'. Similar views were expressed in 1881 by General Gordon, who at that time according to a member of his family 'considered ... that our proper and legitimate means of communication was round the Cape'; he 'would have abandoned the Mediterranean and have withdrawn altogether from Egypt'. When questioned in the House of Commons on 26 June 1882 as to whether he still agreed with the views he had expressed in 1877 Prime Minister Gladstone maintained that he did— 'as far as I can recollect them'. One month later he asked Parliament for £2.3 million to spend on an ostensibly temporary occupation of the Turkish province of Egypt by British forces. Speaking in support of this measure of 'self-defence', one member of Gladstone's cabinet maintained that England had a double interest in the Suez Canal:

> It has a predominant commercial interest, because 82 per cent of the trade passing through the Canal is British trade, and it has a predominant political interest caused by the fact that the Canal is the principal highway to India, Ceylon, the Straits, and British Burmah, where 250,000,000 live under our rule; and also to China, where we have vast interests and 84 per cent of the external trade of that still more enormous Empire. It is also one of the routes to our Colonial Empire in Australia and New Zealand.'

When Disraeli's secret transaction of 1875 became public knowledge the cartoonist Tenniel portrayed the Suez Canal in the pages of *Punch* as a large key. Held by Disraeli, it bore the tag 'The Key of India'. In 1953, seventeen years after the British Occupation of Egypt had been replaced by a Treaty of Alliance due to run for twenty years, *Punch* published a contemporary version of Tenniel's cartoon. Illingworth's drawing depicted the British Prime Minister Eden, and a Sphinx with whom he was clearly not, as his predecessor had equally clearly been, in collusion. The outstretched hand of the Sphinx was expecting to have deposited in it the one feature retained from the original car-toon—the key that Eden was holding, the same key as had been held by Disraeli, held in the same way, inscribed with the legend 'Suez Canal'. To what it was still the key was not made clear, for it had lost its tag. It had become a key unto itself, its purpose as mysterious as the East.

"O, WHITHER HAST THOU LED ME, EGYPT?"

Punch 25 February 1953, reproduced by permission

The one hundredth anniversary of the occupation of Egypt failed to coincide by one year with the twenty-fifth anniversary of the Suez Crisis of 1956. The latter affair has subsequently become as symbolic in its way as the Canal itself, to such an extent that television documentaries made to mark the occasion were shelved on the grounds that the morale of the British people was already low enough in the autumn of 1981.

This near-coincidence of anniversaries was marked by a symposium held at the University of Leeds during Michaelmas term 1981. The majority of the essays collected in this volume were first delivered as papers at that symposium. The volume as a whole begins with the occupation of Egypt by Great Britain and her first sustained contact with that part of the world. It ends, as the final chapter makes clear, with the period following the crisis of 1956 when greater powers than Britain have become more interested in a different part of the Middle East, for different reasons, and have both adopted different approaches to and given different explanations for securing what they perceive as their interests in that region. Together, these essays help to redress the balance of attention hitherto given to the Suez Canal itself, and to place in perspective the real significance of that waterway. They reflect the range of issues, problems, and responsibilities with which their presence in this part of the Middle East brought the British face to face. They reveal, in terms of politics, culture, and nationalism, both British and Egyptian; in terms of diplomacy, trade, and strategy; and in terms of historiography, how complex were the Anglo-Egyptian and the broader Anglo-Arab relationships for which 'the Canal' and 'Suez' were symbols, totems—the easy shorthand myths manipulated and manipulating to obscure the difficult and very different realities.

Acknowledgements

The editor would like to acknowledge the contributions of the following: John E. Duncan, of Mansell; Christine Steele, for the index; the editor of *International Affairs*; Professor E. Kedourie; and Punch Publications Limited.

Notes on Contributors

Dr Steele is Senior Lecturer in Modern History at the University of Leeds. His publications on aspects of Irish and British history in the nineteenth century include *Irish Land and British Politics* (1974) and a chapter on 'Imperialism and Leeds politics 1850–1914' in D. Fraser (ed.), *A History of Modern Leeds* (1980).

Dr Wilson is a Lecturer in Modern History at the University of Leeds.

Dr Eran currently works in the Israeli Embassy in Washington. His doctorate was awarded in 1981 by the London School of Economics for a thesis on the 1936 negotiations between Britain and Egypt.

Dr Whiting teaches Modern History at the University of Leeds. He did research at Nuffield College Oxford, and has taught at Sussex and Heriot-Watt Universities. His book *The View from Cowley: the Impact of Industrialization upon Oxford* is to be published by Oxford University Press.

Dr Lerman was awarded his doctorate by the London School of Economics in 1982. He has contributed to *Middle Eastern Studies* and to publications of the Institute for the Study of Conflict.

Professor Kedourie, Professor of Politics at the London School of Economics, is a Fellow of the British Academy and the editor of the journal *Middle Eastern Studies*.

Professor Warner has been Professor of Modern History at the University of Leicester since 1977. Educated at the Universities of Cambridge and Paris, he has also taught in Australia. He is the author of *Pierre Laval and the Eclipse of France* (1968) and *Iraq and Syria 1941* (1974), and reviser of David Thomson's *England in the Twentieth Century* (1981).

Dr Spiers is the author of *Haldane: an Army Reformer* (1980) and *The Army and Society 1815-1914* (1981). His post at the University of Leeds is funded by the Ministry of Defence.

Britain and Egypt 1882–1914: the Containment of Islamic Nationalism

DAVID STEELE

I

The British occupation of Egypt from 1882 down to 1914 is explicable by reference to the pursuit of national and imperial security and reputation. Under this heading, a number of considerations determined the attitude of successive governments. To list these at this stage without suggesting which were of greater importance, there was the concern, real if overstated, to safeguard access to the Suez Canal as extremely useful, though not indispensable, to Britain's communications with India. There was the undisputed necessity of trying to co-operate with France over Egypt in order to stand favourably with her at a time when comparative isolation from the great powers of Europe, while preferable to a country unused to conscription and used to low taxation, was liable to seem perilous. There was the historic commitment to the integrity of the Ottoman Empire, to which Egypt belonged as a tributary state. There was the virtual certainty that if the French were left to act alone, they would take the opportunity of realizing an old dream and making Egypt their colony. There were British residents, traders and investments, other than in the Canal Company, to be assured of continuing protection. Then, initially, the second Gladstone government had very much in mind the desirability, not to put it more strongly, of showing the public that Liberals were quite capable of firmness and decision in sustaining British interests and prestige, a capability which their handling of recent events in Afghanistan, South Africa and Ireland had called in question.

Later administrations, Liberal and Tory/Unionist, found their freedom of action limited as a result. Ending an occupation repeatedly stated to be temporary was unpopular with too many people in the House of Commons and the constituencies. Staying on was justified by the plea, ever more convincing to British ears, that Britain had gone into Egypt not least to preserve and develop reforms already introduced under Western pressure, which a premature departure would jeopardize. Lord Cromer enlarged and advertised this genuine obligation until it appeared to dictate British policy. Lastly, the Egyptian crisis of 1882 brought this country into conflict with Islamic nationalism, which was to be the enduring theme in Anglo-Egyptian relations for the next three-quarters of a century. The British Agent and Consul-General in Egypt, Sir Edward Malet, sent this message to the Foreign Secretary, Lord Granville, on the British victory at Tel-el-Kebir over the troops of Arabi Pasha: '... You have fought the battle of all Christendom, and history will acknowledge it. May I also venture to say that it has given the Liberal party a new lease of popularity and power?'[1]

The British were not then inclined to underrate the strength inherent in combined Islamic and national sentiment. The severest test their imperial authority had undergone in its steady nineteenth-century expansion came in the Indian Mutiny of 1857–9. The origins of that extensive military and civilian rising in North-Central India remain the subject of controversy. Involving both Moslem and Hindu, it nevertheless focused on the Mogul king of Delhi, whose Moslem dynasty, now pensioner of the British, once dominated the sub-continent. Thereafter the official British view saw in Islam the most dangerous potential instigator of revolt against European influence. The French concurred. Looking back on the British invasion of Egypt, Wilfrid Scawen Blunt, the well-connected Tory romantic and poet who befriended Egyptian, Indian and Irish nationalists, but especially the first, stressed in a note to his published diaries for 1882 how prevalent were the Anglo-French apprehensions of an uprising across the Islamic world from North Africa to India, with Egypt as its epicentre: '... the dread of a general conflagration in the East is perhaps the best excuse that can be made,' he wrote, 'for our Government's action in pressing on ... an immediate violent solution of its difficulties in Egypt.'[2] Almost seventy-five years later, Sir Anthony Eden ordered a second British invasion because he and his French counterpart felt impelled to repress the idea, then personified by President Nasser, of a religiously inspired Arab nationalist revolution to extrude Western influence from the Middle East and North Africa. Reverting to 1881, Britain's approach to Islamic nationalism differed significantly in other respects from that of France.

Shaikh Mohammed Abdu, the Moslem cleric, theologian and revolutionary, who figured prominently in early Egyptian nationalism said that the tribulations of Egypt under the British, compared with those of Algeria and Tunisia, were 'as light to darkness'.[3] Twenty years previously, Gladstone expressed naive surprise at the tone of the French statesman, Gambetta, with whom his government was working closely on Egypt, where the Egyptians were concerned: 'I cannot but be struck by the total absence ... of any indication of the spirit of a true Liberal.'⁴ The Third Republic ruthlessly applied a double standard in its dealings with colonial peoples. The animosity stirred up by the displacement of native landholders to make room for French settlers had no counterpart in Egypt. More importantly, the British adhered to the lessons of their Indian experience in another respect, and were careful not to exasperate Islamic opinion, while watching it vigilantly for signs of political danger. In religious, unlike agrarian, policy, they were guided more by expediency than by principle.

II

The three commanding personalities who did so much to decide Britain's relationship to Egypt over several decades each had an aristocratic and Christian outlook. Their regard for social morality and order actively disposed them to secure the rights of the fellaheen, the Egyptian peasantry largely owning as well as occupying the cultivated land along the Nile and in its delta. Otherwise the peasants might have suffered more from the rapacity of Levantine and European moneylenders who often enjoyed the protection of the capitulatory regime established before the occupation. On the other hand, all three felt differently about Islam and the various challenges it posed.

Gladstone is the first of the three Englishmen through whom British motives for being in Egypt during this period can be conveniently examined. To begin with, at any rate, he took Parliament into his confidence to an extent now unusual. Strongly sceptical of the authenticity of the Egyptian national movement facing him in 1882, he would only concede that in time 'something may be founded there which may give hope for the future—something which may tend to show that the desire for free institutions is not wholly confined to Christian races, that even in a Mohammedan people, where circumstances are certainly less favourable ... a noble thirst may arise ... for these blessings of civilised life ... achieved in so many countries in Europe'.⁵ The small likelihood of this evolution, in his view, influenced Gladstone's subsequent anxiety to withdraw British forces from the country as soon as it could be arranged. Quoting his revered Burke— 'in politics the space afforded to abstract reasoning is extremely limited'—he invited the Commons to conclude that, on the facts presented to them, Egypt was not a nation, but merely a Turkish province. He recognized 'the full ... privileges of national freedom', including the option of constitutionalism, only in a people who had never submitted to conquest; else 'they must stand the consequences of that submission'. Having long lost their national identity and self-respect, the most the Egyptians might reasonably expect was the

3

restoration 'by degrees' of their independence.[6] This speech helps to clarify the comprehensive limitations written into Gladstone's two Irish Home Rule bills and his insistence that he envisaged no more than qualified autonomy for Ireland. Egyptian nationalism, therefore, was premature and superficial, analysable into three elements pursuing their own sectional aims: the pure militarism, as it seemed to him, of Arabi and his fellow officers; the equally self-centred ambitions of a few large landowners of mainly Turkish descent; and 'I admit ... a certain element of strength in the religious fanaticism of the professional clergy, so to call them ...'.[7] It was a seriously mistaken interpretation of the movement which Britain was about to put down forcibly, yet one not entirely devoid of truth. It followed, for Gladstone, that the British had no duty to remain in Egypt and take on the close supervision of an inherently doubtful and protracted development towards full nationhood.

It did not follow, for him, that Britain should eschew a general oversight of Egyptian affairs. That was a continuing necessity if, as he maintained, intervention had averted a genuine threat to the safety 'not only of all Englishmen and all British subjects, but of all European people throughout the whole East'.[8] He told Lord Shaftesbury, the embodiment of the Evangelical conscience, that the hostilities in Egypt had been 'before God and man ... an upright war, a Christian war'.[9] Speaking in February 1884 he thought 'sufficiency of control' obtainable through a political link such as functioned well in India between the Raj and the princely states, one that gave the British representative 'all the power necessary for efficiency, but ... no more'. In those states, he went on, the inhabitants lived under a native administration which 'depend upon it, they love far more than foreign domination. Few ... are the peoples so degraded ... that it shall be a matter of indifference ... whether they are governed by those ... with foreign interests ... sympathies and ... objects'. He agreed in the description of this arrangement, conferring 'plenary power to do what out purpose requires', as a protectorate; though, for compelling international reasons, he excluded formal use of the term.[10] Cromer, styled Agent and Consul-General like his predecessors before the occupation, was by then engaged in making an informal protectorate of this kind work under difficulties unknown to Indian experience. As those problems intensified, so Gladstone's parliamentary candour diminished. Among them were Britain's involvement with other great powers, and with Turkey over Egypt as part of the Ottoman dominions.

At the heart of the European complications lay France with her large stake in and designs upon the country. Gladstone inherited from Lord Salisbury, as Foreign Secretary in 1878–80, the institutionalization of the Anglo-French interest in Egypt through the dual control of her finances. It was established in 1879 to save Khedivial rule from collapse under the pressure of its accumulated debts to Western bankers and investors in their loans. The open partnership was reinforced by a secret understanding between the two powers to co-operate in Egyptian policy. Gladstone complained bitterly of this understanding as inhibiting Britain's exercise of of her judgment.[11] He did not, however, learn of its existence on paper until after the naval bombardment of Alexandria in July 1882;[12] had he been informed sooner, it seems unlikely that he would have refrained from authorizing that step. Be that as it may, he told the House of Commons bleakly on the day after he had been enlightened: 'The effect of breaking with France must have been a sharp conflict in Egypt ... and ... I believe, a general European war.'[13] Bismarck had predicted that Britain and France would fight over Egypt as Austria and Prussia had fought over Schleswig-Holstein in 1866.[14] The implication was clear: one or other of the two great liberal states of Europe would suffer a defeat similar to Austria's in its results, to the benefit of the Hohenzollern and Romanov empires. An accident of French domestic politics left Britain to mount unaided the naval and military operations foreshadowed in the two governments' joint note of January 1882, warning the Egyptian nationalists not to subvert the political and financial settlement of 1879 instituting the Dual Control and replacing Khedive Ismail by the more compliant Tewfik. In consequence of France's sudden abstention, the British moved into a position of superiority in Egypt deeply resented by the French. For the next twenty-two years, the British sought to placate France, while resolved neither to restore the equality which she had enjoyed under the Dual Control, nor to let her slip into Britain's place in the event of evacuation. On both points, Gladstone's own inclinations coincided with those of his Cabinet and public opinion. It was inconceivable that France should be allowed to profit from the expenditure of British blood and treasure, when she had abandoned Britain on the brink of intervention. Economically, the French did very well out of British appeasement: but the political sore festered until the Anglo-French Entente of 1904 compensated France elsewhere.[15]

The Turkish dimension of the Egyptian imbroglio was peculiarly embarrassing for Gladstone. Notoriously anti-Turkish on religious and political grounds, he nevertheless accepted in the context of Egypt, as in several others at different times, the indefinite need to prop up a ruler, Sultan Abdul Hamid II, whom he amiably described as 'that Arch-liar and Arch-cheat ...'[16] When the British invaded, Gladstone explained to his admired friend, the German theologian Ignaz von Döllinger, that they did not intend to keep Egypt, Ottoman territory, 'either forcibly or virtually', because, for one thing, they were not prepared to accelerate the break-up of Turkish dominions.[17] He wrote to Lord Granville, a few days afterwards: 'I am averse to establishing Egyptian independence on account of the heavy shock it would impart to the general fabric of the Ottoman Empire, about which I ... have been steadily conservative ...'[18] Yet the British invasion delivered a severe blow to the Sultan's prestige, all the more so since it looked as if the Egyptian nationalists would have reached an accommodation with him, had he and they been free to do so. Instead, the British tried to persuade the Sultan to act on behalf of the European powers, but in reality of Britain, in suppressing the Egyptian revolution, despite the opposition of France, uneasy lest such an appeal to the authority of the potentate at the head of Islam should inspire new hope among his defeated co-religionists in Algeria and Tunisia. Abdul Hamid procrastinated, with good reason; he, too, had a public opinion to reckon with. 'Arabi Pasha is now regarded, even at Constantinople, as a hero and champion of Islam' reported the British ambassador to Turkey.[19] This outweighed the Sultan's dislike and apprehension of the Egyptian nationalists' constitutionalism and veiled republicanism. After the occupation, the British Liberal government worked fruit-lessly to reach an agreement with the Sultan, as suzerain of Egypt, neutralizing the country, whose financial liabilities it arduously rene-gotiated with the states representing her creditors. The renegotiation was eventually achieved in the London Convention of 1885: but not unnaturally the Sultan viewed neutralization of part of his empire—particularly when urged by a government under Gladstone, of all men—as an unacceptable encroachment. Salisbury was to succeed where Gladstone failed, and win, on another basis, adequate Turkish recognition of the British position in Egypt from 1882.

Gladstone's attitude to Egypt's nationalists did not change with the advent in Cairo of the British ambassador to Constantinople, Lord Dufferin, as special commissioner charged to advise on and superin-tend the post-war reconstruction of the Egyptian state. Dufferin had not liked the crushing of 'Arab independence', which was his inter-pretation of the movement in Egypt.[20] He strove to ensure the fairest treatment possible for Arabi and his principal associates, who were put on trial by the Khedivial authorities, proceedings which the British openly supervised. Gladstone had not been on the side of leniency. 'I shall be very glad if he can be hung without *real* inclemency', he wrote of Arabi.[21] As for longer-term measures, Dufferin's report of February 1883 proposing the erection of representative bodies, starting at prov-incial level, has widely been taken, as by the modern Egyptian his-torian, A. L. al-Sayyid, for 'a perfect example of double talk'.[22] The functions of these bodies were, it is true, consultative, except for the general assembly's right of assent to taxation; the membership was indirectly elected and, at the national level, diluted by nomination. A more telling criticism is that both the Khedive's supporters and the British preferred the tradition of what Dufferin called 'irresponsible centralized bureaucracy', which was the inheritance of the Turco-Egyptian dynasty and aristocracy as well as of Cromer and many of his officers with their Indian background. The organic decree enacting Dufferin's proposals was for long successfully worked in the spirit of the old Chamber of Notables, instituted by Ismail in 1866, of which Dufferin justly observed, 'the wants and instincts of the mass ... were as little represented, as was the Irish nation by the Protestant Parliament'. On the other hand, Dufferin explicitly rejected the conventional wisdom of Europeans who claimed to know the country and pronounced the native Egyptians, the great majority, incapable of self-government.[23] His own expectations of the system were extremely modest. Believing the British occupation likely to last for some time, he thought the structure he had devised might be 'fairly useful ... a convenient channel through which the European element in the government might obtain an insight into the inner mind ... of the native population'.[24] It was an intelligent provision, if years passed before it began to operate as he meant it to do.

Bent on getting British troops out of Egypt without having to send them in again, Gladstone backed Khedivial rule, even unaccompanied by any but cosmetic liberalization. 'It is madness to suppose', he said to his Boswellizing private secretary, Edward Hamilton, in 1884, 'that we can undertake the Government of Egypt ... a Mahometan country, in the heart of the Mahometan world, with a population antagonistic to Europeans ...'[25] Dufferin's report warned of the 'hatred and suspicion' which an attempt at direct rule would elicit; it also emphasized what the revolution in Egypt had obscured, that the Turco-Egyptian ascendancy was as 'chauvinist' as the rest of the country.[26] In the circumstances, Gladstone found something to say for the exiled Arabi. The Dual Control and the deposition of Ismail, he remarked in the Commons, had implanted in the Egyptians 'that fatal ... idea' of alien dictation and exploitation, which Arabi turned to account: 'and so long as foreign domination continues in Egypt, the danger will recur'.[27]

Gladstone was up against obstacles which to others looked insuperable. Firstly, Dufferin saw clearly that 'the Khedive makes no way with the people', and the consequent impracticability of evacuation.[28] Childers, the Chancellor of the Exchequer, suggested recruiting in Britain for the Khedivial service; Sir William Harcourt and some Cabinet colleagues favoured disbanding the Egyptian army and increasing the garrison of Queen's troops.[29] The Prime Minister reacted sharply to the suggestions 'in which ... I see the seed of every possible

7

future difficulty'. He was flatly opposed to 'strengthening the military and governmental hold of England over Egypt'.[30] Secondly, however stubbornly Gladstone argued that the British ought to have no direct responsibility for the internal administration of the country, the moral and political burden was unavoidable with the army of occupation standing behind the special commissioner, or the Agent and Consul-General, and giving him ultimate mastery. Gladstone could not but admit this. The despotic character of the Turco-Egyptians aroused sincere misgivings in Britain over the policy of evacuation. 'We shall, I hope, do our best to eliminate the Turkish ... rulers of Egypt ... substituting a reasonable proportion of ... Englishmen,' wrote Childers in the letter that provoked Gladstone's vehement reaffirmation of his intentions. Even the faithful Hamilton confided to his diary, if not to his chief, 'It seems rather inconsistent that we should be building up a government by Turks whom we are always rightly denouncing as impossible rulers.'[31] W. S. Blunt intimated to Hamilton, for the Prime Minister's information, that he would rather see Egypt annexed by Britain than the Turco-Egyptians relieved of the novel surveillance to which they were subject.[32] The third obstacle to evacuation was the Mahdist revolt in the Sudan. Although Gladstone and the Cabinet decided—or, in accordance with form, advised the Khedive—to relinquish the territory, they could not wish away the aggressive Moslem state that rose up on the Egyptian frontier and had to be kept out. As Cromer later commented, the Mahdists furnished him with a very good argument to counter demands, from whatever quarter, for evacuation.[33]

The fourth, and arguably the most serious obstacle to British withdrawal, was the persistence after 1882 of the type of Islamic nationalism that brought about British intervention. In an essay on its origins, Professor Elie Kedourie contends that the two Moslem divines who stand out in the beginnings and growth of the movement—Shaikh Jemal-al-Afghani and Shaikh Mohammed Abdu—were very probably freethinkers utilizing Islam as the vehicle of modernization.[34] When masonic lodges, stemming from the highly political freemasonry of France, not from the British variety, appeared in Egypt, they were associated with free thought and political liberalism, as also in Turkey and Persia. Under Khedive Ismail, the lodges seem to have had a common membership with secret societies which discussed the modification, indeed the replacement, of traditional Moslem autocracy in the light of Western concepts and institutions. Shaikh Mohammed Abdu believed that in the West the work of freemasonry, 'one of the pillars of European progress', had been completed with the overthrow of monarchs and popes who had resisted 'knowledge and freedom'. He said that he and his master, al-Afghani, belonged to freemasonry 'for a political and social purpose'.[35] Whether or not the two divines embraced free thought or are classifiable as modernists in Moslem theology, they unquestionably devoted themselves to grafting Western liberalism on to Islamic political culture. Professor Kedourie cites al-Afghani exhorting the fellaheen to throw off the Turco-Egyptians who battened on them; calling, in a sermon in Cairo, for 'a revolution to save the independence of Egypt and establish its liberty', and denouncing the new Khedive Tewfik as 'compelled to serve—consciously or not—British ambitions'.[36] On al-Afghani's expulsion from the country by Tewfik, Mohammed Abdu stayed to take part in the coherent national movement that developed out of the masonic lodges and secret societies in the early 1880s. It was not exclusively composed of native Egyptians. The directing political intelligence behind Colonel Arabi Pasha, who may be described as a simple soldier, was that of a remarkable Turco-Egyptian aristocrat, Sami al-Barudi Pasha, a general, politician and poet, premier in the nationalist ministry of 1882 with Arabi as minister of war. What, in a little more detail, did these men stand for?

The answer explains why they posed a threat to the stability of the whole Moslem world, and hence to British interests. Al-Barudi said in June 1882: 'From the beginning of our movement, we aimed at turning Egypt into a ... republic like Switzerland—and then Syria would have joined—and the Hejaz ...'[37] The ideas of Rousseau's *Social Contract*, with its Swiss inspiration, had been circulating among the Egyptian intelligentsia for many years. A standard work, published in 1869, by the Egyptian who first framed an Arabic equivalent for the expression 'social contract', passed every aspect of social reform under review beside its advocacy of technical westernization.[38] According to al-Barudi, objections from some leading Moslem clergy who were 'behind our time' stopped the nationalists from proclaiming these aspirations, but they intended to realize them 'upon the first occasion which presents itself'.[39] Meanwhile, they meant to invoke the Ottoman Sultan's name 'as long as he can be useful to them', and no longer. The entry of Turkish troops fulfilling Britain's wishes would be the signal to declare a republic.[40]

The Suez Canal was, as Dr D. A. Farnie points out in his book *East and West of Suez: the Suez Canal in History*, a secondary consideration in 1882.[41] Paramount for Gladstone's government was 'the dilemma we find ourselves confronted with, the risk of losing our prestige among the Mussulmen on the one side, and on the other ... the risk of incurring the enmity of the Arabian race'.[42] Their republican and pan-Islamic aims overshadowed the published political and social programme of the Egyptian nationalists which was congenial to British liberals. Imperialism and liberalism were united: but they would have been less so had the attack on Egypt featured as something other than 'a Christian war'. The nationalists could not distance themselves from Islam or conceal the anti-Christian and anti-European nature of their movement. These characteristics were apparent when Shaikh Mohammed Abdu visited Britain in 1884. Exiled from Egypt after the invasion, he rejoined al-Afghani in Paris, where they ran an Arabic newspaper, *The Indissoluble Bond*, banned in Egypt and India, to disseminate Islamic nationalism. It printed an account of the meeting between Mohammed Abdu and Lord Hartington, the member of Gladstone's Cabinet most strongly in favour of prolonging Britain's stay in Egypt. Asked by Hartington whether the Egyptian people really were not glad of the judiciously reforming British presence, he replied, 'Not one ... considers it agreeable to be subjected to rule by people of alien race and religion'. Pressed to say whether the peasant masses were capable of distinguishing between foreign and native government, he claimed for the fellaheen: 'Even ... illiterates ... are not unaware of the precepts of their religion, one of the most important being that no Moslem should be indebted to anyone of a different faith. In ... the homilies of their preachers, in the mosques, they have the equivalent of an elementary education'; moreover, the unlettered majority was in the habit of having the Arabic newspapers read and expounded to them by the literates found in every small town. Thus they learnt to equate 'natural feeling and religious tradition with patriotic fervour'.[43] In another interview, with John Morley's *Pall Mall Gazette*, the Shaikh said that benevolence was no substitute for freedom: 'the fellaheen are overtaxed, but ... you might abolish all taxation, and they would not bless you if ... you took it as an excuse to stay ...'. The occupation had taught native Egyptians that 'there are worse evils than despotism'; the Turco-Egyptians were 'our brothers in religion ... if you would only leave us alone with them, we should know how to get on ...'.[44] He made too much of the nationalist Arabic press at this date, but it soon bore him out: what he said about the Moslem clergy and the fellaheen was substantially true. Cromer liked to assert that nationalism was largely confined to the towns. Gladstone noted how he contradicted himself when badly frightened by the state of the country,[45] as he was in his trial of strength in 1893–4 with Tewfik's successor, Khedive Abbas II, who identified the nationalist cause with his own.

III

Lord Salisbury was a man with very few illusions, and a keen appreciation of the decisive power of ideas. He declined to suppose that the Egyptian nationalists were as unrepresentative as Cromer and later

Alfred Milner encouraged British politicians and journalists to think. 'Relief from our hated presence', he wrote on becoming prime minister in 1885, 'is the one benefit we have to offer'[46] to the Sultan, to France, and not least to the Egyptians. A. L. al-Sayyid ascribes the surprising governability of Egypt under the British for many years to the belief that 'autonomy lay just round the corner'.[47] It would have been there had Lord Salisbury had his way. He once said to Cromer, 'the East is decaying for want of revolutions'. 'A somewhat remarkable statement from a Conservative statesman', mused the puzzled official.[48] Salisbury made that comment before his first premiership. As a young MP during the Crimean War, he savaged the pretence that the British Empire did not depend, quite as much as the Russian, on the use of force to maintain itself and expand. He condemned his country's 'repression of nationalities' then,[49] and in the 1880s did not hide his perception of what Britain was doing to the Egyptians. He cautioned the Gladstone government in July 1882 against launching 'something very like a crusade'.[50] Examining its results after some eighteen months, he listed the calamities that had befallen Egypt between the bombardment of Alexandria and British advice to give up the Sudan. Britain's two most damaging errors had been the destruction of the Egyptian army and her treatment of the Khedive, 'so ostentatiously' diminished in the eyes of his Moslem people as to be impotent without the British. 'Is that,' he finally inquired, 'a process . . . likely to leave our name imprinted on their minds . . . with affection and respect?' In the same speech, Salisbury exposed Britain's predicament, shortly to be his in government: how could she safely evacuate the country?[51]

On taking office, he set about the problem with the aim of enlisting Turkish collaboration. Like Gladstone, Salisbury was a very reluctant friend of the Turk: but the Sultan's religious authority, as Caliph, and his overlordship of Egypt were valuable political assets. The mission of Sir Henry Drummond Wolff to Constantinople produced the Anglo-Turkish Convention of 1885, in the sixth article of which the Sultan consented to legitimize the British occupation of Egypt as temporary but indefinite.[52] The two governments were to agree on the timing of Britain's withdrawal when they considered the Egyptian administration to be in good order and the frontier with the Sudan secure against the Mahdists. In return, Britain had enabled the Sultan 'to recover his prestige as suzerain of Egypt and as Commander of the Faithful, which recent proceedings . . . tended to impair'.[53] From Sir Henry's further labours at Constantinople issued a second Anglo-Turkish Convention in 1887, by which the British would leave in three years, retaining a right of re-entry in the event of internal unrest. Moving the troops to Malta or Cyprus might allow Britain, Salisbury hoped unrealistically, 'to watch over Egypt . . . without offending the

Mussulman population by floating the infidel flag among them'.[54] France chose to see this agreement as an unlimited extension of Britain's hegemony in Egypt, and not as a far-reaching modification of her actual position there. 'Baring's hand ... of course after evacuation ... will be practically powerless,' Salisbury recognized later.[55] Under threat of a French occupation of Syria, Abdul Hamid II gave way, and refused to ratify the second convention. It was the turning point of Salisbury's Egyptian policy. He did not despair of evacuation, and meditated it intermittently. By occupying Egypt, Britain had been drawn, to a greater extent than she desired, into great power rivalries. In the freedom of private correspondence, he exclaimed to Wolff, 'I heartily wish we had never gone into Egypt. Had we not done so, we could snap our fingers at all the world.'[56] This was to exaggerate Britain's ability, then or at any previous period of her modern history, to detach herself from international realities; but Egypt certainly made it more difficult for her to stand aside. Once more or less resigned to a lengthy occupation, he looked to the Egyptians, rather than to his diplomacy, to create the conditions for a British retirement.

Cromer quickly ceased to anticipate, as Salisbury never did, that Egypt would one day outgrow British tutelage, assuming that it was not first ended by a treaty satisfactory to France. Salisbury commented in 1892: 'If Egypt goes on improving as rapidly as she is ... now, the time will come when she will insist on being free from Turkey, or England, or anybody else.'[57] It was this clear-sightedness that perturbed Cromer, who lacked Salisbury's profound historical sense. Salisbury's support for Cromer did not preclude criticism. He knew the Anglo-Indian mentality too well. 'There is,' he told one of his Cabinet in 1888, '... a little difficulty in setting the Egyptian government on its legs again by the aid of European employés—when the best of our officers start from the principle that they will not, even nominally, obey anyone of a different colour ...'.[58] Pending the national awakening he expected in Egypt, he wanted every care shown for the susceptibilities of Islam and the Khedive. Shifting the British garrison of Cairo to Alexandria, which was not done, commended itself to him as removing from the capital 'a challenge to Islam' and giving the Khedive more semblance of power, 'It would be a question of shadows; but shadows go for a good deal ...', he wrote, thinking not only of the Egyptians but of the Sultan and of France.[59] It was, however, plain to him that Egypt could not be lifted out of the current of popular nationalism running through neighbouring countries.

Salisbury's weakness, and Cromer's strength, lay in the intensification of British imperial sentiment. Salisbury's letters exude a Gladstonian dislike of 'Jingoes'—a word he used to denominate those members of his own party to whom Gladstone applied it. If they were a considerable nuisance, he felt able to cope with them. The wider public opinion of Britain was a different matter. Gladstone's Egyptian war had stimulated what Salisbury interestingly designated 'the national or acquisitive feeling . . . it has tasted the fleshpots and it won't let them go'.[60] When the second, and abortive, Anglo-Turkish Convention was under negotiation, he confessed, 'I greatly dread that the English Chauvinist will insist on more.'[61] Although—indeed, because—Gladstone thoroughly approved of that agreement, Salisbury assured the Tory publicist, Alfred Austin, that it was 'as un-Gladstonian as anything can be'.[62] He himself exploited British nationalism to the utmost of his impressive talent for popular oratory in the case of Ireland. Since he defined the essence of Toryism for its supporters in all social classes as 'its association with the honour of the country',[63] he was awkwardly placed over Egypt.

The Canal Convention of 1888 settled the status of the waterway to the satisfaction of the great powers, not of the Egyptians. In effect, the Canal was neutralized.[64] As Salisbury's nephew and chief lieutenant, A. J. Balfour, put it to the Admiralty: 'Our occupation of Egypt would assume quite a new complexion if it carried with it . . . the complete control of the Canal in time of war.' [65] If and when war did supervene, Britain might plead overriding necessity and close it to her enemies. Until then it was unwise to provoke the powers collectively. The Canal was not Britain's first priority in Egypt. 'At present they dislike our occupation,' continued Balfour, referring to the Powers, '. . . principally because they dislike *us*.' There was no objection on the part of France, Russia or the Central Powers to letting Britain contain Islamic nationalism in one of its main centres. That was Britain's primary concern in Egypt. A political and military summary of 1904 in Balfour's papers as Prime Minister is starkly revealing. It conveyed the substance of a report written by Cromer at the request of the Foreign Office and after consultation with the British generals commanding in Egypt and the reconquered Sudan. More than twenty years had elapsed since Cromer's proconsular rule began. The conclusion he submitted was 'That no reliance can be placed on the friendliness of the Egyptian government, population or army.' Cromer and the two generals were obliged to assume that the British garrison would have to fight on two fronts, should the forces of a major European power effect a landing when, unless reinforced or withdrawn, the garrison must 'take its chance'.[66] It should be remembered that this report was composed before the Denshawai incident of 1906, which publicly confirmed what Cromer here conceded in secrecy, the sterility of his policy.

13

IV

In his apologia, *Modern Egypt*, published in the year he left his post, Cromer quoted, to show where he stood, the creed of the highly esteemed Punjab school of mid-nineteenth-century Indian administrators, who did not pretend to make themselves liked.[67] He, too, combined outward respect for native institutions and an underlying lack of any sympathy with their religious foundation. From the outset, he perceived in Islam 'a religion which clashes with public and private morality'.[68] At bottom, his was a religious and a daring policy, aiming at the substitution of Christian for Islamic social morality; so he stated in his autobiographical notes.[69] He did not contemplate the actual conversion of Egypt, which to him was irrelevant. On the contrary, he obstructed the establishment of an Anglican Bishopric in Cairo as an irritant to Moslems.[70] Neither the High Churchmanship of Gladstone and Salisbury, nor the Evangelicalism of the Punjab school attracted him. The social importance of religion, not its intrinsic truth, held Cromer's mind. He envisaged westernization as transforming Islam into the broadest of broad churches. Thus Egyptian nationalism would slowly change its politically dangerous nature. Corresponding with his masters in London, he alternated between minimizing the influence of unregenerate nationalism in Egypt, to reassure them and himself, and appraising it more accurately. 'Many ... think,' Salisbury heard from him in 1887, 'that the Arabi movement ... is dead; in a sense this is true ... but I am very sceptical as to the spirit he evoked having altogether died out.'[71] Far from having died out, that spirit was duly to find expression in a crisis that nearly toppled Cromer's administration. A precursor of trouble was 'the recrudescence of Mohammedan fanaticism', he noted in 1890.[72] Whatever he sometimes said, he knew the resurgent national movement had an effective local leadership in the Moslem clergy and the 'Arab squirearchy'—men a little above the level of the peasantry. It was not sensible of him to dismiss these leaders as 'corrupt and ignorant bigots'.[73] They were quietly taking advantage of Khedivial and Turco-Egyptian decline under Cromer's sway to prepare, Shaikh Mohammed Abdu told Blunt, for the re-emergence of 'the fellah party'.[74]

The undeniably constructive side of Cromer's rule yielded a disappointing political return, as Mohammed Abdu predicted it would. Cromer brought with him to Egypt, from India in his case, the idea that a prosperous and contented peasantry readily acquiesced in the wishes of government, whosoever controlled it. To alleviate the peasants' chronic indebtedness and overcrowding on the land, he started with a revolutionary proposal: the limitation of proprietary rights to a life interest, allowing the state to redistribute holdings. If nothing was done, he advised Granville, 'any future Arabi' would have a weapon to hand in land hunger.[75] The scheme he outlined proceeded from a wholly insufficient practical acquaintance with the cultivator and an initial misjudgment of what was possible in Egypt. It did not take him long to learn better. When Lord Kitchener took the post in 1911 that had been Cromer's, the soldierly resolve to curb village usury by law afforded his predecessor wry amusement.[76] Improving the lot of the fellaheen did, nevertheless, lie close to Cromer's heart. It was his heart, and not his head, that prompted him, in a letter to Salisbury's Chancellor of the Exchequer, to imagine himself refusing to pay off 'a farthing' of Egypt's international debts and channelling her revenues into a surplus which should provide the security for loans to finance agricultural canals and roads.[77] No one understood more clearly than Cromer why this was a benevolent fantasy: but it goes some way towards clarifying the ambivalence with which he personally was regarded by educated Egyptians actively committed to ending the occupation. Irrigation was one of his triumphs, perhaps the greatest. The restoration of Egypt's financial health permitted this and other expenditure on public works, and cut taxation appreciably. It also reduced the Continental Powers' scope for interference in her internal affairs through the six-nation Caisse de la Dette Publique, dating back to 1876 and reorganized by the London Convention. This reduction was an objective common to the British, the Khedive and the nationalists. The large, internationally guaranteed loan to Egypt at a moderate rate of interest which Gladstone's ministry arranged with the Convention laid the cornerstone of her reordered finances. The virtuosity of Cromer's fiscal and economic management in lowering taxes and nursing the country into relative affluence appears from the proportion of Egyptian revenue paid over to her creditors—52 per cent in 1881, and 41 per cent, still, of a much higher government income in 1905.[78] Too little of the increased national wealth, however, went to the mass of Egyptians. 'Look at Egypt,' said a Turkish diplomat of liberal views to a British colleague in 1908, '—since you have been there you have made millionaires but you haven't raised the fellaheen one bit.'[79] It was an unfair charge, but indicative of feeling in the Islamic world.

Egypt was 'a nondescript country', Cromer maintained. By this he meant that only if the Canal, the Caisse, the European countries sheltered by the Capitulations, and state enterprises, like the railways, run by Europeans did not exist, could the native Egyptian majority be entrusted with the government of their country. To be realistic, he would prefer the Turco-Egyptian aristocracy to rule, as rather less 'superstitious, rapacious, ignorant and corrupt', had he to choose between them and the nationalists. The former displayed 'some slight

traditional trace of governing capacity'.[80] He did not mention in this
letter to Salisbury the native Christians, Copts, Syrians, and Armenians, or the Jews, on all of whom he drew quite disproportionately for
ministers and subordinate officials. To these minorities he allotted
many pages of his book, *Modern Egypt*, in support of the thesis that
Egypt was and must always be predominantly multi-confessional and
-racial, the Moslem and fellah majority notwithstanding.[81] His reliance on them of course made the minorities more unpopular than
they were historically. In addition, they were conspicuous benefici-
aries of British occupation in terms of personal and economic liberty
and security, hitherto precarious, as generally for native Christians in
Islamic states. Accustomed to live by trade, they furnished Cromer's
Egypt with many of its new rich. The Moslem fellaheen observed their
communal prosperity with rancour; as did the Turco-Egyptian aris-
tocrats who also grew restless as reforms of justice and police eroded
their local ascendancy.

Salisbury admonished Cromer in the late 1880s and early 1890s not
to annoy the French by blatantly exhibiting his domination of Khedive Tewfik in a succession of ministerial changes;[82] but it was the
Egyptians, with more cause for resentment, who showed it to greater
effect. Within a year of taking over in Egypt, Cromer forecast to
Granville the collapse of 'the dummy-minister-plus-English-adviser
policy'.[83] It did not in fact break down, but it required bolstering with
open threats of force in 1893–4. The outcome, if it did nothing else for
Moslem Egyptians, advertised the existence of their nationality. The
young Khedive Abbas II, who had succeeded on his father's death in
1892, exemplified the tendency, noticed by Salisbury, for the Turco-
Egyptians to identify politically with their fellow-countrymen.
Cromer confidently thought 'my poor little Khedive' was, although
'very Egyptian', more impatient of the Sultan's residual sovereignty
and hostile to the Christian minorities than opposed to the British.[84]
The two men collided head on in January 1893 over the appointment
of ministers, the key prerogative which Cromer treated as his own. It
was immediately apparent that Abbas planned a coup by constitutional means in the unrealized hope of being countenanced by France,
and in the expectation of being followed, if a military demonstration
were needed, by his army under its Egyptian officers in defiance of its
commander, Kitchener, and the other senior British officers. The
reconstructed Egyptian army, already tried in battle with the Mahdists, was a source of pride to the British; they believed it loyal to the
real masters of the country and unaffected by memories of the recent
past. 'The system . . . has broken down,' telegraphed Cromer in con-
sternation.[85] Lord Rosebery, the Liberal Foreign Secretary of the
moment, calmed the shocked Cromer, diluted his urgent plans for

military action and faced up to the new situation: 'If ... instead of working with a willing prince for ... an indifferent and not wholly ungrateful nation, we are to carry on ... in the teeth of the prince, the army, and the people, we cannot disguise from ourselves that our occupation has changed its character ...'[86]

Rosebery did not exclude what he knew appealed to Gladstone and most of the Cabinet, a renewed attempt to negotiate the evacuation of Egypt with the Sultan, on the lines of Drummond Wolff's unratified convention of 1887.[87] Describing Abbas's partisans as 'Arabist', Cromer counselled evacuation unless Britain determined on 'the almost irreversible consequences' of standing firm.[88] Rosebery chose the latter course, adopted by the Cabinet in the knowledge that the Tories, a large section of the Liberals in the Commons, and public opinion were with him. Sir William Harcourt went through Rosebery's draft despatch to Cairo, objecting to such expressions, inspired by Cromer, as 'ignorant fanaticism'. They would not, he observed, make a good impression in India or Turkey.[89] Abbas II's submission and his undertaking to comply with British advice discredited him, when coupled with a similar climbdown in January 1894 after the hostility to its British officers he had evinced on a visit to his army. Cromer's demands were accompanied by British troop movements and hints at Abbas's deposition. Meanwhile, the alarm of the important French colony at the popular mood made the task easier by isolating the Khedive from France. In December 1893 the language of the nationalist newspapers was 'very violent' and reminiscent of 1882.[90] The usually tame Legislative Council's report on the budget amounted to 'a strong indictment against the whole British administration'.[91] The instigator was the veteran Turco-Egyptian politician, Riaz Pasha, a respected Moslem figure. Not a liberal, he had been useful to Cromer, who put him in and out of office, as convenient. His alliance with the nationalists was eloquent of the solidarity overcome by imminent force.

The consequences of 1893–4 turned out to be entirely, not almost, irreversible; despite the fact that the character of the occupation did not change as noticeably as Rosebery supposed it must. The British element in the bureaucracy increased considerably, and in 1898 the Ministry of the Interior was the last to come under the control of a British adviser. This was the continuation of a trend: but Egyptians did not forget that the British had begun by seeking to reduce the proportion of European officials employed when the country was subject to the Dual Control, whose numbers had been a nationalist grievance. Cromer prided himself on his tolerance of the advancing native press, relying on an Arabic paper, edited by Syrian Christians, to speak up for him. Attacks on soldiers of the army of occupation met

17

with another kind of response, a special decree of 1895, prescribing 'such penalties ... as necessary'.[92] The reconquest of the Sudan in 1896–7 aroused mixed feelings. The huge territory became an Anglo-Egyptian condominium, reflecting Britain's contribution to the Mahdist defeat. The Egyptian army's creditable performance from the opening of the campaign did not make it better disposed towards the British. At intervals, Cromer's information came near to subduing his political will. 'I always feel here,' he wrote to Salisbury in 1897, 'that I am skating on the thinnest possible sheet of ice, and it is a constant ... astonishment to me that the ice bears at all. The Khedive, if he knew it, is in reality much more master of the situation than he imagines.' What if he were again to defy Cromer over the choice of minister?[93] Abbas II had made a favourite of Shaikh Mohammed Abdu, but fortunately for the British the Khedive never recovered his nerve after the second submission to Cromer in 1894. Nor did the nationalists put much faith in Abbas, if he were to get free of Cromer. Mohammed Abdu thought he should be given little power in an independent Egypt, and restrained by a constitution with ministers answerable to and irremovable except by a genuinely representative assembly. That he had deliberately created 'nothing that can survive of indigenous government' when the occupation ended was the Shaikh's most serious charge against Cromer.[94] This was one way in which the proconsul strove to prevent Egyptian nationalism from reaching maturity.

Another was his educational policy. For evidently political reasons, defensively discussed in one of his published reports, he would not equip the country with a system of state education remotely commensurate with its economic progress and cultural level. In 1897 government schools had places for 11,000 pupils and private schools for 181,000. He denied the imputed unwillingness to see Egyptians trained to displace the British 'gradually'; but the adverb conceded his critics' point. He dwelt on 'the social danger' of expanding the government schools to produce 'a disappointed and disaffected class of half-educated youths'.[95] His real objection went deeper. 'I entirely deny,' he told Sir Edward Grey, the new Liberal Foreign Secretary in 1906, 'that ... in this country moral progress can be ... secured by such instruction as ... is possible ... in the schools ... the Egyptian people ... are heavily weighted by their leaden creed and by the institutions which cluster round the Koran.'[96] As for a national university, which to the Egyptians like the Irish symbolized political maturity, if one were set up it should be effectively reserved for the sons of wealthy families.[97] That small section of Egyptian youth promised to be less nationalist in outlook because a high percentage came from the Christian and Jewish minorities. When in 1904 the Legislative Assembly showed convincingly how the nationalists could breathe life into Dufferin's representative bodies, and asked for a parliament on the Western model, it wanted more Koranic education too. Cromer was caustic in private about 'a fairly extensive programme. Possibly by the year 2004 some portion of it may have been adopted.'[98] In fact, his last years in Egypt were spent fighting Islamic nationalism harder than he had ever had to do. A few months before the end, he gave the Ministry of Education to the rising nationalist, Saad Zaghlul, an unprecedented gesture of conciliation which came too late. Under those conditions his continued distrust of the Egyptian army's loyalties worried him to such an extent that he argued 'the Army has to be kept efficient for service ... At the same time we want to keep it inefficient in order that it shall not be a danger ...'[99] 'The hatred of the Moslem for the Christian,' he assured Grey, 'is so intense that it dominates over all other sentiments.'[100] Grey naturally had his doubts. The Legislative Assembly's renewed pressure for a European-type constitution and its request for government aid towards a national university did not smack of fanaticism in themselves.

Cromer insisted on retiring in 1907 because he rightly believed that even the sympathetic Grey was not persuaded of the Islamic menace to Britain in Egypt. The final report on Egyptian affairs he made for publication was carefully phrased in its warning references to Islamic nationalism.[101] In confidence, his distress and concern were unbounded; he was driven to soliciting the help at home of the Anglican missionaries whose activity in Egypt he had refused to assist. The nationalists' liberalism was spurious, he alleged. They wanted 'not "Egypt for the Egyptians" but "Mohammedanism versus Christianity", and the exclusion of Christians from any share in the administration of the country'.[102] The desire to check this religious nationalism in a salutary fashion accounted for the drastic punishments inflicted in 1906 by a tribunal under the special decree of 1895 to avenge the death of one British officer and injuries to others sustained in an affray with the villagers of Denshawai while out shooting at the invitation of a local notable. The tribunal sentenced four to death, two to life imprisonment, seven to lesser terms, and eight to fifty lashes each. Cromer defended the quite excessive severity on grounds of policy: protection of officers of the army of occupation, and discouragement of Islamic and nationalist unrest. British public opinion was briefly questioning, especially of the sentences of flogging, which it was the boast of Cromer's rule to have abolished in criminal cases. The 1895 decree, however, imposed no restriction on the penalties available to tribunals constituted under it. Egyptian nationalists were outraged. The shadow of Denshawai blighted the sincere experiment in cautious liberalization conducted by Cromer's successor, Sir Eldon Gorst, which was seen to have failed when the Legislative Assembly registered in 1910 the overwhelming national protest against extending the Canal Company's concession beyond 1968. Kitchener, who followed Gorst, went further than Cromer in the opposite direction: '... the Nationalist party is slowly but surely dying', he prematurely announced to Grey in 1912.[103]

V

Edward Hamilton wrote of Gladstone in January 1885: 'The prevalent idea is that Mr G. won't trouble himself about foreign matters like Egypt; whereas it is Egypt, and nothing but Egypt, which occupies his thoughts.'[104] Lady Gwendolen Cecil in the unfinished biography of his father and in a slender volume of essays which are a distillation of it reminded posterity of the place which Egypt held in his skilled, patient diplomacy.[105] The classic study of recent years by Robinson and Gallagher, *Africa and the Victorians*, attaches great significance to Egypt in late Victorian and Edwardian imperialism from a British standpoint, but concentrates on factors other than the interaction of religion and politics.[106] In the long view, which this essay has tried to take, the antagonism and incomprehension separating Britain and Egypt may well have been primarily due to the incompatibility of Islam with the religious and political culture of the West. The depth of misunderstanding was profound. So good a Liberal as Sir Edward Grey stated, to his Prime Minister, Campbell-Bannerman, that Cromer 'handled Denshawai delicately', and this when the repercussions had been experienced.[107] Grey's fellow Cabinet minister Winston Churchill, then in his most liberal phase, was adamant that his country derived no vital strategic or economic benefits from the occupation of Egypt: 'we all perfectly well know that our only road to India in war time is by the Cape'.[108] The British, he said in 1910, had to stay in Egypt for reasons of a different order: 'We should hold on to Egypt as we held on to India. It was not that it brought us any advantage, but it was impossible to go back ...'[109] In the period to 1914, public opinion was shaped by religious and political sentiment, two currents that intermingled. One illustration must suffice. Bishop Blyth, the Anglican prelate whose ambition to erect an Egyptian see Cromer asked Salisbury to thwart, informed the *Daily News* that the projected diocese fitted into a larger scheme, avowedly imperialist in conception, for 'a chain of bishoprics' from Cairo to Capetown.[110]

Notes

1. Sir E. Malet, *Egypt 1879–1883*, ed. Lord Sanderson (London, pr. pr., 1909), p. 455, Malet to Granville, 18 Sept. 1882.

2. W. S. Blunt, *Secret History of the English Occupation of Egypt* (London, 1907), p. 375 n. 1.
3. Blunt, *My Diaries, 1888–1914*, 2 vols. (London, 1919–20), II, entry for 12 Nov. 1903.
4. A. Ramm, *The Political Correspondence of Mr Gladstone and Lord Granville, 1876–1886*, 2 vols. (Oxford, 1962), I, pp. 227–8, Gladstone to Granville, 31 Jan. 1882.
5. *Hansard* (3rd ser.), CCLXXII, col. 1590 (24 July 1882).
6. Ibid., CCLXXIII, cols. 1950–1 (16 Aug. 1882).
7. Ibid., col. 1947.
8. Ibid., CCLXXII, col. 177 (12 July 1882).
9. Gladstone Papers (B.L. Add. MS 44545), Gladstone to Shaftesbury, 18 Sept. 1882.
10. *Hansard* (3rd ser.), CLXXXIV, cols. 711–12 (12 Feb. 1884).
11. *Gladstone-Granville Correspondence*, I, pp. 413–14, 427, Gladstone to Granville, 3, 21 Sept. 1882.
12. Ibid., p. 406 n. 1, Granville to Gladstone, 26 July 1882.
13. *Hansard* (3rd ser.), CCLXXII, col. 2100 (27 July 1882).
14. Lord Cromer, *Modern Egypt*, one vol. edn. (London, 1911), p. 102.
15. T. Zeldin, *France 1848–1945*, 2 vols. (Oxford, 1977), II, pp. 118–19.
16. *Gladstone-Granville Correspondence*, II, pp. 101–2, Gladstone to Granville, 14 Oct. 1883.
17. Gladstone Papers (B.L. Add. MS 44546), Gladstone to von Döllinger, 11 Oct. 1882.
18. *Gladstone-Granville Correspondence*, I, pp. 447–8, Gladstone to Granville, 17 Oct. 1882.
19. Sir A. Lyall, *The Life of the Marquis of Dufferin and Ava*, 2 vols. (London, 1905), II, p. 17.
20. H. Sutherland Edwards, *Sir William White: His Life at Constantinople* (London, 1902), p. 205, Dufferin to White, 30 June 1882.
21. *Gladstone-Granville Correspondence*, I, pp. 428–9, Gladstone to Granville, 22 Sept. 1882.
22. A. L. al-Sayyid, *Egypt and Cromer: A Study in Anglo-Egyptian Relations* (London, 1968), p. 33.
23. P.P. 1883, LXXXIII, correspondence respecting reorganization in Egypt, pp. 88–9, 93, Dufferin to Lord Granville, 6 Feb. 1883.
24. Lyall, op. cit., II, p. 26, Dufferin to Sir E. Baring, 12 April 1892.
25. D. W. R. Bahlman (ed.), *The Diary of Sir Edward Walter Ham-*

ilton, 1880–1885, 2 vols. (Oxford, 1972), II, pp. 602–3, entry for 26 April 1884.

26. P.P. 1883, LXXXIII, pp. 87–8, Dufferin to Granville, 6 Feb. 1883.
27. *Hansard* (3rd ser.), CLXXXIV, cols. 706–7 (12 Feb. 1884).
28. *The Diary of Sir E. W. Hamilton*, II, p. 415, entry for 31 March 1883.
29. Gladstone Papers (B.L. Add. MS 44131), Childers to Gladstone, 7 March 1884.
30. Ibid., Gladstone to Childers, 8 March 1884.
31. *The Diary of Sir E. W. Hamilton*, II, p. 491, entry for 9 Oct. 1883.
32. Ibid.
33. Lord Zetland, *Lord Cromer* (London, 1932), pp. 220–1, Baring to Salisbury, 11 Dec. 1891.
34. E. Kedourie, *Afghani and 'Abduh: an Essay on Religious Unbelief and Political Activism in Modern Islam* (London, 1966), passim.
35. Ibid., p. 22.
36. Ibid., pp. 25, 29–30.
37. Blunt, *Secret History*, p. 341ff., Louis Sabunji, Cairo, to Blunt, 18 June 1882.
38. J. M. Ahmed, *The Intellectual Origins of Egyptian Nationalism* (London, 1960), pp. 11–14.
39. Blunt, *Secret History*, pp. 341–4, Sabunji to Blunt, 18, 19 June 1882.
40. Ibid., p. 344ff., Sabunji to Blunt, 19, 24 June 1882.
41. D. A. Farnie, *East and West of Suez: the Suez Canal in History* (Oxford, 1969), p. 292.
42. *The Diary of Sir E. W. Hamilton*, I, p. 293, entry for 25 June, 1883.
43. O. Amin, *Muhammad 'Abduh*, trans. C. Wendell (Washington, 1953), pp. 63–4.
44. Blunt, *Gordon at Khartoum* (London, 1911), pp. 622–6, Mohammed Abdu's interview with the *Pall Mall Gazette* reprinted.
45. Gladstone Papers (B.L. Add. MS 44549), 15 April 1893.
46. Salisbury Papers (A/44), Salisbury to Sir H. Drummond Wolff, 18 Aug. 1885.
47. al-Sayyid, op. cit., p. 202.
48. Cromer Papers (P.R.O., F.O. 633/6), Baring to Granville, 2 Nov. 1883.
49. *Hansard* (3rd ser.), CXXXVII, cols. 1185–6 (26 March 1855).
50. Ibid., CLXXII, col. 1503 (24 July 1882).
51. Ibid., CLXXXIV, cols. 576–7 (12 Feb. 1884).
52. Sir H. Drummond Wolff, *Rambling Recollections*, 2 vols. (London, 1908), II, pp. 287–8.

53. Salisbury Papers (A/44), Salisbury to Sir William White, 11 July 1885.
54. Ibid. (A/55), Salisbury to Baring, 21 Jan. 1887.
55. Ibid. (A/76), Salisbury to Sir Clare Ford, ambassador at Constantinople, 1 March 1892.
56. Ibid. (A/51), Salisbury to Wolff, 23 Feb. 1887.
57. Ibid. (A/76), Salisbury to Ford, 1 March 1892.
58. Ibid. (D/21–28), Salisbury to G. J. Goschen, 4 March 1888.
59. Ibid. (A/76), Salisbury to White, 9 Nov. 1891.
60. Ibid. (A/51), Salisbury to Wolff, 23 Feb. 1887.
61. Ibid.
62. Ibid. (D/1–9), Salisbury to Austin, 5 June 1887.
63. Ibid. (D/15–19), Salisbury to Lord Randolph Churchill, 1 Oct. 1886.
64. Farnie, op. cit., pp. 337–42.
65. Balfour Papers (B.L. Add. MS 49706), Balfour to G. J. Goschen, First Lord of the Admiralty, 5 April 1900.
66. Ibid. (B.L. Add. MS 49698), 'Secret Précis of Case relative to the Garrison of Egypt', July 1904.
67. Cromer, *Modern Egypt*, p. 714.
68. Cromer Papers (P.R.O., F.O. 633/6), Baring to Granville, 2 Nov. 1883.
69. Zetland, *Lord Cromer*, p. 89.
70. Cromer Papers (P.R.O., F.O. 633/6), Cromer to Salisbury, 2 Feb. 1899.
71. Ibid., Cromer to Salisbury, 8 May 1887.
72. Zetland, *Lord Cromer*, p. 199, Cromer to Salisbury, spring 1890.
73. Cromer Papers (P.R.O., F.O. 633/6), Baring to Salisbury, 1 May 1887.
74. Blunt, *My Diaries*, I, p. 111ff., entry for 24 Feb. 1893.
75. Cromer Papers (P.R.O., F.O. 633/6), Baring to Granville, 27 Sept. 1883.
76. C. Boyle, *A Servant of the Empire: A Memoir of Henry Boyle* (London, 1938), pp. 219–20, Cromer to Boyle, 25 July 1912.
77. Zetland, *Lord Cromer*, p. 153, Baring to G. J. Goschen, 9 May 1887.
78. P.P. 1906, CXXXVII, Reports by HM Agent and Consul-General on the Forces, Administration, and Condition of Egypt and the Sudan in 1905, p. 501.
79. C. H. D. Howard (ed.), *The Diary of Edward Goschen 1900–1914*, Camden 4th Ser., XXV (London, 1980), p. 165, entry for 23 March 1908. Edward was G. J. Goschen's half brother.
80. Zetland, *Lord Cromer*, pp. 164–6.

81. Cromer, *Modern Egypt*, esp. ch. xxxiv, 'The Dwellers in Egypt'.
82. For example, Salisbury Papers (A/55), Salisbury to Baring, 23 Jan., 13 Feb. 1891.
83. Cromer Papers (P.R.O., F.O. 633/6), Baring to Granville, 7 Jan. 1884.
84. Ibid., Baring to Salisbury, 15 April, 21 Feb. 1892.
85. Ibid. (P.R.O., F.O. 633/7), Cromer to Lord Rosebery, 21 Jan. 1893.
86. Ibid., Rosebery to Cromer, 19, 27 Jan. 1893.
87. Gladstone Papers (B.L. Add. MS 44290), Rosebery to Gladstone, 16 April 1893.
88. Cromer Papers (P.R.O., F.O. 633/6), Cromer to Rosebery, 28 Jan. 1893.
89. Gladstone Papers (B.L. Add. MS 44203), enclosure in Harcourt to Gladstone, 9 Feb. 1893.
90. Cromer Papers (P.R.O., F.O. 633/7), Cromer to Rosebery, 19 Dec. 1893.
91. Ibid.
92. P.P. 1906, CXXXVII, correspondence respecting the attack on British officers at Denshawai, pp. 691-2.
93. Cromer Papers (P.R.O., F.O. 633/6), Cromer to Salisbury, 6 Feb. 1897.
94. Blunt, *My Diaries*, I, pp. 263, 428-9, entries for 16 Jan. 1896, 29 Jan. 1900.
95. P.P. 1906, CXXXVII, pp. 564-5.
96. Cromer Papers (P.R.O., F.O. 633/13), Cromer to Grey, 8 March 1907.
97. P.P. 1907, C, Reports by HM Agent and Consul-General on the Finances, Administration and Condition of Egypt and the Sudan in 1906, p. 719.
98. Cromer Papers (P.R.O., F.O. 633/6), Cromer, to Lord Lansdowne, Foreign Secretary, 26 Feb. 1904.
99. O. Mellini, *Sir Eldon Gorst: the Overshadowed Pro-consul* (Stanford, 1977), p. 110, Cromer to Maj.-Gen. Sir Reginald Wingate, Sirdar (commander) of the Egyptian Army, 24 July 1905.
100. Mellini, op. cit., p. 108, Cromer to Grey, 5 May, 1906.
101. P.P. 1907, C, pp. 627-32.
102. Mellini, op. cit., p. 126, the Rev. R. MacInnes of the Church Missionary Society, Cairo, to the Rev. F. Baylis, CMS, London, 12 April, 1907.
103. Grey Papers (P.R.O., F.O. 800/48), Lord Kitchener to Grey, 24 Jan. 1912.
104. *The Diary of Sir E. W. Hamilton*, II, p. 762, entry for 5 Jan. 1885.

105. *Life of Robert, Marquis of Salisbury*, 4 vols. (London, 1921–32) and *Biographical Studies of the Life and Political Character of Robert, Marquis of Salisbury* (London, pr. pr., 1949).
106. R. Robinson and J. Gallagher with A. Denny, *Africa and the Victorians: the Official Mind of Imperialism* (London, 1961).
107. Campbell-Bannerman Papers (B.L. Add. MS 41218), Grey to Campbell-Bannerman, 18 Jan. 1907.
108. Blunt, *My Diaries*, II, p. 287, entry for 2 Oct. 1909.
109. Ibid., II, p. 336, entry for 14 Oct. 1910.
110. Cromer Papers (P.R.O., F.O. 633/6), quoted in an extract from the *Daily News*, 16 Feb. 1900, sent by Cromer to Salisbury, 22 Feb. 1900.

I am grateful to the owners and custodians of the MSS on which I have drawn for this essay, and particularly to the Most Hon. the Marquess of Salisbury. In addition to the secondary sources cited in the text and notes, I have made general use of the literature on imperialism, Egypt and the Sudan itemized by H. J. Hanham (ed.), *Bibliography of British History, 1851–1914* (Oxford, 1976), pp. 112–15, 194–9.

Constantinople or Cairo: Lord Salisbury and the Partition of the Ottoman Empire 1886–1897

KEITH M. WILSON

Historiographically speaking, a certain view of British policy and interests in the Mediterranean during the 1890s has dominated the last three decades. The view in question was first put forward in 1954 by A. J. P. Taylor, who pronounced in *The Struggle for Mastery in Europe*: 'the British lost interest in the Straits as their position in Egypt became stronger'. Ten years later, J. A. S. Grenville wrote that Lord Salisbury 'attempted to compensate for Britain's weakness in Constantinople by moving to Egypt Britain's centre of power in the Mediterranean'. Most recently, P. Marsh in 1972 and J. Gooch in 1974 have declared, respectively, that 'the importance of Constantinople to Britain had been reduced by Britain's new position in Egypt since 1882'; 'As Gladstone was replaced by Salisbury, so the occupation [of Egypt] was transformed into a state of semi-permanence by the assumption that Cairo might replace Constantinople as the bulwark against Russia.'[1]

Despite its longevity and general acceptance, this view seems to me to merit considerable revision. The object of what follows is to reconsider the relationship, in British eyes, of Constantinople to Cairo, and the relative importance to Great Britain of the Dardanelles and the Suez Canal. An alternative thesis will be propounded. This is: that Constantinople was, and remained, the key not only to Egypt but to the Mediterranean as a whole; that the British position in Egypt was never regarded as a satisfactory alternative to or compensation for Russian influence at Constantinople; that British foreign policy, and British priorities, possessed a greater degree of continuity than the accounts first cited suggest; that the policy of the Mediterranean Agreements, which is supposed in those accounts to have ended at some point between 1895 and 1897, remained in being; and that Lord Salisbury, having devised a radical solution to the Eastern question, tried unsuccessfully to implement this in the course of his third and last administration.

I

The Admiralty, impressed with the growth in size and quality of the Russian Black Sea fleet, and the War Office, in possession of disquieting intelligence about Russian intentions, met in March 1892 in the form of the Directors of Naval and Military Intelligence to consider the question of a possible Russian attempt to seize Constantinople and what naval and military action would be necessary to meet such a case. Their conclusion was that 'Great Britain, unsupported, cannot prevent the coup de main without endangering her general naval position'.[2] Upon his receipt of this joint conclusion, in June 1892, the Prime Minister produced the following memorandum. Salisbury wrote:

> The protection of Constantinople from Russian conquest has been the turning point of the policy of Great Britain for at least forty years, and to a certain extent for forty years before that. It has been constantly assumed, both in England and abroad, that this protection of Constantinople was the special interest of Great Britain. *It is our principal, if not our only, interest in the Mediterranean Sea*; for if Russia were mistress of Constantinople, and of the influence which Constantinople has in the Levant, the route to India through the Suez Canal would be so much exposed as not to be available except in times of the profoundest peace. There is no need to dwell on the effect which the Russian possession of Constantinople would have upon the Oriental mind, and upon our position in India, which is so largely dependent on prestige ... the matter of present importance is its effect on the Mediterranean; and I cannot see, if Constantinople were no longer defensible, that any other interest in the Mediterranean is left to defend ...

He went on to wonder whether there was any point in retaining a British fleet in the Mediterranean at all: 'There is nothing (except Constantinople) in the Mediterranean worth the maintenance of so large and costly a force.'[3]

Egypt, which had not even been mentioned in the joint report, and to which Salisbury had referred only once, and that incidentally, continued to be regarded as entirely subordinate to Constantinople by the Liberal government which took office within weeks of the production of Salisbury's memorandum. In the course of exchanges between the new Prime Minister, Rosebery, his Foreign Secretary, Kimberley, and the service departments which came to the conclusion that there was nothing Britain could do to prevent the Russians from swooping down suddenly on Constantinople, Egypt was never mentioned. Typical was the comment passed by Rosebery in connection with the purpose of the presence of a British naval squadron in the Levant. It showed, he said, 'that we're keeping a vigilant eye on the Eastern Question of which Constantinople is the vital point, and on the Sultan'.[4]

When the Conservative Party returned to power in July 1895, Salisbury was quick to point out, to the German ambassador, that, if Russia gained possession of the Dardanelles, she would be at all times in a position to place in danger in the most serious way the interests of England in the Mediterranean. He enlarged on this a month later, pointing out explicitly that if Russia was able to issue forth from the Black Sea into the Mediterranean that very fact would expose Egypt, which would then be 'difficult to hold'.[5] In November 1895, Salisbury's nephew and colleague, A. J. Balfour, on behalf of the newly-established Defence Committee of the Cabinet, asked the Admiralty: 'What consequences would flow from a Russian occupation of Constantinople to British naval interests?' The DNI, on 12 November, produced the following answer:

> The power of the Russian fleet to issue from the Dardanelles at any moment, as if from their own port, within 600 miles of the Suez Canal, would give them either the command of the eastern Mediterranean, or compel a superior English squadron to be kept in those waters—but not with the present advantages ... The transfer to Russia of the present English command in the eastern Mediterranean would mean the gradual reduction of English commerce, *the waning of English influence over the Canal and Egypt*, and the loss of touch with India through the Mediterranean ... The interests of the empire, India, and all Britain's eastern possessions required, that as long as England can keep it so, Russia should be vulnerable through the Black Sea—to secure this, the Dardanelles and Bosphorus must either be kept unarmed, or in the hands of Russia's foes. Once the Black Sea is a Russian lake with the Dardanelles as her safe outlet, Russian influence and power will extend through Asia Minor and Syria, and England will be separated from India by the distance of the Cape Route.

Asked what measures should be taken to counteract these effects of a successful Russian occupation of Constantinople, Admiral Beaumont recommended 'the occupation of the Dardanelles peninsula'. Evidently expecting this to fail, he went on: 'Failing that ... the next best move would be the absolute and permanent occupation of Egypt, and the determination to hold it against all comers!' The significance of the exclamation mark is not absolutely clear. It may have marked the realization that he was about to contradict himself; it may even have indicated that, in what he was about to say, he was not being entirely serious. For having convincingly demonstrated how vulnerable Egypt would be, and how little therefore of a good thing even if it were 'the next best thing' would be 'the absolute and permanent occupation of Egypt and the determination to hold it against all comers', he next claimed that this 'would be the means of our retaining the command of our most important communications. In fact, by taking Egypt absolutely, we would secure what we have so long sought to maintain by keeping Russia out of Constantinople.'[6]

The next full appreciation of the position appeared one year later. It too was asked for by the Defence Committee. In a memorandum on naval policy of 13 October 1896, the Director of Military Intelligence Sir J. Ardagh wrote that the effect of opening the Straits to Russia alone would be:

1. To convert the Black Sea into a military harbour, from which the squadrons of Russia could emerge, and into which they could retire at will.
2. To give Russia an even more complete command over Turkey than she now has: to exclude all the other powers from influencing the Sultan; and to leave him no alternative but complete subordination to Russia.

As he understated it, 'this arrangement would be disadvantageous to British interests'. As regards the strategic value to England of Egypt and the Suez Canal, the DMI had this to say:

From its geographical position Egypt is valuable to us as a half-way house to India, as giving a potential control over the Suez Canal, as assuring overland passage for communication with India, in case the Suez Canal is blocked, as giving access to the whole basin of the Nile, of which we already hold the head waters in Uganda, as securing the only overland portion of the telegraphic communication with India and the East entirely in British hands, as possessing in Alexandria a magnificent harbour with a minimum depth in the approaches of 30 feet, and a seaborne trade of over two million tons, nearly one half of which is British . . .

Egypt's security, however, 'depends to a great extent upon the maintenance of naval supremacy in the Mediterranean', and Ardagh admitted that this did not exist, making reinforcement from England, impossible (though permitting evacuation to India), whilst Russia had created a Black Sea fleet 'only excluded from the Mediterranean by a barrier of which she practically holds the key'. The DMI was convinced that, if war broke out, the Suez Canal would be blocked. In one contingency, he intended to block it himself: 'If we were at war with France, and our commerce had to take the Cape route to India, we should block the Canal in order to deprive neutrals of the advantage which the shorter route would give them. If we were at war with Russia, that power would block the Canal, in order to interrupt our route to India.' At this point, Ardagh emulated Beaumont eleven months previously, and concluded:

> Balancing the advantages and disadvantages it now appears to be the wisest policy to remain, and in the words of Eothen 'plant a firm foot on the banks of the Nile and sit in the seats of the faithful'.[7]

Had 'the faithful' been supplied with, and read carefully, the passages preceding what was in context a remarkable statement, they would certainly have vacated their seats well in advance of the arrival of Sir John and his staff.

The Director of Naval Intelligence produced a memorandum of his own on 28 October 1896. This time, Admiral Beaumont was at least consistent:

> If the course of time is to see Russia in Asia Minor with a naval base in the Eastern basin of the Mediterranean, France still in alliance with her, or herself established in Syria, there would be only one way in which England could not only maintain herself in the Mediterranean at all, but continue to hold India, and that is by holding Egypt against all comers and making Alexandria a naval base.
>
> If England leaves Egypt she will not get back even now, and much less then, and notwithstanding what is said in these papers, the Suez Canal cannot be blocked unless it is guarded as well, nor can it be commanded by ships at the Suez end, unless Suez is held, but all this can be done, and Europe defied, if Egypt is strongly held and Alexandria, Malta, and Gibraltar are naval bases. This is England's policy of the future ...[8]

Of this it can be said that the first series of 'ifs' was much smaller (Beaumont himself said that 'the advance of Russia to the Sea, and her establishment as a first-class naval Power both in the Mediterranean and the Far East appears to be certain') than the second series, from 'all this can be done, and Europe defied ...'. It can also be said that Admiral Beaumont's recommendations did not commend themselves. They were not converted into, did not become, 'England's policy of the future'. What he said should be done and could be done was not done. No steps were taken to make Egypt the place where England would have made what surely would have been, in Beaumont's own words, 'the last stand'. Nothing was done about Alexandria, for instance. In May 1901 the Military Intelligence Department informed the Cabinet that Egypt would be isolated during the opening phases of a war with a maritime power. She would be 'liable to an attack by sea', which would have to be met by a British establishment of 4,239 all ranks. The Egyptian army of 13,000 was 'but of doubtful loyalty': it had mutinied the previous year. The situation was not improved by the fact that in a war with Russia and France, 'all troops east of Suez . . . that could be spared from the local defence of coaling stations etc., would be needed for the defence of India'.[9] In February 1903 the Director-General of Military Intelligence, Sir W. G. Nicholson, appended to a memorandum by Balfour which contained the statement 'it appears that there is at the command of Great Britain no effective naval or military retort to a coup de main on Constantinople' a report from Kitchener, the GOC in Egypt, that the present garrison there 'is inadequate to safeguard that country from an over-sea raid of 5,000 European troops'.[10] So much for holding Egypt 'against all comers'.

It can be, and has been, too easily assumed that reports by branches of the service departments were automatically translated into policy. It has also been assumed that such reports as have been quoted extensively above have a greater degree of internal consistency than is in fact the case. The bulk of the argumentation of these reports weighs *against* the conclusion that the maintenance and development of a British position in Egypt could equalize or in some way offset Russia's development of a position of influence and control at Constantinople. Given the state of Egyptian defences as indicated by the reports of 1901 and 1903, the point of the bulk of the argumentation would appear to have been taken, in practice.

The conclusion that there was a switch of emphasis on the part of Great Britain may also have been encouraged by another assumption —that the British reconquest of the Sudan, which commenced in the spring of 1896 and culminated at the battle of Omdurman in 1898, must in turn have constituted the 'speedy and avowed revision of our foreign policy' which was one of the questions which it seemed to Salisbury in June 1892 were raised by the joint report of he DNI and DMI which he had just received.[11] The question of the Sudan, which was at any rate in the opposite direction to Constantinople, will be disposed of in due course. At this point it is necessary to address certain

31

other items which might appear to belie or to contradict the thesis that Constantinople remained the key to, and more important to the British than, Cairo.

The first item is the British Cabinet's refusal, late in 1895, to allow the British fleet to be sent through the Dardanelles in order to forestall a Russian descent upon Constantinople. The Rosebery administration had also rejected this course. On the later occasion, however, this refusal was the reverse of the decision which the Prime Minister and Foreign Secretary, Salisbury, wished to be taken. He described himself as 'cut to the heart', made bitter jokes to the effect that 'if our ships are always to be kept wrapped in silver paper for fear of their getting scratched, I shall find it difficult to go on defending the Naval Estimates in Parliament', and was scathing about 'the theological way' in which the First Lord of the Admiralty, Goschen, was 'absolutely confident' in his advisers' counsels.[12] Salisbury referred to this incident in a letter of 19 October 1897 to Sir Phillip Currie, the ambassador at Constantinople:

> I confess that since, some two years back, the Cabinet refused me leave to take the fleet up the Dardanelles, because it was impracticable, I have regarded the Eastern Question as having little serious interest for England.[13]

The second item is Salisbury's rejection of an overture from the Turkish government, made in London on 5 February 1896, which proposed negotiations for the conclusion of a convention on the basis of the maintenance and protection of the Sultan's rights over Egypt, and the adoption of measures to secure against all attack the freedom of communication between Britain and India. This overture, which reached the French ambassador in Constantinople before it reached the Turkish ambassador in London, was described by the former as admitting for the first time Britain's permanent occupation of the valley of the Nile. (Cambon ascribed this to Abdul Hamid's 'duplicité ordinaire' and as a bid to gain time in the Armenian question; it is more likely that the Sultan was attempting to play off England against Russia, whose ambassador at Constantinople, Nelidov, was pressing him to make arrangements with Russia equivalent to those of the Treaty of Unkiar-Skelessi of 1833; at any rate, Cambon immediately sent his wife to Cairo so that, under pretext of joining her, which he did two weeks later, he could try to counteract any such development by promoting a reconciliation between the Khedive and the Sultan.)[14] The Russian ambassador in London, de Staal, could only account for what he also took to be the Sultan's invitation to resolve the Egyptian issue in a sense favourable to England on the grounds that 'Abdul Hamid n'a plus la possession complète de ses facultés mentales'.[15] Salisbury, however, told the Turkish ambassador that he did not think much benefit would ensue from the reopening of the question, and further cooled the Turkish ardour by saying:

> With regard to the basis of negotiation which His Excellency had suggested, and which seemed to imply that our chief interest in Egypt consisted in the preservation of the through route to India, I said that no proposals could be entertained by H.M. Government which did not provide adequate security for the good government of the Egyptian people.[16]

Two weeks later, the Sultan announced his intention of dropping the question of negotiations about Egypt, 'for the present'.[17]

The third item is the series of public and private statements made by Salisbury in the last six months of 1896 to the effect that the British attitude towards Russia was undergoing a change. These include the letter written to Iwan-Muller of the *Daily Telegraph* on 31 August 1896 in which he said 'I do not know that I can sum up the present trend of English policy better than by saying that we are engaged in slowly escaping from the dangerous errors of 1848–56';[18] the Guildhall speech of 9 November 1896, in which he declared: 'It is ... a superstition of an antiquated diplomacy that there is any necessary antagonism between Russia and Great Britain';[19] and the 'wrong horse' speech made on the opening of Parliament in January 1897, in which he stated: 'I am bound to say that if you call upon me to look back and to interpret the present by the past, to lay on this shoulder or on that the responsibility for the difficulties in which we find ourselves now, the parting of the ways was in 1853, when the Emperor Nicholas's proposals were rejected. Many members of this House will keenly feel the nature of the mistake that was made when I say that we put all our money upon the wrong horse.'[20]

The final item is another sentence from Salisbury's letter to Currie of 19 October 1897. This goes: '... the only policy which it seems to me is left to us by the Cabinet's decision to which I have referred [is] to strengthen our position on the Nile [to its source] and to withdraw as much as possible from all responsiblities at Constantinople.'[21]

So far as the first item is concerned, it must be made clear that Salisbury's difference with his colleagues was not over *policy*, but rather over timing and over the assessment of the point reached in the developing situation in the Near East. Salisbury failed to persuade them of one thing only—that a Russian strike at Constantinople was imminent, and that giving Currie carte blanche to summon the fleet was therefore advisable. The Prime Minister admitted that he could not answer the questions 'Does Russia want to do it? Will she have the audacity to do it?'; but it seemed to him that the prudent course was to assume an unfavourable answer to those questions, and 'to take our precautions'. Goschen in particular considered Currie's telegrams, to which Salisbury referred him, concerning the danger to Europeans in Constantinople, as alarmist, and did not attach as much significance as Salisbury appeared to do to the commissioning of the Black Sea fleet in mid-November. The First Lord of the Admiralty stated the point at issue in a letter of 22 December: 'It was one possible movement, namely to pass our fleet alone through the Dardanelles, to which some of us were strongly opposed … No doubt action has become more and more difficult as Russian policy has developed itself more openly. Still is that policy a descent on Constantinople? Surely not.'[22] If the Russians *had* descended upon Constantinople there is no doubt as to what the unanimous response of Salisbury's Cabinet would have been. For on 19 February 1896, Salisbury recorded the Cabinet's agreement that the country might go to war 'in defence of the Straits to prevent them from being appropriated by Russia'.[23] Salisbury had seen the Austrian ambassador, Count Deym, at the beginning of February, and had told him that although Britain was unwilling to do as the Austrians wished,[24] and to go *further* than the common declaration of Mediterranean policy made in 1887, she was perfectly willing to renew the Mediterranean Agreements as they stood. The reluctance to undertake more binding engagements than already existed, said Salisbury, was *not* to be taken 'as a declaration that Great Britain would not act in defence of the Ottoman Empire against Russian aggression'.[25] Deym conveyed both to Goluchowski in Vienna and to his colleague Hatzfeldt in London accounts of these conversations which leave no doubt as to Salisbury's message. To the former, Salisbury was reported as saying that before the danger of Russia taking possession of Constantinople came about, 'English public opinion could have changed again and it was even to be expected that, as soon as the Russian threat to Constantinople became real, a revolution in public opinion would take place; therefore he did, on no account, intend to say that England would not go to war with Russia over Constantinople, but simply that he could not take the responsibility today of obliging her to do so.'[26] To Hatzfeldt, Salisbury was made to appear even more categorical:

> le comte Deym aurait alors demandé au Ministre, si le gouvernement anglais, en éludant les conséquences de l'ancien accord, entendait par là manifester l'intention de suivre en Orient une politique différente de celle qui avait été jusqu'alors convenue. Mais Lord Salisbury aurait nié cette intention *de la manière la plus formelle*, ajoutant que le comte Deym ne devait pas conclure de ses déclarations, qu'une intervention active de l'Angleterre contre une pénétration éventuelle

de la Russie en Orient appairait comme une chose définitivement
exclue pour l'avenir . . .²⁷

Following the Cabinet of 19 February, Salisbury again saw Deym and
maintained that he had 'said nothing which could throw doubt upon
the continuity of English policy in the East of the Mediterranean'; 'it
must not be assumed that [public feeling in England against the
Sultan of Turkey] would go so far as to make England indifferent to
the fate of his dominions also; or that they would see without concern
the control of the Bosphorus and the Dardanelles pass into the hands
of Russia'. Indeed, Salisbury 'thought it probable that a sight of any
attempt, if ever it was made, to make Russia master of the Straits, so
that her fleets could issue from them, and other fleets could not
penetrate them, would create a violent revulsion of feeling in England,
and as strong a desire for resistance as was aroused by the approach of
the Russian armies to Constantinople in 1878'.²⁸

The second item, the rejection of the Turkish overtures for a resolution of the Egyptian question, is also less straightforward than it
appears. For on 20 February 1896, in a letter to Cromer in Egypt
recounting an encounter with the French ambassador who had been
instructed, as Salisbury well knew, to raise the matter of evacuation
and who found that Salisbury still had plenty of cold water left, the
British Prime Minister nevertheless stated that with regard to the
removal of troops: 'I am not quite certain that, if we reserve a power
of re-entry and keep a garrison at Cyprus, something might not be
done.'²⁹

The third item may be treated in two ways. In the first place, there
are the statements from Salisbury over the same period of time, to the
opposite effect. For instance, when at Balmoral in September 1896 the
new Tsar, Nicholas II, advanced the view that the Straits should be
under Russian control, Salisbury countered:

> I asked him how he thought Rumania would like that arrangement
> . . . I asked him how he thought Italy and France would like the
> introduction of a new Naval Power into the Mediterranean . . . I
> pointed out that Italy, with her long line of maritime coast, had a
> deep interest in the question whether she would have to defend it
> against one Power or against two. France was mistress of the Med-
> iterranean so far as the States bordering on it in any one of the three
> Continents was concerned, and the introduction of Russia to the
> Mediterranean would be a challenge to that supremacy . . . I told
> him that Waddington [the French ambassador in London] had
> been very earnest in assuring me that on that point the policy of
> France was unchanged from what it was at the time of the Crimean
> War . . .

This was hardly encouraging. More was to follow, however, as Salisbury brought up the objections that Austria would have to the Tsar's proposal *as it stood*, Austria's impression being 'that the master of the Straits would have full control over the present Turkish dominions lying between Bulgaria and the Aegean Sea, and that Austria could not allow herself to be surrounded by Russia'. For good measure, Salisbury added that there would be something of 'bassesse' in British conduct if Britain left Austria in the lurch: 'I did not see how we could abandon the allies by whom we had stood so long.'[30] Again, later in the year, Salisbury wrote privately to Currie in Constantinople:

> As time goes on, the prospect that we shall ultimately keep the Straits out of the hands of Russia becomes fainter and fainter. But we must continue to hold the old language—for though our hopes may be fainter our views of policy are unaltered.[31]

He supplemented this, on 15 December 1896, with 'a line as to the Straits' for the benefit of the ambassador:

> It is for the moment a question between the alliance of Austria and Russia. Russia wishes for the whole passage—though for the time she might be contented with the Upper bit of the Bosphorus—Austria would look upon the concession to Russia of this limited instalment as involving the whole concession in the end—I do not believe that Austria would acquiesce in any portion of the Straits being surrendered to Russia ... It follows from this view that we cannot declare our advocacy of such a policy without forfeiting the alliance and provoking the distrust of Austria. She is our only real friend in Europe ... Therefore I shrink from any action which would weaken the tie that binds England and Austria together. It must show a definite and certain advantage sufficient to outweigh the loss of that alliance. A tentative adhesion to a policy of which, even if Russia accepted it, the future would be very doubtful, could offer no such advantage.[32]

In the second place, the particular extracts cited above from the letters and speeches of Salisbury are unrepresentative of the sense of the whole. For having condemned Palmerston to Iwan-Muller for making war with Russia, for insulting Austria, for ostentatiously making friends with France, and for setting up as an article of political faith the independence and integrity of the Ottoman Empire, Salisbury went on: '*But* the feud with Russia remains ... It is much easier to lament than to repair. It may not be possible for England and Russia to return to their old relations ... We may, without any fault of our own, find ourselves opposed to Russia on this question or that, in consequence of past commitments.'[33] In the Guildhall speech is a passage less well known, less frequently cited, but arguably of greater weight. It is where Salisbury commends the restraint of the powers in dealing with Turkey, for here he took the opportunity to point up the consequences of a lack of restraint—namely a European war—fear of which he had already smelt on Nicholas II at Balmoral.[34] He told his audience:

> you have to remember that if the result of your conduct is a war in the east of the Mediterranean it will not hurt you very much. It may affect some of your commercial and political interests, but no part of the territory of the Queen will be affected and no subject of the Queen will be less safe in his industry and his possessions. But if a war is aroused in the east of the Mediterranean, and spreads to the European empires which adjoin the Turkish Empire, vast populations will be threatened in their well-being, vast industries will be arrested, probably great territorial changes will be set on foot, and perhaps the vital existence of nations may be threatened. You cannot expect nations who are in *that* position to look upon the problems presented to *them* with the same emotional and philanthropic spirit with which you, in your splendid isolation, are able to examine all the circumstances.[35]

This was primarily for the ears of the Russian ambassador. The spectre of European war was meant to give the Russians cause to pause. The same applies to the 'wrong horse' speech, in which the very same threat was made. A mistake might have been made but, as Salisbury characteristically went on: 'It may be in the experience of those who [have backed the wrong horse] that it is not very easy to withdraw from a step of that kind when it has once been taken—*and that you are practically obliged to go on.*' Amongst other things, as Salisbury pointed out, 'We are still signatories of that Treaty' (the Treaty of Paris) and 'I do not see that we can take any other course except to exert what influence we may possess with the other Powers of Europe to induce them to press on the Sultan such reforms as may be necessary ...'.[36]

The final item, the sentiments expressed in Salisbury's private letter to Currie of 19 October 1897, is outweighed in importance by this language in the House of Lords on 19 January 1897, together with a statement in the same chamber on 19 March 1897. Salisbury might write of withdrawing as much as possible from all responsibilities at Constantinople: 'Of course this last can only be done gradually by reason of past engagements';[37] yet Salisbury, speaking as Prime Minister in the House of Lords, had on two occasions clearly given Parliament to understand that Her Majesty's Government regarded those 'past engagements' as binding both in the present and the future. In particular, on the second of these occasions, Salisbury had conspicuously taken issue with Lord Kimberley, who in a speech at Norwich had repudiated and utterly refused to accept a policy which was based upon the integrity of Turkey. Salisbury, recalling that Kimberley was a member of the government by which the integrity of Turkey was made part of the public law of Europe, said of the latter's 'momentous statement':

> ... if his declaration of the policy solemnly declared by his Party and the Foreign Minister in whom they trusted, before Europe, and agreed to by England in the face of Europe, is to be given up because only during two years there have been actions on the part of the Turkish Government which deserve the deepest condemnation, I think the policy was either very lightly adopted or very lightly abandoned ...

'This is the first time,' he continued, 'that a man who has been Foreign Minister and will probably be Foreign Minister again, declares in the face of Europe that he will disregard the signature of his country, and, not with the consent of the other Powers, but in their face, will tear up the engagements to which he has come.' Salisbury declared: 'I feel bound ... to separate myself as strongly as possible from that declaration.' The engagements into which the federation of Europe had entered must be respected:

> They must not be treated as pieces of waste paper to be torn asunder at will in obedience to any poetical, or rhapsodical, or classical feeling that may arise. It must not be denounced by the Ministers who have been partisans and colleagues of those by whom they were signed ...

He concluded:

> I cannot cavil because the noble Lord chooses to entertain notions which are certainly eccentric amongst statesmen, and which are entirely novel in himself. But I do cavil at the time he has selected to reveal them, and at the mode he has adopted to enforce them on his countrymen. At all events, I wish to say that we have no part in them, and that, whatever measures the Concert, the federation, of Europe may in the future, in its wisdom, think it right to take with respect to the integrity of Turkey, we will be no party to a violation of that integrity without their authority, consecrated as it is by congresses the most solemn, by negotiations the most important, by events which should have pressed their value upon every mind, and having been, in the minds of some of the greatest statesmen we have had—statesmen not belonging to this side of the House—the foun-

dation of European order, and of the policy which this country has consistently pursued.[38]

Such resounding declarations as this, together with the engagements of 1856 and 1878 which they invoked, severely limited the degree to which it would be possible 'to withdraw . . . from all responsibilities at Constantinople'. They place the sentences in question from the private letter to Currie both in perspective and in the shade.

II

The preceding pages sufficiently establish the degree of continuity that there was, in effect, in British foreign policy during this time, as well as the consistently greater importance which the British attached to Constantinople over Cairo. Effect, of course, is one thing. Intention is another. Lord Salisbury would appear, particularly from his parliamentary statements of early 1897, to have been a great man for continuity. In fact, and largely in secret, he stood for continuity *faute de mieux*.

The major problem inherited by Salisbury on his return to power in mid-1895 was that of order within the Ottoman Empire, and in particular the fate of the inhabitants of the province of Armenia. In his address to the House of Lords on 15 August 1895, in answer to the Queen's speech opening that session of Parliament, the Prime Minister summarized the position as follows:

> If, generation after generation, cries of misery come up from various parts of the Turkish Empire, I am sure the Sultan cannot blind himself to the probability that Europe will at some time or other become weary of the appeals that are made to it, and the factitious strength that is given to his Empire will fail it. I have earnestly tried to impress upon the Turkish Government the extreme gravity of the conduct which it has pursued; but at the same time to impress upon it that there is no Government more anxious to maintain the Ottoman Empire than the English Government. If I may speak for a moment of partisan matters, there is no Party more anxious than that with which I have the honour to be connected to maintain the integrity and the independence of the Ottoman Empire, which is sanctioned by treaties. The Sultan will make a grave and calamitous mistake if, for the sake of maintaining a mere formal independence, for the sake of resisting a possible encroachment on his nominal prerogatives, he refuses to accept the assistance and to listen to the advice of the European Powers in extirpating from his dominions an anarchy and a weakness which no treaties and no sympathy will

prevent from being fatal in the long run to the Empire over which he rules.[39]

In Salisbury's approach to this problem there are certain contradictions, certain discrepancies. They admit of only one resolution. For instance: in a series of letters to Sir Phillip Currie, who was calling for 'pressure of some kind' to be applied,[40] Salisbury revealed that he recognized the futility of single-handed naval action. The Sultan would have no motive for yielding to it, he told Currie, 'because he will know that the action of the fleet, that is to say a demonstration in Besika Bay, cannot be translated into anything which will do him actual harm'.[41] Salisbury had 'no aversion to use the Mediterranean fleet *if* anything is to come of it' but found repugnant the more likely scenario of 'a sojourn of three months in Besika Bay and then a retirement leaving nothing accomplished'.[42] As he told the Queen on 5 November, all the disorders in Turkey were inland and out of the reach of ships: there was therefore no field of action for a distant power like Great Britain.[43] On 17 December he wrote to Balfour that coercion of the Sultan 'would be of little use if it were possible'.[44] And yet, at the same time, in letters to the First Lord of the Admiralty, Salisbury was urging that the fleet be allowed to remain in Turkish waters for the sake of its 'effect on the Sultan's mind': the sight of it had, he said, had a very powerful and salutary effect in the Yangtze, and its presence appeared to be 'the only thing which really frightens the Sultan'.[45] Salisbury was to write in 1897 to Currie: 'As we never had the material force to insist upon [the Armenian reforms] the whole proceeding was somewhat illusory.'[46] If 'the action of the fleet' was 'illusory', what was real?[47]

This is merely indicative. There is a much more glaring discrepancy. On 3 December, Salisbury penned two important letters. To Goschen at the Admiralty he wrote:

> I should not think of proposing an isolated advance of the fleet through the Dardanelles in order to carry any point which is pending now. I only proposed it in case either nakedly, or under the pretence of suppressing disorder, Russia menaced a descent upon the Bosphorus. For this present matter ... we may need to coerce Turkey, but it will not be through the Straits ... I prefer Jeddah for our action, especially as we have already a very sound cause of quarrel there.[48]

To the ambassador in Vienna, Salisbury elaborated:

> If the Sultan continues obstinate I do not see any way out of this difficulty except by the use of force. Russia has forbidden us to force our way through the Dardanelles. Nothing then is left but to make

the Sultan feel at some other point of his dominions that he cannot inflict an insult on us without suffering for it. Action at other points of the Ottoman Empire has this advantage over a forcible passage of the Straits by ironclads, that it gives much less opportunity to Russia. The occupation of the Bosphorus by Russia would be an intelligible, and indeed a legitimate measure, if the Bosphorus were threatened from the south-west. But if there is no armed aggression in prospect through the Dardanelles, an armed rescue or defence of the Sultan would lose its meaning. If the 3 or 4 Powers were to appear off Smyrna or Alexandretta or Jeddah, Russia could not reasonably reply by anchoring off Yildiz, and the Sultan would not thank her if she did.[49]

An operation somewhere on the Red Sea or the Persian Gulf had been under consideration since August 1895. On the 12th of that month, Salisbury had described Jeddah to Currie as the most sensitive spot in the whole of the Sultan's body politic: 'the one thing the Sultan dreads is any hostile action in or near Arabia.'[50] The operation was billed by Salisbury as a safer alternative to action at the Straits, inasmuch as being outside the Mediterranean it was less likely to alarm and disturb Russia.

And yet, in August 1895, in the course of a letter instructing Currie to stiffen his tone about Jeddah, to become 'more and more menacing', Salisbury stated that 'the occupation of Jeddah may bring down the Turkish Empire with a run'.[51] In September, whilst admitting that the Russians were nervous lest the disaffection in Turkey spread contagiously and affect Russia's own Armenian population, Salisbury wrote complacently: 'Time is so much on one side that the excitement in Armenia, as it grows, becomes more and more distasteful to Russia. If we emphasise our demand by occupying some territory at Jeddah etc., it will add greatly to the excitement among the population, and to the alarm of Russia.' The fact that 'if [Russia] loses her head, she *may* make a desperate effort to reopen the Eastern Question and pacify Armenia after her own fashion' was a risk Salisbury was clearly prepared to run, a contingency he not only envisaged but welcomed.[52] His Guildhall speech of November 1895 was taken by contemporary foreign observers as an actual incitement of the Armenians.[53]

Salisbury wanted it both ways. The distinction he made, between action at the Straits and action elsewhere, he knew to be false. The Jeddah operation was not safer: it would have had exactly those consequences which the choice of it was supposed to exclude. It would have provided, though indirectly, through the response of the Turkish provinces, what British action at the Straits would have provided— an excuse for Russia to intervene. This in turn would have provided

Salisbury with what he wanted—an opportunity to *counter* the Russian action, which he could do only if the fleet was to hand in Turkish waters.

It was not Salisbury's practice to hold frequent Cabinet meetings.[54] After a meeting on 5 November 1895 the Cabinet was not summoned again until 8 January 1896. This is the less surprising in view of what Salisbury was contemplating. Only to Goschen, who confessed to him on 2 December that he 'should much like to know to what you expect our passing the Dardanelles, if we do pass them, to lead', did the Prime Minister indicate what was in his mind. He replied, the following day:

> ... my belief is that your refusal to give carte blanche to Currie means, or may mean, the surrender of Constantinople to Russia. If Russia gets there much before we do, so as to be able to man the Dardanelles forts with her own men, I take it that the place is impregnable. On the other hand if we get there first we are a good deal the strongest and our voice will be at all events very weighty in the ultimate arrangements that are made.[55]

It is not certain that Goschen registered this point. The importance of it can only be appreciated once it is recognized that, in late November and early December 1895, there was every prospect that, if the British fleet breached the Dardanelles, it would be accompanied, or closely followed, by units of the Austrian and Italian fleets. This prospect vanished on 12 December, and the tone of Salisbury's correspondence with his colleagues reflects this.[56] But until then, when it became clear that Austria would neither precede nor follow England into the Sea of Marmora, the most likely outcome, in Salisbury's view, of placing the fleet in the hands of Sir Phillip Currie was *not* a repetition of the Crimean War, which Salisbury described as a mistake but which both he and the Cabinet were prepared, for sound party political reasons, to repeat. The most likely outcome was the stuff that dreams are made on.

Salisbury's dream was that he was Lord Aberdeen, and that it was to him that Sir Hamilton Seymour had transmitted in 1853 the proposals of Tsar Nicholas I for the partition of the Ottoman Empire, and that he had accepted them. Whilst in opposition, in December 1894, Salisbury had confided to Currie:

> As far as I can judge, matters are coming to a crisis in your part of the world and the Turkish Empire will have to be reconsidered. I should myself very much prefer to give Russia the S[outh] and E[ast] of the Black Sea—and open the Dardanelles to all powers; set up some kind of autonomy in Egypt; take for ourselves the

southern slope of the Taurus with Syria and Mesopotamia—pay off
the French with Tripoli and a hunch of Morocco—Italy with
Albania, and Austria with Salonika. But alas! these are mere
dreams—nobody agrees with me ...[57]

This, nevertheless, was the foreign political vision that Salisbury
attempted to implement from his return to power. The German
ambassador Hatzfeldt was quite correct when he surmised that it was
'peut-être non sans intention' that Salisbury raised with him the question
of the partition of Turkey in July 1895.[58] When Salisbury declared
that he, Salisbury, would have accepted the proposals of Nicholas I;
when he tried to interest Austria in Salonika, France in Tripoli and
Morocco, Italy in Albania; when he told the Germans that it seemed
to him necessary to come to an understanding 'sur une sorte de plan
de partage en Orient et notamment dans le Méditerranée',[59] he was not
only dreaming aloud—he was seeking to establish who else shared his
dream, what chances it had, what 'ultimate arrangements' would best
suit the other parties in his projected redistribution of the territories of
the Porte.

In trying to have control of the fleet given to Currie and thereby
fulfil a personal assurance given to the Austrian ambassador on 16
November 1895 in response to a proposal for collective action at
Constantinople;[60] in speaking publicly in such a way as to incite the
Armenians and alarm the Russians, in considering operations against
what he had long considered to be the most sensitive spots of the
Turkish Empire,[61] Salisbury was trying to engineer the circumstances
necessary for the implementation of a solution of the Eastern question.

This is what he meant by the phrase 'ultimate arrangements'. As he
told Goschen on 3 December 1895, he was 'not at all a bigot to the
policy of keeping Russia out of Constantinople'. He was certainly not
so blindly and obstinately devoted to that policy that he was not
prepared to try to devise a better one. What he saw, in the state of the
Turkish Empire in the second half of 1895, was a chance to put the
clock back, to retrieve the mistake of the Crimean War, to avoid
having to risk repeating that mistake in the future. This would have
the incidental but not inconsiderable advantage of removing objections to forcing the Straits by removing the necessity to do so, for
though Salisbury's confidence, expressed in 1885 that the ironclads
would always get through,[62] never left him, not even at that earlier
date had he failed to recognize the 'great military objections' to that
scheme.[63]

The Russian ambassador in London, de Staal, wrote home on one
occasion during this crisis: 'Les hommes d'état anglais ont rarement la
vision des choses lointaines.'[64] This generalization certainly did not

apply to Salisbury, who had tried to make of the Armenian question a vehicle for the conversion of his dream into reality. This question gave him his chance to avoid committing what he had once called 'the commonest error in politics'—that of 'sticking to the carcasses of dead policies'.[65] His coûte que coûte approach in the early weeks of his third administration to the desiderata outlined to Currie whilst in opposition only six months previously is too much of a coincidence to be a coincidence. It is unrealistic, moreover, to dismiss the contents of Hatzfeldt's despatches on the grounds that he had a taste for intrigue or a tendency to invent, especially when the French ambassador gained much the same impression from *his* conversations with Lord Salisbury at this time.[66] There are tales from the Vienna woods, and there are tales from the Vienna woods.[67]

How close Salisbury came to achieving his goal may be gauged from a letter Currie wrote to him in February 1896, recounting a recent conversation with the French ambassador in Constantinople. Whilst 'talking of what *might* have been', Cambon had said:

> There was a moment, a very short one, when your fleet could have come in without opposition from any quarter, immediately after the outbreak [of disturbances] at Constantinople. If you had stated publicly that you were coming in simply to maintain order, and had invited Russia to do the same, she would have probably assented and would have ordered her Sebastopol fleet to cooperate with yours: and the other Powers would have followed suit.[68]

Salisbury's, then, was not an impossible dream. Like the dream of one Jay Gatsby, who when told 'You can't repeat the past' cried incredulously 'Why of course you can', at this time it must have seemed so close that he could hardly fail to grasp it. Hence his bitterness towards his colleagues for their lack of trust, their cowardice, their obtuseness, a bitterness all the more understandable when it is appreciated that, like Gatsby, Salisbury as we shall see[69] had come a long way. Also like Gatsby, Salisbury held to his dream. He held to it through the Cabinet's refusal to give Currie carte blanche and the defection of Austria in December 1895. He held to it through the early part of 1896, withstanding Austrian pressure to change the Mediterranean agreements into instruments that would commit Britain to a war whose object was the upholding of the *status quo*, for the *status quo* was incompatible with the dream.[70] He held to it through June 1896, when he established that the French had no desire for Syria.[71] He held to it through August 1896, telling the Kaiser who, following a fresh outbreak of unrest in the Turkish capital, had wondered if a pacific solution to the Eastern question might not be found in opening the Dardanelles to all nations and destroying the forts by which they were guarded: 'Our view is, and has been for some time past in favour of opening the Straits to all nations. The opening of the Dardanelles alone would be a less complete and satisfactory arrangement: but it would be acceptable to H.M.G. The strongest objection will be found with Austria.'[72] He held to it through his interview with the Tsar at Balmoral in September 1896, referring him to the proposals of 1853, encouraging him to square Austria with 'compensation and security' in return for Russian control of Constantinople, to which Salisbury raised no objection provided it was made 'part of a general arrangement';[73] subsequently expressing the hope that Nicholas II would not be talked into inaction and still later making an unflattering comparison of him with Nicholas I for failing to rise to the occasion and accept the role cast for him.[74] He held to it through October 1896, when the Jeddah operation (directed towards an area about which the Sultan was sensitive, as Salisbury had written in 1891,[75] because it was an area to which the Caliphate might well be transferred) had to be abandoned.[76] He held to it, following up his bid at Balmoral to persuade the Tsar to consider the deposition of the Sultan[77] by putting forward on 20 October a plan which would allow for the imposition by such forces as the powers had at their command of any decisions at which they arrived unanimously.[78] Having heard on 3 November that Nelidov supported these proposals, hoped that spheres of influence within which each power would be at liberty to intervene could be agreed upon before what he saw as the inevitable early break-up of the Ottoman Empire occurred, and had gone to St Petersburg to persuade the Russian Government to adopt them,[79] Salisbury nevertheless wrote to Currie on 23 November:

> If the question of cutting up the Sultan becomes practical the sovereignty of the Straits may become both for us and for Austria a question of compensation. Of course we must say nothing of such views for the present, as Austria would imagine we were going to desert her, which is certainly very far from being the case.[80]

Having heard on 3 December that Cambon in Constantinople believed that if the outlet of the Bosphorus into the Black Sea were in Russian hands this 'would be generally acceptable as a solution';[81] having heard on 20 December that Nelidov, back in Constantinople after success at St Petersburg, had revealed that his instructions did not specifically mention the maintenance of the integrity of the Ottoman Empire, and that he had 'casually observed': 'it might happen that coercion if it had to be applied would necessitate some interference with the integrity of the Empire and that therefore it might be safer not to make integrity an absolute condition ...';[82] having heard on 24 January 1897 that Pobdonostsev, though not himself of the

45

school which wanted to extend Russia to the shores of the Bosphorus, still could see no reason why Russia and England should not come to a friendly understanding with regard to their respective spheres of influence,[83] Salisbury nevertheless endeavoured to persuade the Austrians, when they renewed their proposals of twelve months previously, to view with equanimity the prospect of a combined naval force sailing with impunity and without Russian interference towards Constantinople.[84]

Salisbury, then, held to his dream of what would have been the best of all possible solutions of the Eastern question. (So, for that matter, did Currie, who was of course Seymour in their mutual dream.)[85] He held to it, refusing to admit that it was already behind him. So *he* beat on, boat against the current, borne back ceaselessly into the past.

Even whilst restating the old, mistaken, Palmerstonian policy in March 1897, Salisbury was careful to condemn Kimberley only for his unilateralism: only for being prepared '*not* with the consent of the other Powers' to tear up engagements. Salisbury himself declared only that 'we will be no party to a violation [of the integrity of Turkey] *without* their authority'.[86] He still wanted it both ways. Unless and until the powers agreed to a partition of Turkey, which in the circumstances that he was at some pains to devise would be the only alternative to war, Salisbury remained a great man for continuity.

III

What would the 'very weighty voice' of England secure, or procure, for her in the 'ultimate arrangements' dreamed of by Lord Salisbury? What would *she* get by way of 'compensation'? What, in particular, was the place, and fate, allocated to Egypt?

In September 1886, when trying to convince Lord Randolph Churchill of the virtues of the plan that he had even then for forcing the Dardanelles, Salisbury had written: 'England will be mad if she does not get something.'[87] In 1895–7 his outlook was equally positive. No more than in the previous decade, however, did he regard the partition of Turkey as an opportunity to obtain Egypt. In August 1885 he had written to Drummond Wolff in Cairo:

> My great objection to fixing a date for our evacuation of Egypt is, that relief from our hated presence is the one bribe we have to offer, the price we have to pay for any little advantages we may desire to secure. If we once part with that, we practically go into the market-place empty-handed.[88]

Ten years later, Egypt was still 'disponible'. As indicated in Salisbury's

46

letter to Currie of 14 December 1894, and as confirmed later by his letter to Cromer of 20 February 1896 contemplating withdrawal of the garrison to Cyprus, Salisbury was not interested in retaining Egypt. For 'the southern slope of the Taurus with Syria and Mesopotamia', Egypt could certainly be given up, and even Constantinople handed over to the Russians, and this latter without the stipulation that the Straits must be open to all nations. As Salisbury told Hatzfeldt in August 1895, he did not regard the Mediterranean as a source of compensation: 'mes convoitises sont ailleurs, plutôt du côté de l'Euphrate'.[89] Mesopotamia was the main 'little advantage' that Salisbury desired to secure. Mesopotamia, the future importance of which to Great Britain was recognized by the Russian ambassador in Berlin, Osten-Sacken, in February 1896, and by the French ambassador in London, Courcel, in June 1896,[90] would overcome the political objections to the evacuation of Egypt which the years of occupation had produced amongst the British public.[91] Hatzfeldt, who joked in December 1896 that Salisbury's interest in a rumoured Russian map dividing Turkey showed that he wanted to know that his desires concerning 'l'Euphrate etc.' had been taken into consideration in St Petersburg according to his wishes, was rewarded with a nod of approval and, according to the ambassador, 'un regard d'intelligence'.[92] Only British control over that part of Arabia would counter the influence of Constantinople in the Levant and compensate for the substitution of Russian for Turkish influence there. This was *the* way to secure not so much the *route* to India as — India itself. British control, or rather the absence of anyone else's control, over the East African and Arabian littorals was of more importance to the British Empire than any position in Egypt. Domination of the Red Sea was more important than control of the Suez Canal.[93] The installation of the Commander of the Faithful in Mecca would, as Asquith's Liberal Government recognized in its turn when embarking upon its war with Turkey in October 1914,[94] render all these objectives the easier of accomplishment.

In 1885 the Liberal Government's proposed expedition into the Sudan to rescue General Gordon paled into insignificance against the prospect of an Anglo-Russian war arising out of an incident on the Afghan frontier; some Cabinet ministers were prepared to resign if an expedition was announced at that time, against that background; others were prepared to withdraw from Egypt altogether; it was, moreover, admitted by all save the Prime Minister, Gladstone, that England's power of offence against Russia was nil—a view that had been expressed by the Intelligence Department of the War Office in the previous year.[95]

In 1895-6 the Conservative Government's priorities were the same as those of its predecessor of a decade earlier. As G. N. Sanderson has handsomely demonstrated, no decision was taken in March 1896 to reconquer the Sudan. The British Government's directive that the Egyptian Army make a 'demonstration' in order to relieve pressure on the Italians in Abyssinia was a move in Salisbury's European diplomacy. Its object was to help maintain good relations with the Triple Alliance, through a gesture that the Italians would appreciate and for which the Kaiser had also asked.[96] In Salisbury's oriental mind, however, it may well have become, as it developed, and once it had been carefully established that there were at that time in the Sudan very few real dervishes, as opposed to the numbers invented for the purpose, an opportunity to impress 'the Oriental mind'; a chance to achieve at small cost and no risk the sort of 'prestige effect' to which he believed 'the Asiatic populations' were peculiarly susceptible; an effort to restore, in the eyes of the whole Moslem world, some of the 'face' that Great Britain more than any other European power had lost through leading the conspicuously unavailing efforts to bring the Sultan of Turkey to order, and thereby bolster the British position in India. For, as Salisbury had written to Monson on 3 December 1895: 'Nothing ... is left but to make the Sultan feel at some other part of his dominions that he cannot inflict an insult upon us without suffering for it.'[97]

The pace of the Sudan expedition was enormously slow. In this connection it must be remembered that operations against Turkey were still being considered until October 1896. The Egyptian Army took two and a half years to reach Omdurman, where at last it found some dervishes on whom to take revenge. By the time Salisbury envisaged going beyond Berber, at the end of 1896, the railway that was to ensure that the long shadow of General Gordon was not cast across what had commenced as a route-march of no more than thirty miles, with orders to retire, offered the prospect of eventual junction with the long-delayed south-north railway from Uganda by means of which the British, and Salisbury in particular, had long intended to approach and dominate an area less important to the Mediterranean than to the Horn of Africa.[98] This is the perspective in which to place, and keep, Egypt.

Notes

I would like to thank Dr E. D. Steele and Dr H. P. Cecil for their help in the preparation of this essay, and Geoff Waddington for his translations of the Austro-Hungarian documents.

1. A. J. P. Taylor, *The Struggle for Mastery in Europe 1848–1918* (Oxford, 1954), p. 368; J. A. S. Grenville, *Lord Salisbury and Foreign Policy* (London, 1964), p. 97; P. Marsh, 'Lord Salisbury and the Ottoman Massacres', *Journal of British Studies*, xi (1972), p. 75; J. Gooch, *The Plans of War* (London, 1974), p. 238. See also A. F. Al-Sayyid, *Egypt and Cromer* (London, 1968), p. 51: Salisbury 'realised that the defence of Constantinople, for England alone, was out of the question, and that England's hope now lay in using Egypt as the core of Mediterranean defence plans, and as the key to India'.

2. Report by Chapman (DMI) and Bridge (DNI), 18 March 1892, para. 8: printed in C. J. Lowe, *The Reluctant Imperialists* (London, 1967), ii, pp. 88–91.

3. Memo by Salisbury, 4 June 1892, printed in ibid., pp. 85–8. My italics.

4. A. J. Marder, *An Anatomy of British Sea Power 1880–1905* (London, 1940), pp. 221–8, 244.

5. Hatzfeldt to Holstein, 31 July, to Hohenlohe, 31 August 1895, in J. Lepsius, A. Mendelssohn-Bartholdy, F. Thimme (eds.), *Die Grosse Politik der europaischen Kabinette 1871–1914* (Berlin, 1922–7), vol. 10, nos. 2372, 1774/2392; subsequent quotations from G.P. are from the French edition, in order to reduce the number of languages involved.

6. Printed in Marder, op. cit., pp. 247–8; my italics.

7. Ibid., pp. 569–77; *Eothen* was a well-known travel book by Charles Kinglake.

8. Ibid., pp. 578–80.

9. J. Gooch, op. cit., pp. 239–40; memorandum by Military Intelligence Department, 31 May 1901, P.R.O., C.A.B. 38/1/6.

10. C.A.B. 38/2/1.

11. See note 2. An effort was made to retrieve all the copies of this report in mid-1892, when a new government was imminent. The officer given this task was told by the principal private secretary to the Secretary of State for War to mind his own business, and that as the government was changing the report had been put away somewhere; the First Lord of the Admiralty said he could not lay his hands on his copy; Lord Salisbury thought his was at home in the pocket of an old gardening coat; Mr Balfour had no idea what had become of his. Lt.-Col. B. A. H. Parritt, Intelligence Corps, *The Intelligencers—the Story of British Military Intelligence up to 1914*.

12. See M. M. Jefferson, 'Lord Salisbury and the Eastern Question, 1890–98', *Slavonic Review*, XXXIX (1960), p. 50.

13. Hatfield House MSS A138/43.

14. *Documents Diplomatiques Francais 1871–1914* (Paris, 1929–62), First Series, xii, no. 301, P. Cambon to Berthelot, 7 Feb. 1896. Currie MSS P.R.O., F.O. 800/114, notes of late January and early February 1896; F.O. 424/186/39, Currie to Salisbury, 10 Jan. 1896; Hatfield House MSS A136/11/18, Currie to Salisbury, 17 Feb., 5 March 1896; F.O. 407/136, Cromer to Salisbury, 2 March 1896.
15. A. Meyendorff (ed.), *Correspondance Diplomatique de M. de Staal* (Paris, 1929), ii, p. 310, de Staal to Lobanov, 21 Feb. 1896.
16. F.O. 407/136, Salisbury to Currie, 18 Feb. 1896.
17. Ibid., Currie to Salisbury, 3 March 1896.
18. G. P. Gooch and H. W. V. Temperley (eds.), *British Documents on the Origins of the War, 1898–1914* (London, 1926–38), vi, Appendix iv.
19. See *The Times*, 10 Nov. 1896.
20. *Hansard* (4th ser.), XLV, cols. 28–9 (19 Jan. 1897).
21. Hatfield MSS A138/43.
22. Ibid., 3M/E, Salisbury to Goschen, 28 Nov., 3 Dec.; Goschen to Salisbury, 30 Nov., 2 Dec., 22 Dec. 1895.
23. Ibid., A84/10, Salisbury to the Queen, 19 Feb. 1896.
24. G.P., 11, no. 2568, Eulenberg (German Ambassador to Vienna) to M.F.A., 23 Dec. 1895.
25. B.D., viii, pp. 4–5, Salisbury to Monson, 4 Feb. 1896.
26. Printed by E. Walters in *Slavonic Review*, XXIX (1950–1), pp. 279–83, Deym to Goluchowski, 6 Feb. 1896.
27. G.P., 11, no. 2664, Hatzfeldt to Hohenlohe, 8 Feb. 1896, my italics.
28. B.D., viii, p. 5, Salisbury to Monson, 26 Feb. 1896; *Slavonic Review*, XXIX, pp. 285–6, Deym to Goluchowski, 5 March 1896. Another minister had told Deym exactly this a few days earlier: G.P., 11, no. 2668, Hatzfeldt to Hohenlohe, 24 Feb. 1896.
29. Hatfield MSS A113/6, Salisbury to Cromer, 20 Feb. 1896.
30. Salisbury's conversations with the Tsar at Balmoral, 27 and 29 Sept. 1896, printed by M. M. Jefferson in *Slavonic Review*, XXXIX (1960), pp. 216–22.
31. Hatfield MSS A138/34, Salisbury to Currie, 23 Nov. 1896.
32. Ibid., /35.
33. See note 18; my italics.
34. Hatfield MSS A138/32, Salisbury to Currie, 5 Oct. 1896.
35. See note 19; my italics.
36. See note 20, col. 29; my italics. A. Cunningham, 'The Wrong Horse? a study of Anglo-Turkish relations before the first world war', *St. Antony's Papers*, no. 17, Middle Eastern Affairs no. 4 (Oxford, 1965), pp. 60–1.

37. See note 21.
38. *Hansard* (4th ser.), XLVII, cols. 1009–14 (19 March 1897).
39. Ibid., XXXVI, cols. 49–50 (15 Aug. 1895).
40. Hatfield MSS A135/29, Currie to Salisbury, 5 Aug. 1895.
41. Ibid., A138/7, Salisbury to Currie, 12 Aug. 1895.
42. Ibid., /11, Salisbury to Currie, 13 Sept. 1895.
43. Ibid., A84/3, Salisbury to the Queen, 5 Nov. 1895.
44. Balfour MSS (B.L. Add. MSS 49690), Salisbury to Balfour, 17 Dec. 1895.
45. Hatfield MSS 3M/E, Salisbury to Goschen, 1, 9 Oct. 1895. On 5 October the Sultan did ask for the fleet to be withdrawn: Marder, op. cit., p. 243.
46. Hatfield MSS A138/43, Salisbury to Currie, 19 Oct. 1897.
47. The mystification of Goschen continued in December when Salisbury claimed that the Cabinet's aversion to any solitary action on Britain's part in the Straits amounted to bidding him to 'sit still' in the Armenian matter: ibid., 3M/E, Salisbury to Goschen, 19, 23 Dec.; Goschen to Salisbury, 22 Dec. 1895.
48. Ibid.
49. Ibid., A119/4, Salisbury to Monson, 3 Dec. 1895. Yildiz was the Sultan's palace in Constantinople.
50. Ibid., A138/7; A138/10, Salisbury to Currie, 27 Aug. 1895.
51. Ibid., A138/7.
52. Ibid., A138/11, Salisbury to Currie, 13 Sept. 1895; A129/34, Salisbury to Lascelles, 17 Sept. 1895.
53. Meyendorff, op. cit., ii, pp. 289–90, 293–4, Lobanov to Staal, 8, 22 Nov. 1895.
54. Balfour MSS (Add. MSS 49778), Hamilton to Balfour, 12 Jan. 1896.
55. Hatfield MSS 3M/E, Goschen to Salisbury, 2 Dec., Salisbury to Goschen, 3 Dec. 1895.
56. Ibid., Salisbury to Goschen, 12 Dec. 1895; A138/19, Salisbury to Currie, 17 Dec. 1895. Marder, op. cit., p. 244, is mistaken about the timing of the withdrawal of the British fleet. This took place in early January 1896: F.O. 195/1910, Salisbury to Currie, 9 Jan. 1896.
57. Salisbury to Currie, 14 Dec. 1894. This letter is to be found on p. 184 of the edition prepared for publication by Dr H. P. Cecil of the fifth volume of Lady Gwendolen Cecil's biography of Lord Salisbury.
58. G.P., 10, no. 2372, Hatzfeldt to Hohenlohe, 31 July 1895.
59. Ibid., nos. 2375, 2381, Hatzfeldt to M.F.A., 3 Aug., to Holstein, 5 Aug. 1895.
60. F.O. 78/4884, Salisbury to Monson, no. 117, 21 Nov. 1895. Late

in February 1897 the Foreign Office received notification that Mr Bryn Roberts, who was following up a recent speech given by Hanotaux, intended to ask the Under-Secretary of State for Foreign Affairs, in a parliamentary question, 'whether in or about November 1895, or at any other time, one of the Great Powers of Europe proposed to the others that the Dardanelles should be entered by or with the sanction of the Powers, with a view of coercing Turkey or with any other view; and, whether H.M.G. considered any such proposal and whether they supported or opposed it'. Two answers were prepared. The first, in the hand of the Permanent Under-Secretary, Sir Thomas Sanderson, read: 'Such a proposal was made by the Austro-Hungarian Govt. in November 1895 in view of apprehended disturbances at Constantinople. Lord Salisbury did not give any specific opinion but merely said that H.M. Ambassador would be authorised to join in any measures which the six Representatives might consider necessary for the protection of European interests.' The second, begun by Curzon and finished by Salisbury, read: 'I regret that I can give the hon. member no information on the first part of the question. No such proposal has been submitted to H.M.G.' Curzon delivered the second answer in the House of Commons on 26 February 1897: ibid., f. 167, f. 168; *Hansard* (4th ser.), XLVI, cols. 1260–1.

61.   Hatfield MSS A76, Salisbury to White, 14 Sept. 1891.

62.   Ibid., A44/34, Salisbury to Drummond Wolff, 1 Sept. 1885: 'If ever we did go to war with Russia we should in one way or another, force a passage.'

63.   Ibid., D/15–19, Salisbury to Lord Randolph Churchill, 28 Sept. 1886.

64.   Meyendorff, op. cit., ii, p. 307, Staal to Lobanov, 18 Jan. 1896. Hatzfeldt gave a different opinion of Salisbury to Hohenlohe on 31 August 1895 (G.P., 10, nos. 1774, 2392): 'C'est un homme qui aime à envisager les problèmes de l'avenir et à les discuter.' The French Ambassador Courcel wrote to Herbette on 20 June 1896: 'Vous savez que [Salisbury], esprit philosophique et meditatif, aime les solutions, les difficultés tranchées, les situations nettes. Le provisoire, dont les Anglais s'accommodent d'habitude presque indéfiniment, l'obsède et lui pèse; il aspire à y mettre fin.' D.D.F. (1st ser.), xii, no. 410.

65.   Printed in K. Bourne, *The Foreign Policy of Victorian England 1830–1902* (Oxford, 1970), p. 409, Salisbury to Lytton, 25 May 1877.

66.   D.D.F. (1st ser.), xii, no. 88, Courcel to Hanotaux, 12 July 1895.

67.   See A. P. Thornton, *For the File on Empire* (London, 1968), p. 23. W. L. Langer in *The Diplomacy of Imperialism* (New York, 1935),

pp. 197–201, and G. N. Sanderson in *England, Europe and the Upper Nile 1882–99* (Edinburgh, 1965), p. 227 are sounder on this than Jefferson in *Slavonic Review*, 1960, pp. 44–60 and J. A. S. Grenville, op. cit., pp. 24–37. Salisbury's minute: 'I never hinted anything of the kind' on Currie's letter of 2 Sept. 1895 (Hatfield MSS A135/42) informing him of Austrian concern that the Germans had received a hint that England might abandon her conservative policy in the East and agree to hand over Constantinople to the Russians, is by no means conclusive. This much-travelled report was a travesty of the conversation it purported to describe. It presented the concession of Constantinople tout court, and not as part of, and dependent upon, the partition that Salisbury had in mind. Salisbury may even have considered that he had done rather more than 'hint': for according to Hatzfeldt, Salisbury had started from the assumption that the Russians would obtain access to the Mediterranean, and had indicated that this was perfectly acceptable to him. G.P., 10, nos. 1774, 2392. In a letter from Salisbury to the Duke of Devonshire on 3 Dec. 1895 is the following passage: '... I always speak quite openly to Hatzfeldt. I have known him well for ten years—and have found him quite trustworthy: and so I speak more freely to him than to the other Ambassadors.' Devonshire MSS 340.2674.

68. Hatfield MSS A136/12, Currie to Salisbury, 20 Feb. 1896.
69. See note 82.
70. loc. cit., Deym to Goluchowski, 5 March 1896.
71. D.D.F. (1st ser.), xii, no. 410, Courcel to Hanotaux, 20 June 1896.
72. F.O. 78/4884, Salisbury to Lascelles, 28 Aug. 1896.
73. See note 30; also Hatfield MSS A138/32, Salisbury to Currie, 5 Oct. 1896.
74. G.P., 12, no. 3078, Hatzfeldt to Hohenlohe, 9 Dec. 1896.
75. Hatfield MSS A76, Salisbury to White, 14 Sept. 1891: 'Arabia is the terror of the Sultan's dreams—the joint in his armour: because it is in Arabia that some day an opposition Commander of the Faithful will be manufactured ... to the Sultan, to whom his position as the first Moslem of the world is everything this rivalry [with Britain as a protector of Islam in India and Egypt] is both exasperating and alarming.'
76. Hicks-Beach MSS, Gloucestershire Record Office PCC 69, Salisbury to Hicks-Beach, 5 Oct. 1896.
77. Hatfield MSS A138/32, Salisbury to Currie, 5 Oct. 1896.
78. *Accounts and Papers 1897*, vol. CI, Turkey no. 2, no. 2.
79. F.O. 78/4724, Currie to Salisbury, 3 Nov. 1896. F.O. 65/1516, O'Conor to Salisbury, 18 Nov. 1896.

80. Hatfield MSS A138/34, Salisbury to Currie, 23 Nov. 1896. Salisbury's determination to use 'material force' is well illustrated by the drafting of his letter to O'Conor of 25 November, F.O. 65/1513.

81. F.O. 78/4884, Currie to Salisbury, 25 Nov. 1896 (recd. 3 Dec.).

82. F.O. 78/4724, Currie to Salisbury, 20 Dec. 1896.

83. F.O. 65/1531, O'Conor to Salisbury, 24 Jan. 1897.

84. B.D., ix (i), pp. 775–6, Salisbury to Rumbold, 20 Jan. 1897; F.O. 78/4884, Salisbury to Rumbold, 27 Jan. 1897. On 11 Jan. 1897, Currie had telegraphed what purported to be an account of a Russian Crown Council of 5 Dec. 1896 at which Nelidov's proposal for the occupation of Constantinople by Russian troops had been 'rejected by a narrow majority' (F.O. 78/4813). Salisbury made no comment on this information, which came from the Italian ambassador at Constantinople. Nelidov, whose positive interpretation of his instructions was well known, was still the man on the spot in the Turkish capital, where both the French and British ambassadors were sympathetic to his scheme. (The Italian ambassador's information was wrong: the Russian Crown Council had adopted Nelidov's proposal: see Langer, op. cit., pp. 336–9. On 15 Jan. 1897, Salisbury refused any kind of financial assistance to Turkey: minute on Currie to Salisbury, 15 Jan. 1897, F.O. 78/4813.)

85. Currie had replied to Salisbury's account of the Balmoral interviews with the Tsar that it was at least 'some comfort that [Nicholas II] admits the possibility of the present misgovernment bringing the status quo to the ground' (Hatfield MSS A136/52, Currie to Salisbury, 15 Oct. 1896); in Dec. 1896 and early Jan. 1897 he was supporting a proposal of Nelidov which the Austrian representative said 'would tend to the disintegration of the Ottoman Empire' (F.O. 78/4724, Currie to Salisbury, 25 Dec. 1896; Hatfield MSS A137/2, Currie to Salisbury, 3 Jan. 1897); he continued well into Feb. 1897 to look for occasions which would merit the release to him of the fleet (Ibid., /9, Currie to Salisbury, 26 Feb. 1897; Ibid., A138/40, Salisbury to Currie, 28 Feb. 1897).

86. My italics; see above, pp. 37–39.

87. Hatfield MSS D/15–19, Salisbury to Lord Randolph Churchill, 28 Sept. 1886. Lord Randolph resigned.

88. Ibid., A44/33, Salisbury to Drummond Wolff, 18 Aug. 1885.

89. G.P., 10, nos. 1774, 2392, Hatzfeldt to Hohenlohe, 31 Aug. 1895.

90. According to Osten-Sacken: 'L'occupation de (Egypt) a beacoup perdu de son importance pour les Anglais, par le fait qu'étant en possession de la mer rouge, ils seront toujours maîtres du passage

du canal de Suez. Aujourd'hui, d'ailleurs, leurs vues sont dirigés sur une autre route des Indes, celle de l'Euphrate et du golfe Persique.' Osten-Sacken even reflected Salisbury's interest in the fate of the Caliphate. (D.D.F. (1st ser.), xii, no. 310, Herbette to Berthelot, 23 Feb. 1896; Hatfield MSS A138/43, Salisbury to Currie, 19 Oct. 1897.) Courcel wrote to Hanotaux on 20 June 1896: 'La possession de l'Arabie et du Golfe Persique établira [England] primauté incontestée sur les populations musulmanes et assoira son règne sur le littoral entier de la mer des Indes, mettant entre ses mains, comme une chaîne presque ininterrompue, toutes les côtes et toutes les peninsules, depuis le cap de Bonne-Esperance jusqu'au detroit de Singapour ... La Méditerranée elle-même, dans les conditions nouvelles que laisse entrevoir l'avenir, perd pour l'Angleterre l'importance qu'elle a eue pendant le XVIII et le XIX siecles ... Angleterre, le jour ou les chemins de fer de la vallée de l'Euphrate seraient construits, voudrait nécessairement exercer sur cette route de l'Inde une influence à l'abri de contestation.' (Ibid., no. 410.)

91. W. S. Blunt, *My Diaries 1888–1914* (London, 1919–20), i, p. 227.
92. G.P., 12, no. 3086, Hatzfeldt to Hohenlohe, 22 Dec. 1896. He concluded: 'il ne serait pas donc guère douteux que le premier ministre anglais soit assez disposé à s'entendre pacifiquement avec la Russie sur le partage de héritage turc, si la Russie lui consent et révanche des dédommagements correspondants sur lesquels il est déjà visiblement fixé lui-même.'
93. Hence the concern expressed in minutes by Salisbury and Sanderson, 6 May 1896, on Currie's telegrams nos. 336 and 350 (F.O. 78/4707) lest Russia establish a coaling station in the Red Sea.
94. F.O. 371/2138/44231, draft by Grey of tel. no. 462 to Mallet, 29 Aug. 1914; draft by Holderness (Under-Secretary, India Office) for Foreign Office, 13 Oct. 1914, India Office MSS, L/P & S/10/558/4051, f. 125.
95. A. B. Cooke and J. R. Vincent (eds.), *Lord Carlingford's Journal—reflections of a Cabinet Minister 1885* (Oxford, 1971), pp. 82–91; C.A.B. 37/13/36; and see Memo on the Mediterranean 14 Dec.(?) 1885 by H. W. Gordon in Hicks-Beach, MSS D2455 PC/PP 51.
96. G. N. Sanderson, op. cit., pp. 242–52.
97. Hatfield MSS A119/4; and F.O. 78/4884, Salisbury to Monson, tel. no. 92, 2 Dec. 1895.
98. G. N. Sanderson, op. cit., pp. 240, 243–6, 249, 253, 256; A. T. Matson, 'A further note on the MacDonald Expedition, 1897–99', *Historical Journal*, xii, no. i (1969), pp. 155–7.

Negotiating the Anglo-Egyptian Relationship between the World Wars

ODED ERAN

Introduction

Egypt's strategic importance for the British Empire was underscored by the events of the First World War and its aftermath. The British Government did not contemplate deviating from the guidelines prescribed by Granville in January 1883, which called for '... the duty of giving advice with the object of securing that the order of things to be established shall be of a satisfactory character and possess the elements of stability and progress'. Furthermore, in early 1884, Granville instructed Lord Cromer, then Sir Evelyn Baring, Consul General, to make sure that in important questions affecting the administration and safety of Egypt, Her Majesty's Government's advice should be followed.[1] This advice was offered generally to able and dedicated British officials, who were employed by the Egyptian Government. Stability and good management became synonymous with security of the Imperial route from Great Britain to the Indian Ocean. The Protectorate declared over Egypt on 18 December 1914 was, therefore, a logical consequence, though it fell short of the demand voiced for total annexation of Egypt to the Empire. Whatever the words of the Protectorate's declaration were, there was certainly no intention in London of changing the nature of the Anglo-Egyptian relationship, neither before nor after the war. Sa'd Zaghlul's demand, delivered as soon as the war ended to Sir Reginald Wingate, then the High Commissioner, for a 'complete autonomy' (probably a euphemism for independence) came almost as a surprise.[2] Preoccupied with a shattered Europe, Lloyd George and Balfour had no brief for these demands or the conveyors of them, but they were forced to deal with the events which followed and which were described by Egyptian historians as the '1919 Revolution' and by British diplomats and politicians as 'riots' and 'disturbances'. It was the cumulative impact of various factors which led to the events of 1918–19. For the Egyptians it was the combination of the sacrifices in human and material resources they had made during the war, the sentiment created by President Wilson's 14 points and the strange coalition between the ever-scheming Egyptian monarch and the newly-founded party, the Wafd. Great Britain emerged victorious, though bruised, from the war, with a weakened resolution to invest in protecting the Empire. The quality and number of British officials willing to serve in Egypt fell sharply, as did British steadfastness in preserving the stability and determination to work for long-term solutions. From the end of the First World War, Great Britain was to conduct a battle of retreat. There was no change in the premises underlining Egypt's importance to the Empire, but the new attitude was one of considering the security of the Imperial route from a very narrow point of view—one which separated the Canal from the rest of Egypt.

The Milner Mission and his
Negotiations with Zaghlul and Adli

Following the events of 1919, His Majesty's Government decided to send a mission to inquire into the causes of these disorders and to report on the form of constitution which, under the Protectorate, would be best calculated to promote peace, prosperity and development of self-governing institutions and the protection of foreign interests.[3] When the conclusions of the mission, headed by Lord Milner, were published, it soon transpired that they seriously deviated from the mandate given to it. Milner, an imperialist in his views, came under the influence of J. A. Spender, editor of the *Westminster Gazette* and member of his mission, Gilbert Clayton, then adviser to the Egyptian Ministry of the Interior, Valentine Chirol, then *The Times* correspondent in Cairo, and Cecil Hurst, Legal Adviser to the Foreign Office and also a member of the mission. The common denominator among these four persons was the view that Egypt's acquiesence in Great Britain's retaining forces on its soil could be obtained in return for reducing Great Britain's involvement in the Egyptian administration.[4] This quid pro quo, coupled with reduction of forces and their being deployed in agreed zones, was the basis for the treaty policy which the mission advocated pursuing. It should be emphasized that members of the mission were not unaware of the adverse effects for Egypt and the Egyptians resulting from a further decline in Great Britain's influence. They admitted almost explicitly to sacrificing the Egyptians and especially the fellahin and the poorer classes to the old abuses.[5] All the various rounds of negotiations which followed have to be examined in the light of the conclusions reached by the Milner Mission. These conclusions reflected the incompatibility between maintaining a policy based on conceptions which dictated firm control

Oded Eran

in Egypt, and the lack of will to face the consequences of such a policy. Conversely, the Sudan was the one issue on which the Commission was unequivocal in its opposition to any concessions and to any alterations in the way the country's affairs were conducted. No British negotiator made any major deviation from the guidelines on the Sudan laid down by the Milner Commission.

In the 1919 Versailles Peace Conference, Zaghlul utterly failed in enlisting international support and sympathy for his demands. He was thus forced to negotiate with Milner. The latter submitted to Zaghlul, on 17 July 1920, a memorandum, the main points of which were as follows: (1) Great Britain would guarantee Egypt's integrity and independence. (2) No political treaties would be signed between Egypt and third countries without Great Britain's consent. (3) Egypt would confer upon Great Britain the right to maintain forces on Egyptian soil, 'place or places' to be determined. (4) Great Britain would support Egypt's request to abolish the Capitulations. (5) Egypt would agree to the appointment of Judicial and Financial Advisers.

Zaghlul countered on the very same day with his own draft.[6] He requested Great Britain's recognition of Egypt's independence, abolishment of the Protectorate and withdrawal of forces within a certain period. Zaghlul agreed, however, to a British military post on the 'Asiatic side' of the Canal, i.e. Sinai. In his draft, Zaghlul agreed to Great Britain's exercising the Capitulation on behalf of other powers. A defence pact would be signed for 30 years. Milner, who admitted in a letter to Zaghlul five days later to making concessions '... as to the wisdom of which we felt very doubtful ...', had to inform Zaghlul that his, Milner's, document represented the full length to which his government was willing to go, a phrase which became worn out during the next 16 years of negotiations. Failing to reach an agreement with Zaghlul, Milner had turned to Adli Pasha and soon, on 18 August 1920, delivered to him too a memorandum, containing the following points: (1) Great Britain would recognize Egypt's independence as a constitutional monarchy in return for Great Britain's right to safeguard its special interests and represent Capitulatory Powers. (2) Egypt could have independent representation in foreign countries. (3) The location of the British forces stationed on Egyptian soil should be determined in a treaty. (4) The offices of the Judicial and Financial Advisers would be retained, though in a reduced form. (5) Possible termination, within two years of a treaty being signed, of foreign officials' employment. (6) Closing down of Consular Courts.[7] In a separate letter bearing the same date, Milner made it clear that the status of the Sudan could not be negotiated, though he assured Egypt on the question of water supply. Between July and August 1920, Milner had agreed to limit the presence of the British forces in Egypt

58

to one area only, had reduced the function of the Financial and Judicial Advisers and was willing to let Egypt terminate the employment of foreign officials within two years following a treaty. The greater concessions offered to Adli were meant to bolster his position since the Foreign Office officials viewed him as the only Egyptian politician who could see an agreement through in face of the Wafd's opposition. Zaghlul, however, torpedoed the concessions, declaring them insufficient and unacceptable.[8] Negotiations between Zaghlul and Milner were resumed, despite the former's disruptive tactics, later in October 1920. Zaghlul demanded the limitation of the functions of the Financial Adviser to the administration of the Caisse de la Dette (a body established in 1876 with the aim of collecting revenues assigned for payment of Egypt's various international debts) and those of the Judicial Adviser to the administration of laws affecting foreigners. He also asked for some commitment that Great Britain would annul the Protectorate. This time Milner stood his ground and refused to make alterations in the August 1920 memorandum.

The 1921 Negotiations

In January 1921, His Majesty's Government decided to invite an official Egyptian delegation notwithstanding that Egypt had not adopted the Milner Mission's proposals. Allenby had used the instructions to invite such a delegation to mount an attack on the Protectorate. Curzon, by then the Foreign Secretary, asked his Cabinet colleagues for support of Allenby's position: 'Why worry about the rind if we can obtain the fruit?'[9] On 21 February 1921 the Cabinet adopted, against Lloyd George's and Churchill's opposition, a resolution which admitted the Protectorate to be of unsatisfactory status, thus giving away the rind prior to ascertaining that the fruit was obtainable. But this commitment, to abolish the Protectorate, was not sufficient. Caught between the wish to support Adli and the desire to reach an agreement backed by Zaghlul, the British Government decided to opt for the first course. Zaghlul, for his part, was determined to undermine Adli both as Prime Minister and as a likely head of the Egyptian official delegation. In this he was aided by Sultan Fu'ad, who was bent on eliminating any centre of power which could challenge his position. Zaghlul's obstructive tactics, however, created a rift within the Wafd's own ranks, and some of his lieutenants, Ali Sha'rawi, Muhammad Mahmud and others, left the party.[10] This did not deter Zaghlul from resorting to violence once the official delegation was composed. When Adli arrived in London in July 1921, this violence had sown the seeds of doubt as to his ability to carry through any agreement in Egypt. Nevertheless, Curzon's draft was adopted by the Cabinet, albeit as the maximum of concessions. This draft proposed the replacement of the Protectorate by a treaty, deployment of British forces in places and for periods to be determined, limited Egyptian conduct of foreign relations, an effort by Great Britain with the other Capitulatory Powers to abolish the Capitulations, maintaining the functions of the Financial and Judicial Advisers to the Egyptian Government, and the subordination of Egyptian forces in the Sudan to the Governor-General. At the talks held in July and August 1921, Adli opposed the deployment of British forces in the cities, pressing for their confinement to the Canal area. He also demanded the curtailment of responsibilities held by the Judicial and Financial Advisers. The Egyptian delegation asked for the annulment of the title High Commissioner, and was reluctant to discuss the issue of the Sudan. Late in August 1921 the two delegations dispersed without achieving much progress. After the Egyptian delegation left for Europe, the Foreign Office and the Residency debated the line to pursue. Scott, Acting High Commissioner, admitted that further concession-making could lead Great Britain to be '... filed out, bag and baggage, with nothing to the credit side'.[11] Yet, knowing that his government was unwilling to provide money and troops in order to enforce a policy, he advocated giving the Egyptians 'complete internal independence' and withdrawal of British troops to the Canal. Selby, then First Secretary in the Residency, repeated the same line of argument—underlining the dangers of more violence, or 'resort to the Irish methods' as he termed it. Referring to a visit in September–October 1921 of four Labour Members of Parliament who encouraged Zaghlul, he wrote: 'If we cannot contain such influences ... we should take the opportunity, professed by the negotiations with Adly Pasha, to "get out" on the best terms we can.'[12] In London, Murray, Head of the Egyptian Department, who dominated British policy towards Egypt for a decade, between 1920 and 1931, was drafting the 'irreducible minimum'. The main points were: (1) Retention of troops in the Canal area. (2) Retention of troops for an agreed period at Alexandria. (3) Right to veto employment of foreigners in Egypt's public services. (4) *Status quo* in the Sudan. (5) Compensation for retiring British officials. Advocating concessions, Murray and Duff Cooper, then in his department, claimed that a policy based on force might create another Ireland, though without an Ulster. Negotiations were resumed on 12 October 1921 but led nowhere. Adli had not budged and Lloyd George decided to '... put his foot somewhere, and he has chosed Egypt for the operation'.[13] On 10 November 1921, Adli was given a draft treaty which he formally rejected five days later. His reasons were the British insistence on military presence at all times and all places, the need to consult the High Commissioner on foreign affairs and the title 'High Commissioner' itself, and that the solution proposed for the problems of the Capitulations and protection of foreigners were incompatible with Egypt's sovereignty. No mention, Adli added, was made of Egypt's 'incontestible' rights in the Sudan. Adli resigned on 11 December 1921. The pattern of British eagerness to reach an agreement with any government in Egypt and the treaty being an issue pitched and tossed between rival politicians in Egypt was already set. It lasted until the end of 1935.

By the end of 1921 the policy based on concession-making to moderate Egyptian politicians in return for their willingness to assume control of the Egyptian Government and co-operate with the High Commissioner was proven bankrupt. In June 1921, Allenby had already revealed his alternative policy. The policy was devised, in fact, by Sir William Hayter, the Legal Adviser to the Egyptian Finance Minister, and was founded on two ideas: first, a unilateral British declaration of Egypt's independence and, second, the protection of British interests through an agreement to be signed within ten years after that unilateral step had been taken. During this period the Egyptians were also expected to enact a new and working constitution.[14] The initial reaction of the British Government was negative but Allenby was undeterred, and the failure of the talks with Adli only encouraged his campaign for the approval of the unilateral policy. In a series of actions, which included Zaghlul's deportation to the Seychelles on 20 December 1921 and allowing Sarwat Pasha to have a preview of his draft declaration and proposal, Allenby had stepped up his campaign to get an approval for his proposal. During January and February 1922, Allenby tendered his own resignation and was joined by other senior British officials in the service of the Egyptian Government. He despatched messages to the Cabinet containing warnings as to the events likely to occur if his proposals were declined. Allenby was invited to come to London for what almost everyone believed to be his last journey as High Commissioner. However, he had his way and finally mustered support for the unilateral abolition of the Protectorate. Four issues remained reserved for the discretion of His Majesty's Government until an agreement could be signed with the Egyptian Government. These four issues were: (1) The security of the communications of the British Empire. (2) Defence of Egypt against all foreign aggression or interference. (3) Protection of foreign interests and minorities. (4) The Sudan.

The Protectorate was terminated officially on 28 February 1922. Allenby's success in swerving the Cabinet was due largely to the Irish situation. Faced with estimates and evaluations of the likely events had he continued to oppose Allenby's proposal, Lloyd George opted for what seemed the easier course. Yet this course resolved none of the difficulties. The Egyptian reaction was at best lukewarm, as the so-called newly-acquired independence did not mean an evacuation of the British forces. For the British, the 1922 Declaration could not provide the legitimization for the military presence in Egypt. It further thickened the confusion as to where, when and how Great Britain's representatives were to involve themselves in Egypt's affairs with the object of attaining the British objectives, objectives which had not been modified. Between February 1922 and January 1924, Allenby saw three Egyptian Prime Ministers resign (Sarwat Pasha, Tawfik Nessim Pasha and Ibrahim Yehia) in circumstances which could not always be defined as falling within the domain of the four reserved points, yet in which Allenby found himself actively involved. Another noteworthy development was the promulgation of the new constitution.[15]

The MacDonald-Zaghlul Negotiations, 1924

Zaghlul returned from his exile on 17 September 1923. A month later, following the general elections in Britain, Ramsay MacDonald became Prime Minister. In January 1924 the Wafd won an overwhelming majority in the elections and Zaghlul became Prime Minister. MacDonald, who—while in opposition—had remarked that a Labour Government would be engaged 'without a moment's delay' with a view to reaching a treaty,[16] faced a request from Zaghlul for such negotiations. Selby, now MacDonald's Private Secretary, wrote to Clark Kerr, Allenby's deputy, that it was necessary to prepare the ground because a breakdown of the negotiations could lead to disastrous consequences.[17] MacDonald himself told Allenby he wanted to have some indication that Zaghlul's aspirations did not conflict too hopelessly with the 'irreducible requirements', these being, according to Murray's opinion, the Sudan and the location of the British forces. A treaty could be signed, Murray claimed, only when British forces were withdrawn from Cairo. For that the War Office officials accused Murray of 'abandoning the substance for the shadow'. MacDonald decided, however, to adopt Murray's views as guidelines for his forthcoming talks with Zaghlul. The latter, on the other hand, made it clear that he was going to London '. . . to obtain the full independence of Egypt and the Sudan . . .'[18] There could therefore be no room for illusion as to the likely results of the diametrically-opposed positions concerning the Sudan. If that was not enough, Zaghlul's attempts to extract a commitment from His Majesty's Government—that the 1922 Declaration was not binding—prior to his going to London should have served as an early warning.

At their second meeting, on 29 September 1924, Zaghlul submitted to MacDonald the following demands: (1) Withdrawal of British forces. (2) No control by the British Government over Egypt and the two offices of Judicial and Financial Advisers to be abolished. (3) No limitation on Egypt's conduct of foreign relations, and (4) Abandonment by Great Britain of its claim to protect foreigners and to defend the Suez Canal. The third and last meeting between the two took place on 3 October 1924 and was a matter of form as there was no possible way to bridge the gap between the two positions. Zaghlul ended by saying that the door was still open but one of them had to get thinner in order to get through, to which MacDonald replied that the British way of dealing with narrow doors and stout men was to widen the doors rather than cutting down the men.[19]

Zaghlul could claim, upon returning to Egypt, that he had not given away any of Egypt's rights; however, he had forfeited an opportunity to reach an agreement with the most sympathetic British Government and Prime Minister he could negotiate with. Was Zaghlul gambling on getting most of his demands, counting on MacDonald's clouding political skies; was he, Zaghlul, intimidated by elements at home against making any concession, especially on the Sudan; or was it a calculated move by a shrewd politician interested only in his political survival? The three propositions are plausible. At any rate, Selby was right and the consequences of the breakdown were disastrous. On 19 November 1924, Sir Lee Stack, Governor-General of the Sudan, was murdered and no further attempts to negotiate a treaty were made until 1927. Allenby, in retaliation for the murder, imposed limitations on Egypt's involvement in the Sudan affairs, thus adding another bone of contention to the negotiations to come.

George Lloyd, who succeeded Allenby as High Commissioner in summer 1925, pursued a course based on the wider interpretation of the 1922 Declaration. In Lloyd's view this instrument went further than declaring Egypt's constitutional independence. It also contained the intention to attain an amicable arrangement with Egypt. In 1926 he acted upon this understanding of the 1922 Declaration and forestalled Zaghlul's bid to become Prime Minister. Lloyd claimed that this would inevitably lead to greater difficulties in the bilateral relations and in Great Britain's capability to carry on its responsibilities assumed in the Declaration. Lloyd's term as High Commissioner was characterized by his attempt to strengthen the British presence in Egypt. In 1926–7, Lloyd conducted protracted negotiations to prolong the contracts of many British officials with the Egyptian Government.[20] On this issue, as on the question of British control over the Egyptian Army, Lloyd found himself at loggerheads with the Foreign Office officials who claimed that the 1922 Declaration was a good horse but not one that should be ridden to death. While Chamberlain

more often than not supported his officials, Lloyd could rely on the
interventions in his favour by Amery and Churchill, whenever he
applied for a Cabinet ruling. The differences between Lloyd and the
Foreign Office were described by Murray in June 1927:

> We believed that it was not only a mistake but quite futile to
> attempt to stand rigidly on the precise letter of a unilateral docu-
> ment drawn up five years ago, because nothing in this world stood
> still, and that therefore we should strive to move forward from the
> 1922 Declaration in the direction in which it clearly pointed.
>
> This, I gathered, was not Lloyd's conception, and he aimed
> rather at recovering the complete status quo ante February 28,
> 1922, in respect of the reserved subjects where he considered that
> our position had been seriously eroded during the last five years.[21]

These differences developed into a Foreign Office crusade against
Lloyd and against the widely-held belief that he had tried to restore
Cromerism. But it was not until 1929, when Labour returned to power
in Britain, that Lloyd was made to resign.

The Negotiations between Sarwat and Chamberlain, 1927–8

The moving force behind this round of negotiations was Chamberlain,
acting upon the advice of the same officials who had advocated vast
concessions for a treaty a few years earlier, namely Lindsay, Murray
and Selby. Lindsay, by then Ambassador to Berlin, provided the
reasons for this renewed effort:

> The irregularity of the British position has always been a source of
> embarrassment to His Majesty's Government in the past and almost
> certainly will be so again in the future. The Great Virtue of a
> treaty—even of a treaty as drafted by Sarwat—is that it gives Great
> Britain a legal title for what she holds. It would be worth the while
> of His Majesty's Government to pay a heavy price and to overlook
> many defects in the treaty itself if, in a negotiated document, Egypt
> would consent to enter the orbit of the Empire.[22]

The Egyptian Prime Minister, Sarwat Pasha, accompanying his
king on a trip to Europe, was asked by Chamberlain on 12 July 1927
to make 'precise indications as to the lines on which negotiations
should proceed in Cairo'. Instead he submitted, on 18 July 1927, his
full draft for a treaty. In it Sarwat confined the presence of British
forces in Egypt to the region of the Canal for a limited period, which
he orally specified to be 3–5 years. He further eroded the functions of

the Judicial and Financial Advisers to mere reporting and he wanted the *status quo ante* 1924 to be restored in the Sudan. The counter-draft proposed by the Foreign Office contained in principle the withdrawal of troops from Egypt's urban centres but, like Sarwat's draft, had no reference to the protection of foreigners. It contained a phrase about the interests of the two countries in the Sudan being served on the basis of the 1899 Convention.

Zaghlul Pasha died on 23 August 1927, and Sarwat asked for postponement of negotiations until the question of the Wafd's leadership had been settled. During the internal debates which went on in the Foreign Office, both Murray and Chamberlain cast doubts upon Sarwat's ability to have the treaty adopted in Egypt. Nevertheless the concession-making process continued, following Lindsay's counsel: 'I can hardly believe that he will be able to put his treaty through in Egypt, and I hope His Majesty's Government will not break a willing horse's back by overloading it. They will never get a better one.'[23] Several reasons caused this futile exercise to be continued. It seems that the main one was Chamberlain's hope to buy time and temporary peace while he was occupied by other problems. As he explained to his colleagues,[24] British interests were under attack in China, in Europe and the Balkans, and at the same time Poland and Lithuania posed grave problems. Relations with the United States were also entering a difficult phase. A new argument was added with the veiled threat that an approach by Egypt to the League of Nations could produce undesirable results for Great Britain. Chamberlain also produced a partisan argument maintaining, correctly as it turned out, that the Labour Party, once in power, would make greater concessions and it was therefore better to pre-empt this by reaching an agreement then.[25] When George Lloyd, the High Commissioner, submitted to Sarwat the revised draft on 3 December 1927, he emphasized that it represented the limit to which His Majesty's Government were willing to go. The process continued, though it became clearer that Nahas Pasha, being a new leader of the Wafd, could not associate himself with a treaty that was not his own doing and that King Fu'ad, loyal to his reputation, was not going to let Sarwat reach a treaty. On 4 March 1928, Sarwat resigned and another round of negotiations came to an unsuccessful end.

The Henderson–Mahmud Negotiations, 1929

In June 1929, MacDonald became Prime Minister, Arthur Henderson Foreign Secretary, and hopes were aroused in Egypt, boosted, no doubt, by Lloyd's dismissal. The preliminary discussions with British diplomats in Cairo held by Mahmud (the Egyptian Prime Minister since June 1928) revealed a significant departure from the final position reached in the talks with Sarwat. Mahmud emphasized the Egyptian desire to join the League of Nations, its desire to see the withdrawal of British forces to the Canal area for a period to be negotiated, and for the relaxation of various measures of control still held by Great Britain such as ending the contract of the two Advisers with the Residency (they had a double contract—with the Egyptian Government and the Residency, simultaneously), and phasing out British officials and police officers. While Mahmud repeated Sarwat's demands for the return of the *status quo* in the Sudan, the Foreign Office's recommendation was to pursue the negotiations: '... *nothing will have been "given away" which was not given away nine years ago when the Milner proposals were published'.*[26] The draft treaty submitted to Mahmud contained, therefore, the elements both of withdrawal east of Tel-el-Kabir (later defined as east of 32°) and restoration of the *status quo* in the Sudan, including the return of the Egyptian battalion, which was ordered back to Egypt following Stack's assassination. Mahmud initialled the draft on 15 July 1929, thus creating a curious situation whereby in Britain His Majesty's Government were unaware of this development while on the Egyptian side only the king was informed of the negotiations and then only on 9 July 1929.

When the debate on the draft ensued in the Cabinet, the military experts expressed once again their opposition to the concessions made by the Foreign Office. They were overruled, however, and on 24 July 1929 the draft was adopted. MacDonald's position at that juncture deserves some attention. While attending the Cabinet meeting during its debate on other items on the agenda, he excused himself when the issue of Egypt came up. Following the leakage of the draft, MacDonald wrote to Henderson: 'Mahmud is a drowning man and if we help him it must be at the expense of our own lives.'[27] MacDonald was, no doubt, expressing his displeasure with the draft's details ('It was the Sarwat mistake over again'[28]), but he was also expressing his assessment that, faced with the Wafd's opposition, Mahmud could not get an approval for the treaty in Egypt. That was apparent to Henderson too, who was conducting conversations with Makram Ubeid of the Wafd while Loraine held talks in Cairo with Nahas Pasha. Mahmud himself resigned on 4 October 1929, leaving behind him yet another unsigned draft for an Anglo-Egyptian treaty.

The Henderson–Nahas Negotiations, 1930

Given Henderson's eagerness to reach a treaty and Loraine's optimistic despatches from Cairo,[29] a new round of negotiations was almost inevitable. The elections in Egypt, in December 1929, produced an overwhelming victory for the Wafd and Nahas formed his government on 1 January 1930. While the new Egyptian Prime Minister refused to commit himself to the 1929 draft treaty, Loraine continued to mislead his government in the belief that the Wafd's objections to it could be removed 'firmly but also good humouredly'. Firmly but consistently, Nahas refused to give any indication as to his views, though a well-educated guess could be made as to their nature. Yet the absence of an early understanding with Nahas did not prevent his arrival in London late in March 1930. The draft treaty he submitted at the opening of the negotiations on 2 April 1930 was rejected by Henderson. The most difficult elements in the Egyptian draft were the exclusivity Egypt claimed in defence of foreigners and their property in Egypt, the removal of the need to use only British services in training the Egyptian Army, the confinement of the British Army in Egypt to the area of Port Fu'ad and only until Egypt would become capable of defending the Canal with its own means. No mention was made of the employment of various British officials which was discussed in previous rounds. On the Sudan, Nahas suggested a 'joint and effective' administration.

The two main issues during the 1930 negotiations were the British forces in Egypt and the Sudan. The Egyptian case for stationing the British forces in one area rested on the Milner Mission's conclusions (as interpreted by the Egyptians) and on an alleged report by Mahmud that during his negotiations the British delegation agreed to such an agreement.[30] Nahas added that Great Britain's demands, which were based, as he claimed erroneously, on wartime conditions, gave a veto power to Great Britain over the defence of the Canal which was an 'exclusively Egyptian waterway'. This, he added, was in contradiction to the 1888 Constantinople Convention which provided that no one nation should have any special right to the Canal (except Egypt's right of property). But Nahas finally agreed to the deployment of 8,000 British soldiers and 3,000 airmen in the area of Ismailia and ten miles westward. In accepting this, the British delegation had gone back on the position held only several months earlier that those forces should be deployed all over the area between the Canal and the 32° line (running about ten miles east of the Canal). There is one possible explanation, but very little evidence supporting it, that the willingness to concentrate all the British forces in one area stemmed from the wish to turn them into a rapid deployment force to be sent to troubled areas in the Middle East.[31] Such an idea could have emerged, given the impact of the circumstances under which four British battalions were despatched in 1929 to quell the Arab–Jewish disturbances. It is more likely, however, that Henderson's eagerness to reach an agreement had motivated the concessions. Among these concessions was the willingness to reopen, 20 years after the treaty came into force, the question whether the Egyptian Army could ensure by itself the safety of the Suez Canal.

The stumbling block proved, however, to be the question of the Sudan, where it seemed that the Egyptian delegation had no room to manoeuvre. Given the relative greater intransigence on this question than on the question of the British military presence on Egyptian soil, it may be assumed that the Wafd, in general, was in 1930 still under the influence of the events in 1924 and the urge to rectify the situation created by Allenby's ultimatum. On the British side, Henderson's hands were tied by the fact that MacDonald was not expected to approve a concession on this issue, nor was King George V. The demands made by Nahas in 1930 included the appointment of an Egyptian as Deputy-Governor, the return of the Egyptian forces to the Sudan and the unlimited right of Egyptians to emigrate to the Sudan. No mention was made of the 1899 Convention. Nahas' constraints in this issue were best illustrated by his wish to interrupt the talks in order to send two emissaries to Egypt to ascertain with his colleagues what concessions he could make.[32] Pressure which was exerted, on the other hand, on Maffey, the British Governor-General of the Sudan, to agree to various concessions proved to be of no avail and he rejected any change in the status or application of the 1899 Convention. On 8 May 1930, the negotiations ended in failure,[33] though the Egyptian side could justifiably claim that, given the experience of previous rounds of negotiations, they established new grounds for future negotiations.

The 1936 Negotiations and the Treaty

Nahas resigned on 17 June 1930, and Ismail Sidki, who became Prime Minister, appealed for the resumption of treaty negotiations. The suspension of the 1923 Constitution by Sidki made his credibility as a party to negotiations the subject of a lengthy debate in Whitehall. It is possible that Sidki's wish to negotiate was an attempt to acquire official British recognition and thereby to strengthen his credibility in Egypt. The single meeting in Geneva between Simon, the Foreign Secretary, and Sidki on 21 September 1932 did not constitute much of a treaty negotiation though it rekindled the heated debate between the Foreign Office and the military establishment over the concessions to be made for a treaty.

Sidki resigned in September 1933 and, following an interval during which Lampson replaced Loraine as High Commissioner, the British representatives in Cairo, imposing their will on the king, brought about the appointment of Tawfik Nessim as Prime Minister in mid-November 1934. By doing that it became imperative for them to sustain their chosen Egyptian premier almost at all costs. In January

1935, the Wafd called for the restoration of the 1923 Constitution. In making full use of his weakness, Nessim, not even consulting the High Commissioner, forwarded the request to King Fu'ad. Soon it became clear to Lampson that the Wafd and Nessim were collaborating. Aware of this collaboration were other politicians in Egypt like Mahmud and Ali Maher, all jockeying for power during the second half of 1935, all calling for reinstating the 1923 Constitution and a full use of the new situation which developed in the Mediterranean and East Africa as a result of Italy's invasion of Abyssinia.

Given the importance of the Suez Canal, the lack of naval bases in the eastern Mediterranean and Italy's presence in Libya, Egypt acquired added strategic importance. Great Britain's need to maintain a secure base in Egypt did not escape the notice of the various rival political parties and figures in Egypt. On 12 December 1935, Nessim submitted to Fu'ad a rescript for the 1923 Constitution's return while Nahas, on behalf of a United Front, submitted a letter to Lampson calling for a treaty negotiation with England on the basis of the 1930 draft. Lampson's advice to London to accept the demand was based very much on the opinion of Keown-Boyd, that a refusal would lead to riots and disturbances on the scale of 1919, the quelling of which would need no less than a division.[34] In East and North Africa, Italy was massing troops, in Egypt the king, the Prime Minister and the various political forces found themselves, though for different reasons, on the same side, and in England Hoare, the Foreign Secretary, had to resign in the wake of the scandal over the Hoare-Laval agreement. Facing these circumstances, the British Government accepted the demand for negotiations and for the first time in the history of these negotiations instructed the High Commissioner to conduct them himself in Cairo. Even before these negotiations started Vansittart, the Permanent Under-Secretary, criticized Lampson for not taking a firmer and clearer line in his dealings with the Egyptians and for continuously speaking of 'the pass having been sold' by his predecessor.[35] In the preliminary debates between the Residency and the Foreign Office in London, Lampson had no difficulty in obtaining various concessions. His proposals for the broader negotiating tactics were approved by the Cabinet in the beginning of February 1936.[36] This contained three stages: (1) Suggesting a 'pool' of British and Egyptian forces for the defence of Egypt until the Egyptian Army could assume such responsibility. (2) A fall-back position of withdrawal from Cairo to Abbassiyya and Hilmiyya (two suburbs of Cairo). (3) And if this (2) proved unobtainable, suggesting 'as our absolute minimum' withdrawal to Helwan (south of Cairo). Lampson was also instructed to seek to attain the objectives listed by the chiefs of staff such as the right to reinforce troops in Egypt in any emergency apprehended by the British, the attempt to remove any time limit on the British forces' stay in Egypt, the exclusivity for the responsibility of defending the Canal, a high limit, if at all, on the size of the British Army in Egypt, exclusivity in training and equipping the Egyptian Army, etc. The chiefs' of staff minimum, consistent with safety of withdrawal from Cairo's centre to the two suburbs, was thus over-ruled. Very little remained of this list by the time the negotiations started on 2 March 1936, following Lampson's and Eden's work. By the end of March 1936, Lampson was already asking for authorization to propose stage (3), that of withdrawal to Helwan, but it was clear that even this proposal would not bridge the gap as Nahas Pasha demanded withdrawal in peace time to the Suez Canal area, though he was suggesting an increase in numbers. When, in mid-April 1936, Nahas rejected course (3) (withdrawal to Helwan), Lampson did not repeat his proposal to maintain liberty of action but rather pressed for more concessions.[37] Abandoning the fall-back positions in the negotiations had, on the other hand, put Eden in a difficult situation in the Cabinet. He was citing the traditional advantages of a treaty, i.e. normalizing Great Britain's position in Egypt, reduction of 'nationalist feeling' and an improved image of Great Britain in the 'public opinion of the world'. To this he added the need to offset Italy's anti-British activities in Egypt. By the spring of 1936 Italy had completed her occupation of Abyssina and on 2 May 1936 Emperor Haile Selassie left his country. On 7 March 1936, Hitler ordered his troops to occupy the demilitarized Rhineland, and Spain was already showing the signs of the troubles to come. Nahas manipulated, in a heavy-handed manner, the international situation which was in his favour and there was no reason for him to accept at that stage the initial British proposals. Eden was, therefore, asking his Cabinet colleagues to give up the demand to retain troops in Alexandria, the opposition to a time limit for the treaty and to the approach to the League of Nations if agreement could not be reached, after 20 years, on the number of troops and positions needed to defend the Canal. Eden warned his colleagues that '... faced with a proof of British hostility to Arabian aims and aspirations, it would be a signal for an outburst in Palestine and Syria. It could hardly fail to have serious repercussions in Iraq and Saudi-Arabia.'[38] This warning, false or true, was amplified by the need to despatch, during May–June 1936, 4,000 soldiers from the garrison in Egypt to quell the new wave of Arab–Jewish riots in Palestine. Towards the end of May 1936, the British Government adopted a new position—that of agreement to withdraw from Cairo if troops could be retained in Alexandria and agreement to refer the issue of British troops and their positions to the League of Nations 20 years after the signature of the treaty, if agreement could not be reached by the parties. Yet Nahas remained adamant. Defence of the Canal, he claimed, was the responsibility of Egypt alone and its sovereignty over the Suez Canal could not be renounced.[39] Given this attitude, Lampson's view was that there were three alternatives: break, delay or compromise. While he did not divulge his preference, he added the following:

> His Majesty's Government can best judge what result a breakdown of treaty talks would have on Arab world. According to our information course of Anglo-Egyptian conversations is being followed closely in neighbouring Arab countries and a breakdown would probably have adverse reaction in these quarters. A hostile Egypt would no longer maintain its present fairly restrained attitude towards anti-British movements in Palestine.[40]

Lampson did not provide evidence to substantiate his statement. The riots in Palestine erupted before, after and regardless of the treaty of 1936, and there is very little evidence showing an interest in the rest of the Arab states in that period as to the progress of the Anglo-Egyptian talks. It was part of an attempt to create an atmosphere of goodwill in the hope of improving the terms of the treaty.[41]

Lampson was invited to London for consultation and his presence there gave impetus to more changes in the British position. The cue was given by Prime Minister Baldwin: '... politically it was most important to conclude a treaty. It would be worth a great deal to us in the Near East if we made an alliance with a country of Moslem population.'[42] Towards the end of June 1936, the Cabinet agreed to a withdrawal from Alexandria as well, after a period of 7–10 years, and to the submission to the League of Nations of any disagreement, after 20 years, of the question whether British troops were still needed for the defence of the Canal. Equipped with these concessions, Lampson was able to reach an agreement on most of the military issues on 6 July 1936. Nahas, too, had made some concessions, such as his agreement to refer to the Geneifa area south of the Great Bitter Lake for the redeployment of the British troops rather than specifying one single locality for that. He, however, was unable to make more serious concessions, even if that had been his wish, given the composition of the Egyptian delegation to the talks. This included persons like Mahmud, who in the past negotiated himself for a treaty and who imposed various demands during the 1936 negotiations. While limiting his flexibility, it had also given Nahas the opportunity to appear as a moderate who had to be inflexible due to pressures exerted by his colleagues.[43]

Solving most of the military problems enabled the delegation to turn their eyes to the Sudan. The original draft submitted by the

British negotiators contained two concessions in comparison to the previous rounds of negotiations after 1924. These were the admittance of free Egyptian immigration to the Sudan and the return of Egyptian Army units to that country. During the negotiations in 1936 the British delegation added another concession, that of saying that nothing in the article covering the Sudan would prejudice the question of sovereignty over that country. Thus the Egyptian delegation could take home a Sudan clause which was a significant improvement from their point of view on the 1930 proposal.

Issues like the Capitulations and the protection of lives and properties of foreigners in Egypt, which in the past loomed large in the negotiations, were settled in a short time in 1936, and the British delegation accepted the principle that Egypt alone was responsible for protecting foreigners. The treaty was signed on 26 August 1936 in the Locarno Room at the Foreign Office in London.

The 1936 treaty did contain acknowledgement of the importance of the Suez Canal to the British Empire and the 'legitimization' of the presence of British forces in Egypt for the defence of the Canal. This presence had been limited in size, in area of deployment and in time — 10,000 soldiers and 400 pilots in time of peace for the duration of 20 years, to be stationed in Moascar and the Geneifa area, south-west of the Great Bitter Lake. For achieving these objectives the British Government had given up any shred of responsibility for what took place elsewhere in Egypt. Furthermore, by being led to believe that the defence of the Canal could be disassociated from the rest of Egypt's other concerns, Great Britain had sown the seeds of the troubles which finally led to the total British evacuation from Egypt in 1954. The perception of being under the pressure of international crises elsewhere in East Africa, the Middle East and Europe induced the British policy-makers to make concessions in order to buy peace in Egypt. This was obviously an element in Lampson's success in extracting these concessions from his government. In fairness to Lampson it should be said that he was quite right in saying that the 'pass had been sold in the past' and that sale had probably taken place in Milner's report. Milner and his colleagues defined British interests as follows:

> The essential British interests are that the Great Imperial Communications which pass through Egyptian territory shall not be jeopardised either by internal disturbances or foreign aggression; that they shall be available in time of war, and for necessary purposes in time of peace; that the struggle for ascendancy in Egypt between rival Powers shall not be renewed; and, finally, that an independent Egypt shall not pursue a foreign policy hostile or prejudicial to that of the British Empire.[44]

Already, in the immediate post-World War period, it was clear that the idea of reduced responsibility in return for 'legitimization of military presence' as a way of protecting British interests was unworkable. And yet, successive British negotiators found themselves negotiating on these premises, unwilling to review them afresh in the light of knowledge and experience gathered.

For Nahas the 1936 treaty was not a victory either. His predecessor's legacy was one of rejecting Great Britain's military presence on Egyptian soil and of rebellion against the forces of occupation. His predecessor had refused to co-operate with the Egyptian politicians in negotiating a treaty and went as far as undermining their attempts at reaching one. Yet he, Nahas, both collaborated and signed a treaty together with the other non-Wafdist leading politicians, a treaty by which British forces were permitted to remain stationed in Egypt though in a much curtailed way. It may be assumed that six years in the political wilderness of Egypt (1930-6) had left their impression on his and his fellow Wafdists' readiness to defy any British presence at all costs. With this sort of political realism they could also view the international circumstances of 1936 as most propitious for attaining the majority of Egypt's goals. The 1936 treaty was therefore a compromise between two rivals who could not attain their declared objectives. Egypt gave up, for the time being, its desire for 'complete independence' and Great Britain achieved, though for a limited period, the right to continue to station its forces in Egypt for the defence of the Imperial line of communication.

Notes

1. Granville's statement can be found in J. C. Hurevitz, *The Middle East and North Africa; A Documentary Record* (Yale University Press), Vol. I, p. 447. Granville's instructions, see in Earl of Cromer, *Modern Egypt* (London, 1908), Vol. I, p. 381.
2. The reports on this meeting on 13 November 1918 are at variance as to the precise words used by the delegation's members.
3. 'Report of the Special Mission of Egypt', F.O. 371/4978, file E 5168/6/16.
4. Ibid.
5. 1,548 British officials and 1,842 other foreign officials were employed by the Egyptian Government in 1919-20, out of 24,500 officials in the public administration.
6. Both drafts in F.O. 848/25.
7. Ibid.
8. *The Times*, 20 September 1920.

9. In a memorandum circulated on 14 February, C.A.B. 24/119, C.P. 2589.
10. See Afaf Lutfi al-Sayyid-Marsot, *Egypt's Liberal Experiment 1922–1936* (University of California Press, 1977), p. 56.
11. F.O. 371/6306, file 11260/260/16.
12. Ibid.
13. Duff Cooper, *Old Men Forget* (London, 1953), p. 105.
14. F.O. 371/6298, file E 7320/260/16. It was forwarded to Curzon already in June 1921 and the latter approved of it but could not see it through in the Cabinet.
15. For a detailed discussion of the new Constitution, see Elie Kedourie, 'The Genesis of the Egyptian Constitution of 1923', in *The Chatham House Version and Other Middle Eastern Studies* (London, 1970), pp. 160–76.
16. In an article he published in *The New Leader*, 22 June 1923.
17. MacDonald Papers, F.O. 800/218.
18. *The Times*, 12 May 1924.
19. F.O. 371/10043, file E 8669/368/16.
20. See Lord Lloyd, *Egypt Since Cromer* (London, 1933), Vol. II, Chap. XI, pp. 194–8.
21. In a letter forwarded by Tyrrell to Chamberlain of 15 June 1927, Chamberlain Papers, A.C. 54/476.
22. From a letter circulated by Chamberlain to the Cabinet on 29 October 1927; C.A.B. 24/189, C.P. 260(27).
23. Ibid.
24. In a Cabinet Committee dealing with the negotiations, C.A.B. 27/351, E.A.C. 27, 2nd Minutes.
25. Labour members of Parliament like J. Clynes and B. Spoor encouraged the Wafd leaders to work against the terms of the draft, promising better terms.
26. Written and underlined by Murray, F.O. 371/13841, file J 1897/5/16.
27. MacDonald Papers, P.R.O. 30/69, 1/272.
28. Ibid.
29. Percy Loraine replaced Lloyd as High Commissioner in late summer 1929.
30. See report on the 5th meeting on 8 April 1930, F.O. 371/14609, file J 1157/4/16.
31. There is one entry in Hugh Dalton's diary to that effect, on 15 April 1930. Dalton Papers, British Library of Political and Economic Science. Dalton was then Parliamentary Under-Secretary in the Foreign Office.
32. Muhamad Salah al-Din and Abd al-Kadr Hamza travelled separately to Egypt in April 1930. The first one was the 'official'

courier, the second was the correspondent of the newspaper *Al Balagh.*

33. During the long negotiations on the night between 7 and 8 May 1930, Nahas shouted: 'There is no joint sovereignty in the Sudan, there in only Egyptian sovereignty', Hugh Dalton Papers.
34. F.O. 141/614, file 1/4049/35.
35. F.O. 371/20097, file J 780/2/16.
36. C.A.B. 23/83, 5(36) and 6(36)6.
37. Lampson discovered by then through Brooke-Popham, the Commanding Officer Royal Air Force, Middle East, that Helwan was not suitable for the Air Force, although it is not clear why the latter withheld his opinion for almost two months. F.O. 371/20104, file J 3193/2/16.
38. C.A.B. 64/32, C.P. 131(36).
39. See memorandum by Nahas of 1 June 1936, F.O. 371/20110, file J 5160/2/16.
40. Telegram of 25 May 1936, F.O. 371/20108, file J 4810/2/16.
41. See Hassan Ahmed Ibrahim, *The 1936 Anglo-Egyptian Treaty* (Khartoum University Press, 1976), p. 25.
42. At the 4th meeting of the Cabinet Committee, on 15 June 1936; C.A.B. 27/607, A.E.C. (36).
43. See Lampson's Diary, St Antony's College, Oxford, entries for 12, 13, 20 and 23 July 1936.
44. F.O. 848/25.

The Suez Canal and the British Economy 1918–1960

RICHARD C. WHITING

From its opening in 1869 until 1956 the Suez Canal was regarded as a key feature of the British economy: in the year of the Canal's inauguration the *Economist* commented quite accurately that it 'had been cut by French energy and Egyptian money for British advantage'.[1] In 1956, in more gloomy conditions, Eden warned publicly of the 'serious industrial dislocation and unemployment' which would come from any prolonged interference with the traffic of the Canal—because of the importance of oil to the British economy 'machinery and much of our transport would grind to a halt'.[2]

In examining the Canal and the British economy in the twentieth century, due account has to be taken of these judgments, but inevitably they reflect different uses of the Canal over time and also suggest an importance which was more apparent than real. In the first contribution to this volume, Dr Steele dealt with the religious and political antagonisms arising from the British in Egypt before 1914. This contribution is concerned with the more prosaic world of trade and shipping, and there is a further change of perspective for, as far as the use of the Canal went, the British crossed swords as much with the French *rentier* capitalists who ran the Canal Company as they did with the Egyptians themselves.

The relationship between the Suez Canal and the British economy can be approached in three ways: by relating the Canal to Britain's trade and to the international economy of which it was a part; by examining the use made of it by shipping companies; and by outlining the triangular relationship between the shipping companies, the Canal company and the British government, the last of course both holding shares in the Company and having an interest in the health of British shipping. Like most three-cornered relationships, this was not always a very happy one.

During the first half of the century the Canal was bound up with many key changes in the British economy and Britain's position in the world. To put it simply, our period begins when the British economy was still a powerful force internationally, reflected in her trade in certain products, most especially coal; the period ends when British economic power and competitiveness had declined and when her shipping industry had failed to respond to a switch from coal to oil as a source of energy and as a cargo. Our period begins when the Suez Canal played a central role in the movement of commodities and in the multilateral payments system to which these movements gave rise; it ends with the closure of the Canal in 1956 which affected the economy not so much in real terms because of the hindrance to the movement of goods and materials, but as a political crisis which diminished confidence in sterling. In my broad conclusion, there is no need to depart from the judgment made by Dr Steele that the Canal was extremely useful to Britain and her trade but was never indispensable. But it does seem worthwhile to investigate how far Britain's use of the Canal was at one with her fortunes elsewhere, or how far it reflected particular strengths which were not evident in the wider, more hostile world. I will begin by examining the Suez Canal, British trade and shipping, before moving on to the rather more historically specific section on the shipowners, the British government and the Canal Company.

The savings in shipping time effected by the Canal remained fairly constant from 1918 to 1956: that is a saving of roughly half on the journey from Bombay to Liverpool via the Cape, between one-quarter and a third to China, with much smaller differences in the trade with Australia, perhaps a day or two.[3] The main value of the Suez Canal in world trade lay in yoking together suppliers of primary commodities from the East with their customers in the more developed West, and acting as a channel for a reciprocal flow of manufactured consumer and capital goods west to east. Among the commodities going southwards through the Canal to the East we therefore find railway equipment, metals, and machinery to meet the demands of hitherto non-industrial countries which in the inter-war period were beginning to develop some industrial capacity.[4] These countries in turn sent raw materials of various sorts to the industrial core of the world economy — ores and metals, textiles, vegetable oils and food. Of growing significance throughout our period in the traffic going northwards through the Canal to the West was oil from the Middle East. Inevitably the countries east of Suez did not have a monopoly in the production of primary commodities — the American continent was a major producer of meat, oil, cotton and copper. The main producers east of Suez using the Canal, India, Burma and Ceylon, sent rice, rubber, tea and various metals and minerals, especially manganese; in the period after the Second World War the export of oil from the Middle East dwarfed all these products. The impact of oil is shown in the changing proportion of Canal cargo to world trade as a whole; when in 1948 oil became more important than all other northbound cargoes added together, the share of Canal cargo in world trade rose from just below 7 per cent which it had been throughout the inter-war period, to just over 10 per cent and it continued to increase thereafter.[5] Britain's use of the Canal showed the same change in importance. For most of the inter-war period about 10 per cent of Britain's imports and exports came from those countries east of Suez which would have sent or received their goods through the Canal. By the 1950s this share had doubled to around 20 per cent, largely because of the much higher imports of oil from the Middle East routed through the Canal.[6]

While the Suez Canal was therefore in a central position for part of Britain's trade it was never in the most important sector in terms of the share of trade. Far more of Britain's trade went along the routes to Europe or to America than through Suez. Although diverging economic patterns suggested interdependence—that is, advanced industrial economies selling manufactured goods were brought into close relationship with fundamentally dissimilar economies supplying primary products—greater trade was to come from convergence, from advanced economies trading with each other. As long as the latter category contained in the main the USA, Britain and Western Europe, the Canal was obviously peripheral to these exchanges, at least in a direct way. We might nonetheless expect trade routes using the Canal to become more important to Britain as she lost ground to other more competitive industrial economies and was forced to search for markets elsewhere.

It was not only the movement of goods but their carriage which was important to Britain. In 1913, British ships had carried roughly 30 per cent of world trade; by 1938, this was down to 12 per cent.[7] The percentage of British ships of the total traffic through the Canal declined much more slowly but declined nonetheless. In 1913, 61.7 per cent of tonnage going through the Canal was British, by 1955 only 28.3 per cent.[8] Much of this decline had occurred after the Second World War; during the inter-war period, Britain remained the major user of the Canal, owning half the tonnage going through in 1938. But it was also true that Britain was able to exploit the growth of northbound oil cargoes in a way which she was not able to with regard to the movement of oil elsewhere: and so while in very broad terms the decline of British shipping through the Canal was part of a declining share in the wider world, the movements were not in step with each other because of the special conditions involved in the movement of oil through the Canal.

However, direct use of the Canal by British shipping as a channel for British trade is not the most sensitive way of measuring the importance of the Canal for this country. This is particularly true at the beginning of our period when the Canal, in having a critical effect on the trading position of other countries, played a vital part in defending Britain's trading position in increasingly competitive conditions. While the Canal brought India closer to Britain, it also effected even greater savings in the journey from Bombay or Calcutta to European ports. At first sight this might be expected to have threatened Britain's mercantile interests, for it meant that continental countries could trade directly with the eastern producers, including India, instead of importing their goods from London. Before the Canal was opened and when most goods from the East went around the Cape, London acted as a doorway to the European continent for goods from eastern countries. The opening of the Canal removed London's position and therefore diminished Britain's entrepot trade, but this was in the end very much to her advantage. The greatly improved ability of the Indian economy to sell goods directly to Europe (and also to the USA) allowed that country to consume British exports; in turn this enabled Britain to remain a free trade country when her diminishing competitiveness in relation to industrial Europe was leading some to doubt the wisdom of that policy. It was because Britain could meet her trading deficits with Europe by sending exports to India, purchases which were in turn financed by sales of primary commodities to industrial Europe, that Britain's international position remained viable, and she could pursue the strategy of maintaining the volume of world trade which was threatened by protection and in which Britain's role in servicing that economy brought her high invisible earnings. As Professor Saul has put it in his important book on British overseas trade, Britain, by keeping open her markets to European producers, prevented them searching further afield where Britain was successfully sending her exports; free trade was thus an indirect form of protection.[9] Since the Indian economy was at the heart of this, the Suez Canal clearly played an important role in Britain's international position at the beginning of this century.

Such a multilateral pattern of trade settlement—insofar as it involved the Suez Canal—was going to be affected by two main factors in the years after 1918: first, Britain's own ability to find markets for her goods east of Suez, and this was going to be shaped at least in part by the extent to which she met European or American competitors in these markets, and at least in part by the degree to which British exporters met indigenous producers in previously non-industrial countries; second, the pattern of demand for commodities in the industrial core was also going to determine the ability of producers east of Suez to absorb exports from countries like Britain.

To begin with the first factor: a major aspect of Britain's industrial decline in the inter-war period can be written in terms of the diminishing demand for coal. Coal had not only been a staple export but had been linked very closely with trading routes through Suez. Ships going out to India before the First World War left partly with manufactured goods and textiles but mainly with coal, some of which was off-loaded at Mediterranean ports, but most of which was not, so that ships were going through the Canal at least three-quarters full. Such use of coal to make full cargoes was valuable for British shipping when meeting government-assisted foreign competition. Although Britain remained in the inter-war period the chief exporter of coal through the Canal (90 per cent of the southbound coal in 1929 was British), the volume of exports diminished dramatically. The amount of coal going through the Canal in 1938 was one-fifth of the average exports between 1911–14.[10] All the countries east of Suez which produced coal themselves—Australia, India, China, Japan and Indo-China—either ceased to import European coal at all or cut their imports to a very low level. Whereas in 1914 the entire coal traffic had been going southwards, by 1938 it was exceeded by that going northwards, in the main exports from French Indo-China to France.

The decline in coal exports had a severe effect on British shipping. Tramp ships carrying coal on their outward journeys did so at a loss because freight values were so low; the decline in the amount of coal to be carried also weakened British shippers against their competitors. The longer-distance coal trades had provided secure cargoes on the outward trips for ships bringing grain and other bulk goods home. Before 1914 they had been able to operate at near peak capacity— much nearer to being fully laden than those ships using the Atlantic routes, for example.[11] The decline of coal exports after the First World War removed this advantage, and made British shipping more vulnerable to lower crew costs of the Norwegian and Greek shipowners.[12] So the basic shifts in international demand for certain products hit Britain hard not merely as a producer but also as a shipper of goods because of the effect on the economies of cargo-carrying.

But Britain also had difficulty in exploiting new trends in southbound Canal traffic which reflected changed conditions of demand east of Suez. One of the most important categories of goods going southwards through the Canal was that of metals and machinery to countries hitherto non-industrial but beginning to develop some industrial capacity.[13] Although this type of product was increasingly important in British exports during the 1930s competition against other European producers using the Canal could not be sustained. In China, British engineering concerns did poorly against European and American competitors; not only were the British much less energetic than their rivals in the marketing of their products and the technical support for them, shifting much of the burden for carrying out these tasks on to hard-pressed agents rather than doing the job themselves, but they also tended to be undercut by quite dramatic margins—often by as much as 20–25 per cent.[14] Contracts for electrical power plants, for example, went with depressing regularity in the inter-war period to the French, the Germans, and the Swiss. But a further aspect of the decline in exports to the Far East was the growth of indigenous competition: exports to Asia declined from 25 per cent in 1913 to 17 per cent in 1937 of total British exports.[15] As Lord Inchcape of the P and O line rather petulantly observed in 1925: 'It appeared to be the aim of both India and the Dominions to manufacture all they require and to import nothing.'[16] At the time, Lord Inchcape's company was finding great difficulty in filling its outward-bound ships with cargo. On one route to the east of Suez in the 1920s, 68 per cent of the cargo space went unfilled.[17]

British companies using the Canal were concerned not only about outward cargoes but also about the homeward trip and the value of the goods they were carrying. Just as freight rates for the outward trip had been forced down by the low prices of coal, so the profits on the homeward journey inevitably reflected the demand for those cargoes. By and large the prices of primary commodities and the demand for them slumped in the inter-war period. Although this was particularly marked in the 1930s, the tendency for supply to outrun demand had already appeared in the second half of the 1920s when production was expanding the trend of world trade upwards. This was true of petrol and sugar, for example, and becoming true for wheat and rubber.[18] Primary products can never be lumped together with any real confidence in order to describe the behaviour of prices, since meat for example, held up fairly well. However, the following figures indicate the dimensions of the slump in demand for certain products. Following the Wall Street crash of 1929, the export price of wheat and rubber fell by 50 per cent, that of copper and jute by 40 per cent. Apart from a very brief recovery in 1937/8, caused by a trade boom in the USA, those countries producing raw materials suffered even more severely than industrial ones.

For several of the shipping companies the decline in demand for primary products caused very real problems. The Orient Line was not one of the biggest users of the Canal amongst the British companies, sending through only one-third of the tonnage of Alfred Holt's of Liverpool, but it did trade mainly with Australia and used the Canal for this purpose: 80 per cent of its revenue arose from trade with New Zealand and Australia, particularly in wheat and wool.[19] The company was hit by the inability of the Australian economy to absorb imports from Britain during the Depression and by the fall in the price of exports from Australia which made up the returning cargoes. In 1931 the Orient company's profits were a quarter of what they had been in 1928, the last year of recovery in the 1920s, and they were unable to pay any dividends to shareholders.[20] Because freight rates were a small constituent of final selling price it was never open to companies to increase cargoes by dropping their freight charges. The Orient company did make such a cut of 10 per cent in 1927 and saw no increased cargo and simply a decline in their profits for their pains.[21]

Problems of demand and price affected not only the trading companies involved with these particular cargoes but also the whole pattern of trading relationships which had exploited the Suez Canal before the First World War. The major users of the Canal east of Suez were India, Ceylon and Burma, taking nearly one-third of the Canal traffic in the early 1930s.[22] Exports from India and Burma declined rapidly in the Depression, being in 1932 practically half what they had been in 1928, and falling faster than other commodities sent northwards through the Canal; particular products were hit spectacularly badly—for example, metals. As manufacturers ran down their stocks, exports of metals fell by 1932 to a third of what they had been in 1928. After the depths of 1932, exports from India and Burma fell no further but failed to show any significant recovery. They did so in 1937/8 with sharp increases in the exports of metals to meet the needs of European rearmament, and the movements of rubber to the USA to meet a cyclical boom there. The most obvious aspect of this upturn at the end of the 1930s was the way in which it was not met by any compensating imports from the industrial west through the Canal, indicating perhaps the effect of indigenous industrialization.

Comparative advantage, like water, does not always flow in the same direction, and the rather chaotic conditions of the early 1930s showed how the closer links with Europe which had been of much advantage to British India in the pre-1914 period (and thereby to Britain herself) could be suffered as a channel for temporary competition in depressed market conditions. India experienced for a brief period increased imports of oil from Rumania and Russia in the early 1930s. The Rumanian economy in particular was heavily dependent upon the export of petroleum products, the prices of which had halved between 1928 and 1932.[23] Dumping of this oil in India meant that established British interests, for example the Burma oil company were heavily undersold while prices were so depressed.[24]

Beyond these rather detailed points, it should be mentioned that the very satisfactory trading relations described at the beginning of this paper had been replaced by a less favourable, bilateral system at the end of the 1930s. Before 1914, Britain had evaded problems of competitiveness in Europe by selling to distant markets, including India, a strategy made possible by India's sale of primary products via the Suez Canal to Europe and the USA. This relationship continued into the 1920s with countries like India continuing to absorb British goods which could not find buyers elsewhere. After 1929 the forces which had been weakening the British side of things—the development of indigenous producers and the competition from foreigners—meant that her exports to India, China and Japan all fell. But also the ability of countries to offset deficits with Britain by sales elsewhere was diminishing in the 1930s, mainly because the USA was ceasing to take in primary products to the same extent as it had done previously. India's trade in the 1930s showed the elimination of deficits with Britain and the diminution of what had been offsetting surpluses with other countries. The same was true of Australia, although in reverse, with reduction of deficits with America and diminution of surpluses with the heavy buyers of wool in Europe, again indicating a move to a more bilateral system of trading relations compared to the multilateral system described earlier. In a difficult world the advantage tended to lie with the Empire rather than with Britain. This was particularly true for India—finding it much harder to trade with foreign countries in the inter-war period than it had done before 1914 she compensated for this at least partially by increasing the proportion of total exports going to Britain at a faster rate than she accepted imports from Britain. In this respect the system of imperial preference relieved the Indian economy of the pressures of a difficult export position in the 1930s.

By the end of the 1930s, then, the Suez Canal was part of a fundamentally different set of trading relationships from those in which it had been located before 1914. In the 1930s the multilateral trading pattern was being replaced by a more obviously bilateral one, and if the Suez Canal was in a sense still an escape route for goods which could not find a market elsewhere the context was a far less buoyant one than it had been before 1914. The Canal was becoming as much a channel for competitive forces from elsewhere as it was a means of indirect protection; European producers were now found in distant markets and indigenous producers were expanding output behind tariff walls. The abandonment of free trade in 1932 was not only a sign that Britain could no longer find a satisfactory place within the international economy, but was also part of a secular trend in which foreign trade as a proportion of total home production was falling.

While the Canal was part of a much less dynamic set of trading relationships by the end of the 1930s compared to before 1914, its traffic did show changes in cargo which preface the rather different role it was to have in the years after 1945, that is as a channel for oil.

Middle Eastern oil was regarded as vitally important to Britain's economic and strategic interests at the end of the First World War because it was seen to have displaced coal as a fuel. This was borne out by 1928 when Western Europe, instead of being an exporter of energy in the form of coal, became an importer in the form of oil.[25] The importance of the Middle East for Britain lay in the possibility of maintaining some independence for the USA, the main supplier of oil to Britain. The Americans' attitude to oil was envisaged by the British as developing in two ways: either, America would outrun domestic supplies and have to look elsewhere because of the growing demand of her car industry in particular; or, the USA would still look elsewhere, but merely in order to corner oil-producing areas in order to protect domestic producers. In either case the British hoped that their increased dependence on oil would not mean increased dependence on the USA.[26] It was regarded as of 'paramount importance for us to obtain undisputed control of the greatest possible amount of petroleum'. Anxieties about the intention of the USA remained throughout the inter-war period. Great attention was given to the movements of any representative of the Standard Oil Co. appearing in the Middle East when concessions were being renegotiated.

The Suez Canal was central to the exploitation of Middle East oil; there was no other worthwhile route from Abadan to Britain, and oil became a major cargo on the northbound route. Whereas in 1937 total traffic going through the Canal had not reached the levels of 1929, oil shipments had surpassed their tonnages of that year, and in 1930 had become the biggest single item of traffic moving northwards.[27] Britain was the chief user of this oil, importing in the 1930s five times as much as the next largest customer, the Italians.[28] The Middle East was very far from supplying the bulk of Britain's fuel requirements in the 1930s—roughly one-quarter of motor spirit came from Persia for example[29]—but its contribution was still important and was also of value, in a rather unrepresentative way, for British shipping. By way of contrast to the partially laden ships leaving Britain for Suez and eastwards on conventional routes, ships carrying oil from the Middle East were fully employed. The British Tanker Company, a subsidiary of Anglo-Persian Oil (subsequently BP), increased its tonnage through the Canal in the 1920s and by 1938 was carrying more than the conventional shipping companies like P and O and Alfred Holt's. The British Tanker Company was also responsible for carrying a high proportion of all the oil going northwards—between 75–80 per cent in the later 1930s.[30] But the success of the British Tanker Company should not be taken as representative of the responsiveness of British shipping as a whole to new cargoes and new trade balances; in fact, British shipping failed to exploit new possibilities for tanker operation in the inter-war period which might have compensated for the damage done by the decline in coal exports. The position of the British Tanker Company as a subsidiary of Anglo-Persian is not representative of what was going on elsewhere because oil companies only met a proportion of their own shipping requirements: roughly half the oil was carried by independent shippers at the end of the 1930s.[31] It would have been logical for those hit by the contraction of coal exports to have switched to tanker operation, but the British failed to do so; in 1939, Britain owned only one-quarter of the world tanker fleet as against a half in 1913.[32] If we wish to see the oil cargo of the Suez Canal as representative of British shipping in the wider world we need to look at the southbound rather than the northbound traffic. Here Britain lost out very badly to the Norwegians. In 1913, Britain had enjoyed a monopoly of the north–south oil trade, carrying 86 per cent of the traffic, their nearest rivals the Norwegians carrying only 6 per cent.[33] By 1933 the roles were reversed, the Norwegians carrying twice the amount of the British ships. The north–south trade in oil was of course far less important than that going in the reverse direction but British weakness in the former was more in line with what was happening elsewhere, since by the end of the 1930s the Norwegians carried one-quarter of the oil imported into Britain.

If oil was of increasing importance in the inter-war period it became even more so after 1945 owing to a very marked increase in imports of oil by Britain—oil consumption roughly doubled between 1946 and 1955[34]—and it was this which underlined the anxieties of certain politicians about the closure of the Canal during the crisis of 1956. Of the 125 million tons of oil imported into Western Europe from this area about half went through Suez, very little went around the Cape, the rest going through pipelines to the Mediterranean.[35] The Canal was blocked from 31 October 1956 until the end of March 1957. The event would seem to present the concrete example of a case so often pursued experimentally by economic historians: to assess the importance of a particular element in an economy by removing it and assessing the costs arising. The test case in this instance proved that the Canal was not terribly important to the British economy as far as the movement of real goods was concerned; according to the two leading authorities, Worswick and Ady, the closure of the Canal had very little effect on the performance of the British economy.[36] There was some petrol rationing, perhaps an element of growth forgone, but no sign of an actual cut in industrial production because of a shortage of fuel. The main result of the Suez crisis on the economy was as a political crisis affecting sterling. As a result of Britain's belligerent stand over Suez there was a flight from sterling which required recourse to the IMF. Since the balance of payments position at the time of Suez was no worse than it had been previously, this was very much a crisis of confidence. As such it had internal as well as international consequences: in order to bring money back into Britain the bank rate was pushed up to the then high level of 7 per cent. This was deflationary, and although not operated long enough to produce high unemployment, did precede a period of a year to 18 months when growth in national income was negligible.

The Suez crisis insofar as it affected oil at all concerned its shipment and not its supply. Despite the changing significance of the Canal as it switched from being a channel for coal to being one for oil, the market conditions for the latter were not markedly different from what they had been for the former before 1914; that is, it was a buyer's rather than a seller's market. The switch to a seller's market which did focus attention on supply did not occur until after the end of our period when the importance of the Canal as a channel for oil had been much diminished. In 1956-7, alternative supplies of oil came from Venezuela and from accumulated stocks in the USA. By November 1956, tanker companies were beginning to meet diminution of supply through having to re-route Middle East oil around the Cape. This meant increased costs for maintaining these supplies: the freight rates for oil, always subject to very sharp fluctuations, shot up in November 1956 soon after the closure of the Canal: for a ship going around the Cape the charges in December were over 80 shillings per ton, whereas before the blockade the rate had been about 55 shillings, which included the dues payable for using the Canal.[37] The same basic problem had of course been faced at the beginning of the Second World War when it became clear that oil could not be carried through the Suez Canal into the Mediterranean; to meet the doubling of the distance from Abadan to Britain by going around the Cape meant greater demand for tankers. The main intention in this instance was to switch to some degree to supplies from the USA since, for every million tons of oil so transferred, there was a saving of 36 tankers.[38]

In 1956, of course, this meant that supply problems were solved at the cost of much higher freight rates paid to American tanker operators and of the need to pay for a much higher proportion of oil imports in dollars. Even if the impact of the Suez crisis was not very marked in real terms, a higher cost for oil in terms of higher freight rates had to be paid. But, even if to satisfy some bizarre counter-factual position, had the Canal not been re-opened in March 1957, it is difficult to envisage that any serious problems would have been presented for the supply of oil. For at the time of the Suez crisis the importance of the Canal for oil tankers was diminishing. The main reason for this was the change from refined to crude oil as the main cargo, which made possible the introduction of the supertanker, which was much too large to use the Canal when laden with oil; these ships were, however, very economical in operation and could compete with smaller tankers using the Canal even when they had to go around the Cape. To some degree this switch was accelerated by the crisis itself. Because previous to the crisis there had been a surplus of tankers, the advantage of using the larger tankers had not been fully appreciated. The crisis, by giving the larger vessels regular employment, therefore played a part in the development of the larger tanker which diminished the importance of the Canal.[39] After the crisis, in fact, the practice developed of sending the supertankers through the Canal in ballast on their outward journey and bringing them back fully laden via the Cape. Nonetheless, after the Canal was re-opened, traffic returned to it; it was still cheaper for many ships going to Europe to use the Canal rather than to make the much longer trip around the Cape. Although the Canal had therefore become more important for British imports by the 1950s over the inter-war period, this does not indicate any degree of indispensability. This flowed from two main conditions: for most of our period the commodities flowing westwards through the Canal were being sold in a buyer's market—supply problems were not acute. It was of further significance that the main saving effected by the Canal—in shipping—occurred when the world capacity of shipping was in surplus. Particularly in view of this second circumstance, the re-routing of shipping around the Cape, although not in itself desirable, was not a major problem.

The Canal therefore had a certain importance for a particular section of British trade; but what of the costs of using it? Ships travelling through the Canal, whether laden or in ballast, had to pay dues on their cargo space (not on its value or volume) to the Suez Canal Company. Although for many shipping companies there was little alternative to the Suez route in normal trading conditions, since the saving in time exceeded the saving in dues achieved by going around the Cape,[40] many resented the level of dues they had to pay. This particular matter is best studied in the context of the inter-war period, which saw both depression and some recovery in world trade. It is difficult to give a precise figure for the proportion of freight costs represented by Canal dues. On the Australian run they appear to have fluctuated between 5–8 per cent of costs and were less important than port charges elsewhere on the route. In general, most European trade with Australia went through the Canal, and all wool shipments used this route, the main exception being some tramp ships using the Cape on their homeward trips to avoid Canal charges.[41] For an oil tanker on the Swansea–Abadan route, the costs of using the Canal were higher—about 25 per cent of total costs for the voyage.[42] It seems to have been true that the costs of using the Canal were not sufficiently great to warrant the charges made by British shipowners during the depression that the Canal dues were damaging their competitiveness.[43] The Suez Canal Company found it perverse of the British to complain about the loss of trade to the Far East and to plead for a reduction in dues when these represented about 1–2 per cent of the value of goods transported and when the loss of competitiveness was of much greater dimensions.[44] This reply to Britain was all the more persuasive when Britain's competitors among the other Western producers were also users of the Canal. And so while it could be claimed that the Canal Company, in making their charges, could exploit a monopoly position and that the Canal ought to become an international waterway, a tax of between 1 and 2 per cent on between 10 and 20 per cent of British trade was hardly serious.

In certain conditions the dues could become burdensome for shipowners; for example, those having to pay dues on passenger space in off-season sailings found that Canal tolls could amount to between 20 and 25 per cent of gross earnings,[45] and with sharp fluctuations in tanker freight rates, dues could assume a significant proportion of costs.[46] And so, while before about 1950 there was little choice for moving oil from Persia except through the Canal, the possibility of sending the product of the more northerly fields in Iraq out to the Mediterranean by pipeline did present itself, and one factor in embarking on the heavy capital costs of constructing a pipeline was the possibility of avoiding dues charged by the Canal Company.[47] When the Iraq pipeline was constructed in 1935, the oil moving through the Canal actually diminished (instead of its annual increment slackening), and thereafter the pipeline carried about 70 per cent of the load going through the Canal.

The dues paid by ships using the Canal benefited two main interests, the Egyptians and the French. The Canal Company had to respond to the wishes of the Egyptians to gain some material benefit from the Canal, in the form of taxation and royalties. The company itself was Egyptian in title and subject to the legal jurisdiction of the Mixed Courts; inevitably it felt some of the pressure of Egyptian nationalism. Demands for its expropriation in 1935 were not fulfilled,[48] but in the following year the hostility of the Egyptians towards foreign influence was expressed in an agreement to increase the Egyptian directors and staff and for it to pay an annual royalty of £200,000 to the Egyptian government,[49] an arrangement which officials at the Board of Trade felt was 'a present to the Egyptian government at the expense of the British taxpayer'.[50]

But while royalty payments caused some annoyance in official circles, the anxieties of the British shipowners lay far more with the level of dues charged, and in this regard their resentment was directed

more to the French than to the Egyptians.[51] Although the Company
was nominally Egyptian, for most practical purposes, in its locale and
personnel, it was French: more importantly in its policy it appeared to
be serving the interests of French *rentiers* rather than meeting the needs
of the shipowners whose activities provided its profits. Company
shares, quoted on the Bourse, were a popular investment and it is not
difficult to see why, given the high dividends paid to shareholders.[52]
As a standard textbook on British shipping commented, on a dividend
of 60 per cent in 1939 'this, for a public utility company whose assets
are sand and water, and therefore indestructible, may not be considered too bad'.[53]

Complaints about the dues were channelled through the British
directors on the board of the Canal Company, the London Committee
as it was called. However, the British interest lacked direct control
over the company. Although the British shipowners were the chief
users of the Canal, their government held only 44 per cent of the shares
and the British directors made up only one-third of the board. There
were practical difficulties in mobilizing shareholding strength, since
the government shareholding required the sending of over 1,000 nom-
inees to any meeting. It was also not at all clear that the further 10–15
per cent of shares held in private hands would be used in the interests
of the British shareholders,[54] since any reduction in dues drastic
enough to appease the shipowners threatened the profits of the company and therefore the dividends of the shareholders. This consideration did not weigh heavily with the government. While the Treasury
was 'reluctant to agree to a reduction in dues which is not absolutely
necessary to shipping',[55] it was bound to encourage any move to
improve the position of the shipping industry. While the income from
its shares had grown impressively during the inter-war period from
£798,566 in 1921 to £2.4 million in 1936,[56] this was very small in
relation to total revenue,[57] and the Treasury regarded the shares as a
political rather than a commercial asset. Hence when, in 1924, one of
the British directors urged the government to exploit the opportunity
provided by the division of shares to increase its own holding, on the
grounds that the shares were 'a magnificent investment, not only for
the Treasury but for the Empire',[58] he found little support for his
scheme.

But while governments saw their purpose as to promote British
interests within the Canal Company, through securing adequate representation on the board, reductions in dues and a large share of the
orders for work carried out on the Canal,[59] pursuit of the strictly
economic aspects of the use of the Canal inevitably were constrained
by wider political considerations. Thus it was considered unwise of a
British director to raise the possibility of a re-negotiation of the conces-

sion to the Company at the time of the Anglo-Egyptian treaty negotiations.[60] Re-negotiation of the position of the company with the
Egyptians, it was felt, lay only through Egypt finding the obligations
incurred in the 1936 treaty too heavy to bear.[61] More direct pressure
on the company was also tempered by concerns for Anglo-French
political collaboration.[62] The British government's anxieties about the
Canal Company only played a leading part in the development of the
1956 crisis when the wider context of the struggle with Arab nationalism became threatening. The onus for securing reductions in Canal
dues therefore fell on the British directors, and while Inchcape of the
P and O, Cadman of Anglo-Persian managed some continuous reductions in dues throughout the 1920s (without serious loss to the profits
of the company), they had to meet the continued reluctance of the
French directors to make any major reductions. As one of the British
directors put it, 'none of the French directors knew or cared anything
about shipping';[63] they were concerned primarily to protect the value
of what was not surprisingly a very popular investment in France, and
as was pointed out in the 1930s, 'in these hard times shares that pay
45 per cent are pearls of a great price which the owners will not lightly
dissolve in a glass of wine out of mere altruism'.[64] The French also
pointed to the interruption of earnings during the First World War
and the subsequent depreciation of the franc as reasons for dragging
their feet over reductions in dues. While the point about depreciation
had some force, the company was always able to protect or augment
their profits quite considerably by exploiting changes in currency
values. During the 1920s, in fact, the company held large sums in the
form of Treasury Bills in London to protect themselves against falls in
the value of the franc.[65]

The dividends paid by the company appeared quite astronomical
when British shipowners were facing very real hardship, and while it
was clear that reductions in Canal charges would not have changed
the pattern of demand for British goods, the earnings of the company
appeared excessive. They appeared all the more so during the depression following the Wall Street crash when dues were reduced by only
10 per cent at a time of the virtual collapse of world prices—and for
the British in particular the fall in the value of the pound after 1931
meant that in real terms the costs of using the Canal had increased.

In 1931 the British shipowners made a real effort to get Canal dues
reduced, one which showed not only some passivity on the part of the
government but also divisions of opinion amongst British shipowners.
This was supplementary to the pressure put on the company by the
London Committee of the British directors, and was generated by the
Liverpool Steamship Owners' Association, led by Holt's, a leading
user of the Canal, who found rather to their alarm in 1931 that the

costs of using the Canal were nine times higher than their tax liability.[66] The Liverpool companies brought in Bevin of the T & GWU to help make their case and questions were asked in the House. They clearly felt that their position as traders in real goods was being undermined by the *rentier* interests of the French shareholders in the Canal Company. The Liverpool group led by Major Cripps of Holt's were dissatisfied with the British directors of the Canal Company, regarding them as a 'self-appointed oligarchy', although the feeling was mutual, Inchcape of the P and O making disparaging references to 'those people in Liverpool' as he tried to curb the agitation against the Canal Company.[67] Perhaps more seriously, the British directors were in the main representative of liner interests and Suez Canal dues apparently pressed rather less hard on them than on the tramp owners. Inchcape was not disposed to support the opposition against the company led by Alfred Holt's, and the government was able to evade serious criticism of its own passivity by the apparent division amongst the shipowners. Inchcape was unable by private negotiation to secure a reduction in Canal dues—it was only the threat by Holt's to take the company to court in Egypt for having to pay dues in gold rather than in paper francs which led to the eventual 10 per cent reduction in dues.[68]

Some companies, including Shell, during the very depressed conditions in the early 1930s sent ships around the Cape to avoid transit dues through the Canal. In 1936 the British directors, trying to get further reductions in charges after the depreciation of the pound, reported to Anthony Eden, the Foreign Secretary, that

> the view is held amongst our shipping colleagues that the Suez Canal is no longer so important to shipping as it used to be. The use of motor propulsion, which concidentally increases efficiency, the reduction of port fees in South Africa and possible reductions in the price of coal were all factors which tempted shipowners to use the longer route.[69]

The temptation to send ships by the Cape was never strong enough for the switch to be permanent. At the height of the depression the increase in shipping going around the Cape was only a very small proportion of that continuing to use the Canal; and by the mid-1930s the shipping going via the Cape (particularly on the Australian route) was beginning to return to the Canal, as speed once more became of some importance and Canal dues could be absorbed more easily in improved freight rates.[70] The diversion, in fact, was rather less than occurred when the Italians used the Canal very heavily during their war in Abyssinia in 1935.

The British had no real power over the Canal Company then, which was regarded as serving the financial interests of the French investor even though it was largely British traffic in real goods which created that wealth. The Canal remained of importance to the British economy even when the role of the Indian economy had diminished and was replaced by the export of oil from the Middle East. Britain remained the leading user of the Canal down to 1964.[71] Because of savings in distance it effected there was no alternative route in normal trading conditions; but the monopoly position in which this placed the company did not exert any major effect on British trade since the 'tax' involved was small. The behaviour of the company had nonetheless attracted considerable criticism for failing to keep the Canal's development in line with the traffic it bore—it was never widened to allow two ships to pass in transit and tended to become congested during active trading. Hence, as Dr Farnie has suggested, at the time of the Company's nationalization in 1956, 'No capitalist organisation had ever been sacrificed with such speed or unanimity'.[72]

Notes

1. Quoted in M. Fletcher, 'The Suez Canal and World Shipping 1869–1914', *Journal of Economic History*, XVIII (4) (1958), p. 564.
2. Quoted in G. Worswick and P. Ady, *The British Economy in the 1950's* (Oxford, 1962), p. 39.
3. Figures for 1918 in Fletcher, loc. cit., p. 559, and for 1956 from *The Economist*, 4 August, p. 528.
4. Flows of commodities are given in *Compagnie Universelle du Canal Maritime de Suez* (The Suez Canal) (London, 1952), tables 4 and 5, pp. xi, xiii.
5. For the share of oil as a cargo see graph 10 in *The Suez Canal*; for Suez cargo in world trade see D. A. Farnie, *East and West of Suez: The Suez Canal in History 1854–1956* (Oxford, 1969), table 3, p. 754. Dr Farnie's is probably the most thorough survey of the place of the Canal in international, political and economic affairs, and provides a very full bibliography of printed sources.
6. Tonnages are given in the Board of Trade *Journal*, 8 March 1928, pp. 293–4; 23 March 1933, pp. 443–6; 26 March 1936, pp. 449–52; 14 February 1953, pp. 324–9.
7. S. G. Sturmey, *British Shipping and World Competition* (London, 1962), table 9, p. 89.
8. Farnie, op. cit., table 1, pp. 751–2.
9. S. B. Saul, *Studies in British Overseas Trade* (Liverpool, 1960), p. 200.

10. See 'Coal Traffic via the Suez Canal' in P.R.O., F.O. 423/68, pp. 22ff.
11. See A. J. Sargent, *Seaways of the Empire* (London, 1918), pp. 64, 67.
12. S. G. Sturmey, op. cit., pp. 73–4.
13. For figures see *The Suez Canal*, op. cit., table 4, p. 41.
14. Board of Trade, Committee on Industry and Trade, Evidence, vol. 3, pp. 1419ff.
15. A. Kahn, *Britain in the World Economy* (New York, 1943), pp. 210ff.
16. P and O Company report in *The Economist*, 12 December 1925, p. 1006.
17. *The Economist*, 10 December 1921, p. 1003.
18. J. W. F. Rowe, *Primary Commodities in International Trade* (Cambridge, 1965), pp. 79, 85.
19. *The Economist*, 27 December 1930, p. 1237.
20. *The Economist*, 24 December 1932, p. 1210.
21. *The Economist*, 24 December 1927, p. 1154.
22. The position of these three countries is analysed in P.R.O., F.O. 423/67, pp. 129ff.
23. *The Economist*, 5 August 1933, pp. 268–9.
24. *The Economist*, 10 June 1933, p. 1260.
25. Farnie, op. cit., p. 570. The growing importance of oil from the Middle East is discussed fully in Chapter 30.
26. See the discussions on petroleum policy in P.R.O., POWE 33/13 and 33/298.
27. See *The Suez Canal*, op. cit., p. xiii.
28. 'Analysis of Merchant Traffic for the Year 1937' in F.O. 423/67, pp. 43–4.
29. See 'Sources of Motor Spirit' in P.R.O., POWE 33/398.
30. S. H. Longrigg, *Oil in the Middle East* (London, 1968 edn.), p. 65.
31. S. G. Sturmey, op. cit., pp. 262ff discusses the economics of tanker operation.
32. Ibid., table, p. 75.
33. See the note on British and Norwegian tankers of December 1934 in P.R.O., F.O. 423/64.
34. M. F. G. Scott, *A Study of United Kingdom Imports* (London, 1963), pp. 33–40.
35. *The Economist*, 22 September 1956, pp. 982–4; 3 November 1956, p. 440.
36. Worswick and Ady, op. cit., p. 39.
37. *The Economist*, 1 December 1956, p. 809.
38. See the discussions in P.R.O., POWE 33/604.

39. S. G. Sturmey, op. cit., p. 264.
40. A. J. Sargent, op. cit., p. 83.
41. K. Burley, *British Shipping and Australia* (Cambridge).
42. Information for 1922 kindly supplied by J. K. Taggart of British Petroleum. Figures for dues as a proportion of cargo value (13 per cent in this case) relate to crude oil and not to the refined end product, and so exaggerate the incidence of canal dues.
43. Concern was felt specifically about competition from Japan and the west coast of America in markets which were, as far as Britain was concerned, east of Suez. As was pointed out by Harrison Hughes, director of Harrison's and a member of the London directors of the Suez Canal Company,

    > This trade [i.e. from Japan and America] would always have the advantage of not having to pay any canal dues at all and it was in effect a growing trade, the effect of which we were only just beginning to feel. P.R.O., MT9/2038.

44. *The Economist*, 17 June 1933, p. 1321.
45. *The Economist*, 17 December 1938, p. 636.
46. *The Economist*, 14 May 1938, p. 382.
47. Note by Sir John Cadman of Anglo-Persian, in 'The oil situation in the Middle East', P.R.O., POWE 33/328.
48. Farnie, op. cit., p. 604.
49. Ibid.
50. See 'Agreement between the Egyptian Government and the Suez Canal Co. on maximum dues', P.R.O., MT9/2627.
51. Thus during the negotiations between the Canal Company and the Egyptian government in 1936 the British directors on the company were more concerned to secure a commitment to a continuing reduction in dues—which was made public in a French press release—rather than with the fixing of a maximum level of those dues, and establishing their payment in Egyptian piastres. P.R.O., MT9/2627.
52. For a list of receipts and dividends of the Canal Company 1870–1955, see Farnie, op. cit., pp. 755–6, table 4.
53. R. H. Thornton, *British Shipping* (Cambridge, 1939 edn.), p. 111a.
54. These problems were discussed in a memorandum of HMG on the Suez Canal in P.R.O., F.O. 423/65, and in P.R.O., MT9/2038 on Canal dues.
55. Treasury note of 5 December 1930 in P.R.O., MT9/2038.
56. Farnie, op. cit., p. 757, table 5.
57. Total revenue was £845 million in 1935; since the government

had no intention of selling its shares, their market value was irrelevant to the assessment of their economic benefit.

58. Letter of I. Malcolm to Ramsay MacDonald, 4 June 1924, in Malcolm Papers, P.R.O., T206/1. The Treasury 'were not impressed by the purely financial merits of the case'.

59. These basic aims were set out in a government memorandum of 1937 on the Suez Canal, reproduced in P.R.O., F.O. 423/67.

60. The treaty of 1936 permitted Britain to protect her interests in the Canal not as an occupying force but as 'an allied power admitted under treaty'. Although nationalist opinion in Egypt criticized the treaty because of the financial burdens of constructing barracks in the Canal zone, it nonetheless 'elevated Egypt to full equality with Britain'. Farnie, op. cit., pp. 605–6.

61. P.R.O., F.O. 423/67.

62. From 1926 the Treasury wanted the payments to ordinary shareholders to be paid in gold rather than paper francs, which was cheaper for the company. This would have brought a gain of roughly £40,000 to the Treasury. The prosecution of the case aroused considerable fears in the Foreign Office about the 'political disadvantage' of legal action against the company. Note of Foreign Office to Sir Ian Malcolm, British Director of Company, 1 December 1927, P.R.O., T206/5.

63. In 'Memorandum of H.M.G. on Suez Canal'. In P.R.O., F.O. 423/65.

64. Ibid.

65. See reply of President of Company, 10 May 1924, to Inchcape, reproduced in Malcolm Papers, P.R.O., T206/1.

66. This campaign is dealt with in Farnie, op. cit., chapter 31 and in P.R.O., MT9/2038.

67. The comments of Cripps are in a note from Sir Ian Malcolm to the Foreign Office, 19 November 1931, and those of Inchape in a memorandum delivered at a meeting of the London Committee, 9 November 1931. Both in P.R.O., F.O. 423/65.

68. In 'Memorandum of H.M.G. on Suez Canal'. In P.R.O., F.O. 423/65.

69. P.R.O., F.O. 423/65.

70. *The Economist*, 12 June 1937, p. 638.

71. Farnie, op. cit., p. 744.

72. Ibid., p. 723.

British Diplomacy and the
Crisis of Power in Egypt:
the Antecedents of the British Offer
to Evacuate, 7 May 1946

ERAN LERMAN

A 'retrograde' nationalist attitude would be out of place in the post-war world: this was the message that Terence Shone, the British Chargé d'Affaires in Cairo, sought to convey to Mustafa Nahhas, the Wafdist Prime Minister, and to Amin Uthman, Nahhas' Finance Minister, confidant and go-between with the embassy, in a meeting of 23 September 1943. The immediate purpose of the message was to restrain some of the Wafd's nationalist legislation and 'xenophobic measures'.[1] The views expressed by Shone had, nevertheless, a wider significance: the Egyptians were not unaware of the prospect that the Wilsonian principle of nationalist self-determination might not be as central in the new post-war era as it had been after 1918.[2] Yet within a year from the end of the war, the British position in Egypt was seriously challenged, and to some extent compromised, by the nationalist stance taken up by the Egyptian government in the 1946 Treaty Revision Negotiations: the 'retrograde' pattern of relations was not broken.

Nor could it easily be broken. Britain's position in Egypt was, indeed, based on an international obligation to protect the Suez Canal region against aggression; yet it was, at the same time, based on the exercise of power over Egyptian politics. Thus the dialogue with Egypt could not be based on rational solutions to generalized problems: power made the British Embassy into a reluctant party in the internal struggle between monarchy and mass party, king and constitution in Egypt. This in turn made the settlement of bilateral issues inseparable from the fortunes of that struggle and from the ambitions and designs of the parties. Despite the trappings of constitutional parliamentarism, power in Egypt resided not in the ballot box but in three sources of influence over internal affairs: the king's constitutional authority to appoint and dismiss governments; the ability of those who sought office to resort to agitation and popular disruptions; and the ability of the British Embassy to call, at a crisis, upon the British forces—stationed in Egypt by right of the 1936 Treaty and of the needs of war—to suppress, if need be, both the king's designs and the agitators' activites. It is in the context of this reality that the effort to revise the 1936 Treaty ended in failure and in acrimony.

Responses to this reality were complex. The last High Commissioner and the first Ambassador to Egypt, Miles Lampson—Lord Killearn since 1943—seemed to relish the exercise of British power and to favour continued intervention in the internal struggle in Egypt. During the war years, backed by Churchill, he moved to reassert the embassy's power over the making of governments in Egypt—a power which young King Faruq seemed determined, since December 1937, to exercise himself unhindered by popular opinions (which still largely tended to support Nahhas' Wafd) or by British advice. Faruq's favoured Prime Minister, Ali Mahir, was forced to resign, on suspicion of pro-Axis sympathies, in 1940; on 4 February 1942, at the height of the Axis tide, the ambassador took dramatic action—the famous 'tanks' incident at Abdin—to impose a Wafdist government on Faruq. In April 1943 and again a year later, Lampson moved to prevent Faruq from dismissing Nahhas—and was again backed by Churchill in his willingness to use force if necessary. His philosophy as explained to a meeting of the Middle East Defence Committee at the height of the April 1944 crisis was simple:

> So far our influence in Egypt has been predominant, and the Egyptians, who were not yet capable of directing wisely their own affairs, had had to conform to our wishes.' In the long view, British interests required that we should retain this influence. If we allowed the King now to turn out the Wafd, whom we were known to support, it would establish a dangerous precedent.'[3]

The interventions of 1940, 1942, 1943 and 1944 thus served to reassert British influence in a country which Lampson, in effect, deemed to be prematurely independent.

But whereas the dramatic interventions did succeed, not even Lampson could see them as a permanent solution to the problems created by British involvement. The constant quarrel between the Wafd and the palace; the calls upon the embassy to intervene in petty affairs; the attempts by those outside office to win British attention by engaging in anti-British agitation on the 'national aspirations' (mainly British evacuation and the unity of the Nile Valley—all of these factors contributed to the deepening exasperation with which British authorities regarded their political involvement in Egypt. Lampson himself occasionally reacted with unsuppressed anger to Egyptian political conduct during the war, and suggested (in most secret messages to Eden or Churchill) a return to direct British control and the incorporation of Egypt in the Commonwealth:

> I know that this would not be easy (to put it mildly) ... but what is the use of winning the war if we cannot impose what we think best in *our* interest on a feckless crew like the Egyptians? My advisers are aghast at what they regard as my flights of fancy (they are too polite to call them dementia!): but I refuse to believe myself that we should not get away successfully with whatever we want here if we are prepared to see it through.[4]

Such radical solutions, however, found no favour at the Foreign Office. The Egyptian Department's hope was to reduce the more entangled and absurd aspects of the Anglo-Egyptian relationship—such as the opposition's use of anti-British agitation for the national aspirations in the efforts to threaten and cajole the embassy—by limiting the interventions to the minimum of absolute wartime necessity: to loosen the British grip on Egyptian affairs rather than tighten it. In concrete terms, this meant that a limit was set to what the embassy could do to keep the Wafd in power. The Wafd, sensing danger, tried to pre-empt the palace designs by provoking a crisis, but were defeated in the manœuvre and dismissed on the morning of 8 October 1944 while Shone, on strict orders from London, stood by; rather than wrest Faruq's powers from him, as Lampson wished to do, the Foreign Office chose to allow the king to exercise them—and to bear the responsibility for the consequences.

The impact of this decision was not immediately felt. The new Prime Minister, Ahmad Mahir—leading a coalition of four 'minority parties', the Sa'dists, the Liberals, Makram Ubaid's Kutla (Bloc) and the Watanists—was friendly to the embassy, both because of his hope to establish his own power, independent of palace control, and because of more personal considerations—a yearly subsidy of 2,000 Egyptian pounds from the embassy helped him pay his gambling debts.[5] In February 1945, Ahmad Mahir, who had previously advocated Egypt's entry into the war, readily accepted Churchill's and Roosevelt's suggestion that Egypt should declare war and join the United Nations in their conference at San Francisco. This decision, however, was regarded by extreme nationalists as akin to treason; and Mahir was assassinated on 24 February, on his way from the Chamber of Deputies to the Senate to argue for the declaration of war. He was succeeded by his Foreign Minister, Fahmi Nuqrashi, with whom he had left the Wafd in 1937 to establish the Sa'dist Party. Unlike Ahmad Mahir, however, Nuqrashi was not a friend of the embassy; despite their life-long association (they stood trial together in 1926 for complicity in the murder of Sir Lee Stack, but were acquitted), Ahmad Mahir chose in January 1945, in consultation with Lampson, to keep Nuqrashi out of the Ministry of the Interior—the second most powerful post in Egypt—so as to avoid friction with the British.[6] In power, Nuqrashi grew steadily less amenable to British requests—whether over economic issues, such as the establishment of an Anglo-Egyptian airline, or over political questions, such as Treaty revision.

Nuqrashi came to power—and held it—amidst widespread expectations that he was not equal to the task and that he would be replaced. shortly by a coalition or a non-party Cabinet led by one of the better-known independent politicians. Inside the Cabinet, Makram and the Kutla, as well as the Watanists, were restive, and outside it the Wafd was actively mobilizing opinion against the Cabinet. In such internal adversity, Nuqrashi carefully avoided any close co-operation with the embassy which might be used against him by his powerful enemies. This situation—and Nuqrashi's personal inclination to procrastinate over decisive issues, and to adhere to a rigid interpretation of Egypt's national rights—exacerbated Nuqrashi's relations with Lampson; the changing nature of the global balance of power provided the Egyptian government, moreover, with wider diplomatic options, including the possibility of an appeal to the UN Security Council, the Assembly, or the International Court of Justice, to challenge the British position in Egypt.[7] The implications of the loosening grip were becoming clearer; and while the British position was not under immediate threat of elimination, there was less and less hope that a new and friendly framework for it could be built with the consent to the Egyptian government then in power.

There were several possible ways out of that impasse. One of these—and an option which was given considerable thought in the context of the future of the Suez Canal—was the 'internationalization' of the position. The notions of the Canal Company reverting to French control (as before the war) and ultimately to Egyptian hands (in 1968) were hardly welcome to the Foreign Office. The Military Sub-Committee of the Reconstruction Secretariat (after 1943 renamed the Post-Hostilities Planning Staff), Britain's strategic post-war planners, were inclined to endorse 'U.N. bases' and an 'international utility company' as solutions to the twin problems of defence and control of the Canal; so were the FO Reconstruction Department and such experienced diplomats as Sir Kinahan Cornwallis (who suggested trilateral—British, American, Russian—control in the Middle East).[8] But these ideas were never put to the test; neither Lampson's temperament nor the nature of his position in Egypt led him to favour or pursue such internationalist notions, and Sir Maurice Peterson—the under-secretary superintending the Egyptian Department—wrote to

Cairo in April 1944 to assure the ambassador that 'Egypt is the last place in which we shall resort to premature experiments'.[9] The Cabinet Committee on the Suez Canal's future reached similar conclusions, if from a different angle: the Treasury representative, Osbert Peake, wrote that 'international management would be bad management' and that an Anglo-Egyptian understanding would be preferable. Significantly, Attlee was the only member of the Committee who held out, in March 1945, for internationalization.[10] Once in power, however, the Labour Government did not alter the basic British commitment to 'political predominance' in the region—in the words of Bevin's report on the Conference of British Representatives in the Middle East, which he had convened in London in September 1945.[11] But in a changing world the mere assertion of British predominance was no longer sufficient.

Lampson had his own ideas as to the manner in which this predominance should be exercised; in line with his past attitudes, he rejected any signs of weakness ('I often find myself rubbing my eyes and wondering whether we have won this war in order to lose whatever we have got? To my untutored mind it just does not make the very beginning of sense!' he wrote in an internal embassy minute in April 1945).[12] As tensions with Nuqrashi mounted, and following some tentative exchanges of views with friendly palace officials, Lampson put it to London on 30 May 1945 that the time had come to have Nuqrashi replaced by Husain Sirri, the pro-British independent politician who had been Nahhas' predecessor in power.[13] His advice was rejected; but by the end of June 1945, Lampson again lost patience: he wanted some show of determination to put an end to the Egyptians' 'inflated mood'. In the Foreign Office, where a policy of friendly relations with Faruq was preferred to a course of confrontation, the ambassador's mood caused some alarm; Coverley-Price, who handled Egyptian affairs in the Egyptian Department, even suggested that it was time for 'the removal of the resentment and uneasiness inherent in the continuation of the Lampson regime'. The head of the Department, Patrick Scrivener, had to warn him against raising this delicate subject; as he may well have anticipated, Churchill's first reaction to Lampson's advice was, as it had often been, that the ambassador should be supported. But having 'parried one attempt to get Nokrashi sacked', Scrivener found no difficulty in parrying another.[14]

Within weeks Churchill was out of office and Lampson left without his most powerful supporter. Now not only his wilder suggestions, but even his more calculated counsels were rejected. 'Winning the peace,' wrote Scrivener on 20 June, '... does not include a return to Cromerism in Egypt.'[15] If Nuqrashi could not be dismissed, Lampson suggested, British purposes—which, at the time, were to secure delay in the revision of the 1936 Treaty until Britain's strategic desiderata could be better defined—could perhaps be served by a subtle game of hints to the effect that the British, if pressed to negotiate, would have to insist on Wafdist participation in the negotiations, hints which would deter Nuqrashi from taking premature action. 'A little involved,' Lampson wrote apologetically, 'but quite worth bearing in mind in this convoluted country.'[16] Scrivener, however, was no longer interested in intricate manœuvres and in threats of intervention; in line with the Department's past counsels, his preference was for a deal with the king—if this could secure an end to the prospect of continued involvement and interference in Egyptian squabbles. The new Egyptian envoy in London, Abd Al-Fattah Amr (a young man, once the world champion in squash racquets, who earlier in 1945 had been Lampson's favourite go-between with the king) had precisely that suggestion to make.

Amr's argument was simple; it was well founded in some of its aspects; and it was what the Foreign Office evidently wished to hear. Parliamentary rule in Egypt, Amr said, had degenerated into a game of corruption and intrigue among the political parties; only once that game was swept aside, and the monarch's powers fully restored, could Anglo-Egyptian relations be improved; and removed from Egyptian internal squabbling, steps could be taken towards essential social reform. On his first brief for Bevin, on 10 August 1945, Scrivener adopted much the same line.[17] The wish to convince Bevin that there was a viable alternative to Lampson's practices in Egypt may account for these sudden indications of trust in Faruq's good intentions and good judgment; but the trust may well have been sincere. As Nuqrashi seemed set to press ahead with Treaty revision, the new superintending under-secretary, Sir Robert Howe, chose to speak frankly with Amr rather than to engage in the manœuvre of hinted threats to Nuqrashi, as Lampson had suggested. That frankness with Amr proved costly: once Amr, and subsequently the palace, realized how urgently the British wished them to restrain Nuqrashi, they steadily raised the price which was to be extracted in return from Nuqrashi's restraint. That price was the political destruction of the Wafd.[18]

As it turned out, the palace was neither powerful nor determined enough to pursue the demise of the Wafd themselves; they went about it directly, by purchasing, for a while, the loyalties of the Ikhwan al-Muslimun,[20] and by pressing Lampson to convince Nahhas that he would never be Prime Minister again.[21] This, in spite of London's wishes, was more than Lampson was willing to do: he was content to watch the Nuqrashi regime to to ruin under internal pressures. In the process, however, no control was left over Nuqrashi's actions, and the Egyptian Government, with Makram deliberately urging Nuqrashi to take a course which would entail his fall, finally forced the issue of Treaty revision upon the British by formally requesting, on 20 December 1945, that the 'caractère transitoire' of the 1936 Treaty should be recognized and negotiations for a new Treaty start forthwith.[22] Several of the premises underlying Amr's plea—as endorsed by Scrivener— were thus shattered; Faruq's co-operation was extremely limited, and such actions as he did take to accommodate British wishes were ineffectual. He had no real interest in delaying the revision—he himself wanted the British troops, a potential threat to his own powers, out of Egypt—and he was willing to use violence to promote his purposes. This was not fully realized, however, at the time,; it was only by the end of 1946, when the trial of the assassins was evidently becoming a farce, that the embassy began to realize that the murder of Amin Uthman, on 5 January 1946, and the attempts on the life of Nahhas, may have been ordered by the palace (it seems now that Faruq's 'iron guard' of officers—including Anwar Sadat—organized by Faruq's physician, Yusuf Rashshad, carried out these as well as other violent activities).[23]

Lampson acutely felt that the embassy was losing control over events, and that the Nuqrashi Government was unlikely to acquiesce in any treaty that would allow the British to keep troops in Egypt; he wanted the negotiations to be held in London, so that the embassy would not be faced with 'instructions quite incapable of achievement even to the Archangel Gabriel'.[24] This defeatism further weakened Lampson's standing in London; but the point about Nuqrashi's attitude was taken. The Foreign Office did not relish negotiating with Nuqrashi—or with any 'minority' delegations, from which the Wafd was absent—any more than did Lampson. Unlike the ambassador, however, what the Egyptian Department wanted was not an imposed solution but a deal; Lampson was instructed to suggest to Faruq that if he could create a representative government by eliminating 'the personal problem presented by Nahhas', the British would acquiesce in that.[25] This final stab Lampson refused to inflict on the man he had kept in power during the crisis of 1942; and it was in connection with the manner in which he asked Faruq to replace the Nuqrashi Cabinet (Amr alleged in London—but later admitted he was wrong—that Lampson had tended 'formal advice') that the palace finally undid its hated rival at the embassy: on 4 February 1946, an interesting date, Lampson was informed of Bevin's decision to appoint him as co-ordinator of reconstruction activities in South-East Asia.[26] Faruq's Chef du Cabinet, Ahmad Hasanain (who died two weeks later in a car accident, leaving no clue as to the ultimate purpose of his man-œuvres) then proceeded to wreck Scrivener's strategy as well. Anti-British agitation grew apace—and Nuqrashi was finally asked to resign, not because he failed to restrain it but because he cracked down on it too hard. The man appointed to replace him, Ismail Sidqi, had virtually no popular support at all, and his Cabinet—supported by the Liberals only (with Sa'dist acquiescence) and sustained by palace pressure—was not what Scrivener had hoped to see in power. The royal rescript appointing him described the previous week's violent demonstrations as 'a wholesome expression of the people's eagerness to realize their just aspirations'. Scrivener admitted to Winant, the US Ambassador in London, that he was 'at his wits end' trying to understand this turn of events.[27]

The Treaty revision negotiations thus began at a time of crisis; or rather their start had induced a crisis of British policy and power in Egypt. It was a crisis made all the more puzzling, to an experienced observer such as Scrivener, by the relative lack of popular resentment against the British. Intelligence assessments, Scrivener noted, indicated 'that the present agitation is *not* nation-wide, and indeed confined to a comparatively small number of politically active Egyptians and their tools'. From a conversation with a schoolmaster, Smart concluded that the student agitators were isolated in Egyptian society; the US Minister, Pinkney Tuck, reached a similar conclusion.[28] Yet the Egyptian political classes, in pursuit of their internal struggles, were challenging the British position at its most basic form: the presence of British troops, stirring up emotions in favour of 'Al-Gala'', evacuation. The vehemence of this political challenge was, in part, a result of Wafd's growing frustration at being kept out of power, and the loss of the restaining influence which Amin Uthman (and Lampson's hints of a possible change in the future) had exercised on Nahhas: in January 1946, MI5 reported, Nahhas decided to adopt 'a more virile tone of anti-British propaganda' and perhaps even toy with a pro-Soviet line.[29] The palace had in the past used the organization of the Ikhwan Al-Muslimun to strengthen their own hand in the internal game (and so did Siraj Al-Din when the Wafd were in power). But the services of Hasan Al-Banna came with a financial and political price-tag; the political price being adherence to a nationalist programme and, in the specific case of Sidqi's purchase of Hasan Al-Banna's help, in February 1946, the release of the demonstrators arrested by Nuqrashi.[30]

But fear of the Wafdist (and Communist) challenge, and the need to placate the Ikhwan to gain their help against that challenge, were not the only reasons behind Sidqi's conduct. He had to shake off the memories of his own repressive measures in 1930–3; and he was also quite aware that even demonstrations hostile to the government would strengthen his hand in the negotiations. A British personality assessment of Sidqi, written in 1945, described him as the most able and cunning statesman in Egypt, yet 'apt (under the influence of ambition, resentment or concupiscence) to keep his nose too close to the scent of his object'.[31] The observation held true—as regards vices, but not virtues—for Sidqi's young master as well. So it was in this case: the Sidqi Government allowed large-scale demonstrations (in which Wafdists and Watanists, Ikhwan and Communists all took part) on 21 February—but these turned into a riot, after an incident involving British lorries: British people and property (including Army camps) were attacked; some thirteen Egyptians were killed and over one hundred wounded from British soldiers' fire. The embassy reacted angrily, demanding punishments, compensations and a commitment to keeping the order; and the British commanders in Cairo were willing to make an official military demarche to Faruq—a course rejected by Bevin, at the advice of the Egyptian Department, as too reminiscent of February 1942.[32]

Sidqi, however, was not easily deterred; he accused the British of having triggered the mob violence by the lorries incident ('irritating verbiage', wrote Scrivener), and while he used the Ikhwan to disrupt the Wafd's call for a three-day strike, he did set 4 March as 'Martyrs' Day'.[33] Faruq, anxious to see the British troops, rivals to his own power in Egypt, leave, backed Sidqi's tactics. The 4 March demonstration in Alexandria, sarcastically described by the US Consul-General, Hooker Doolittle, as 'a splendid foretaste of national dignity and reasoned capacity for self-rule', led to extensive violence, damage to property, and an incident in which, Doolittle wrote, 'statemen from the slums beat up three and lynched two British [military] policemen'.[34] But these events, while doing little to improve Egypt's reputation in Britain or the US, did serve their demonstrative purpose. On 16 March, Bevin instructed Bowker, the Minister in Cairo, to demand the maintenance of law and other—or the British would take forceful action to protect British lives; it was, as Sidqi complained, an ultimatum.[35] But Sidqi, while in fact curbing all further demonstrations, was still defiant in his letter of response: 'Le vrai problème, qui est à l'origine de toutes les difficultés, est celui de la présence des troupes Britanniques dans le pays.'[36]

In a frank admission that the Department's tactics had misfired, Scrivener wrote on 23 February that Faruq, 'having successfully, as he supposes, got rid of Lord Killearn ... imagines he can defy us';[37] but this admission did not amount to a suggestion of return to Lampson's policies. In his 'swan song', written on 6 March 1946, Lampson renewed (in a generally gloomy survey of the situation) his call for active intervention: 'Can we allow Egypt to disintegrate at her own sweet will? ... Can we, in short, admit any diminution of our predominance? With all deference I gravely doubt it.' He felt that a show of determination would suffice, 'For with powder in the gun I maintain that in the East it is usually unnecessary to discharge it'—and that the course of conciliation with the Wafd, rather than a competition with it for nationalist merit, should be forcefully urged on the king. But while Scrivener was impressed by Lampson's assessment (coming as it did after the failure of his own), Howe, who superintended the Department, still urged the wisdom of non-interference.[38] A policy which began as an attempt to transcend Egyptian party politics became an attempt to placate the stronger party, the palace; Lampson's strong advice, not to negotiate with any delegation unless the Wafd participated, went unheeded.[39] This policy of non-intervention was reaffirmed by the Cabinet on 18 March: the new ambassador, Ronald Campbell, was authorized to negotiate with Sidqi's delegation as it stood—Liberal, Sa'dist, Kutla and independent politicians, but no Wafdist representation—if Faruq and Sidqi would pledge themselves against repudiation of the Treaty, once signed. There seems to have been no understanding, in the Cabinet, of the nature of the political game of nationalism in Egypt.[40]

Sensing this lack of British resolve, Sidqi put it to a decisive test. Whereas the British Cabinet refused to interfere in the composition of the Egyptian delegation, Sidqi—upon learning of Campbell's wish to start negotiating at an early date (as Sidqi had asked him to do) assisted by the senior embassy staff—asserted his right to reject the British choice of negotiators. The embassy officials, he said, were unequal in rank to the Egyptian delegation (headed by Sidqi himself, it included four other former prime ministers—Abd al-Fattah Yahia, Ali Mahir, Husain Sirri and Nuqrashi); moreover, the Egyptian public saw them as perpetuating the 'Colonialist' attitudes and actions of the Lampson regime. In this line, again, Sidqi was backed by Faruq.[41] The choice of arguments was significant. The rational issue of rank would have sufficed for Sidqi's immediate purpose; by adding the emotional issue of attitudes to the discussion, Sidqi challenged—successfully, since Campbell does not seem to have demurred—the very continuity of British authority in Egypt. Jacques Berque's assessment of Campbell—'as weak and timid as his predecessor had been imposing and dictatorial'—is typically distorted; a fairer comment was Tuck's observation that Campbell was more of an ambassador than a high commissioner.[42] On 6 April, Campbell suggested to London that 'some small evidence of genuine warmth' might make British representations more effective: 'any blunt speaking that may be necessary will have a better background than that created by an inferiority complex'.[43] But attentiveness to Egyptian psychological attitudes— over the embassy staff issue—led Campbell to avoid some of the blunt speaking he had already been instructed to do. The explicit attempts by Sidqi's Foreign Minister, Lutfi al-Sayid, to inform Campbell that with his arrival no obstacles remained to the fulfilment of all Egyptian wishes, in turns 'annoyed and disgusted and amused' the ambassador.[44] But by accepting Sidqi's argumentation about the Lampson regime, Campbell implicitly based his own position in Egypt on precisely this promise of a new British attitude.

This shift of attitude at the embassy coincided with increasing apprehension among the British military commanders: in a dramatic departure from their previous far-reaching desiderata in Egypt, they concluded on 22 March that with their troops in the cities vulnerable to attacks, it might be best to indicate willingness to settle for 'what the Egyptians will accept', in the hope of calming down the atmosphere—and later obtaining, by suasion, 'some measure of our strategic requirements'.[45] This was a failure to perceive that considerations of political power, rather than of emotional atmosphere, lay behind much of the Egyptian campaign for evacuation. Moreover, Sidqi used the fears that social and economic discontent, aggravated by Soviet propaganda, might combine with the specific political frustrations of the Egyptian political classes (whose 'mental processes were English', claimed Sidqi—'sez you!' wrote Scrivener—yet felt they were not being treated as equals) in order to convince Campbell that a crisis might erupt unless the Egyptian national aspirations were satisfied.[46] Campbell was impressed; the embassy, he wrote on 25 March, fully endorsed the commanders'-in-chief recommendation to settle for 'what the Egyptians will accept'—and to concede, therefore, the principle that 'HMG have no intention of maintaining forces in Egypt against the wishes of the Egyptian people'.[47]

These were momentous conclusions to have been reached within weeks of a major crisis and, in Campbell's case, within days of arrival in Egypt. Scrivener was suspicious: 'I think we must be on guard against being bluffed out of Egypt by Sidki and the King', he wrote in response to Campbell's ideas.[48] His own reaction to the events of February had been rather the opposite of Campbell's: the violence only demonstrated the need for firm control, he argued, and it was 'totally fallacious' to assume that British concessions would bring about an end to the demonstrations—'Egyptians will riot about anything'. In international terms, he felt, it would be 'unpleasantly symbolic' if Britain lost the position in Egypt—and to set an example of behaviour when no other power did so would be 'akin to suicide'. An alternative strategic base in British East Africa was being considered; but if it proved impossible or insufficient for its purpose, Scrivener felt, 'we ought to stand fast in Egypt, and face riots and the Security Council if necessary'. These views were expressed in the Egyptian Department's brief for Bevin, submitted on 17 March 1946.[49]

Underlying this basic divergence of views between Campbell and Scrivener was a basic difference of political and even philosophical perception. Campbell tended to see Egyptian politicians—and mainly Sidqi, a personal friend since Campbell's spell in Cairo some fourteen years earlier—as expressing general Egyptian aspirations which, if satisfied, would cease to be a source of tension in Anglo-Egyptian relations. Scrivener tended to see the 'national aspirations' as devices—not necessarily reflecting the will of the mass of the people, the Fallahin—which Egyptian politicians used in their struggles for power and which were likely to be used, whatever concessions were made, as long as these struggles persisted. the continued presence of British troops in Egypt thus became not just an importance issue in itself—as indeed it was—but also, in the circumstances, a test of political premises: would Britain's power in Egypt come to rely on Egyptian goodwill, or would Egyptian goodwill and co-operation be secured by resolute indications of British power. Unless the circumstances were to be changed by direct British action, which Lampson had vainly hoped would happen, or unless Britain chose to forgo all interest in Egypt, which was unlikely, some choice between these *principia negata* had to be made—although it took some time, and some acute disappointments, before the stark nature of the choice became quite clear in London. Bevin's initial attitudes indicated a refusal to admit the inevitability of the choice: he refused to believe that the Egyptians would indeed insist on evacuation; he told both Campbell and Amr that Britain would require a garrison in the Canal Zone; but at the same time he sought to square the vicious circle by sending to Egypt as the actual head of the British delegation (Bevin himself, in response to Sidqi's representations, was to be the nominal head) the Secretary of State for Air, Lord Stansgate, who as William Wedgwood Benn had been a radical advocate of Egyptian nationalism in the House of Commons at the time of Zaghlul.[50] While Bevin's precise motives are unknown, he evidently felt that by sending a friend of Egypt to Egypt he would help Campbell in creating an atmosphere in which blunt speaking would be better heard. But Sidqi's strategies were based on politics, not on atmospherics—a point which Stansgate, by the very nature of his mission, was ill-equipped to realize. Events were to prove that the decision to ask Stansgate to go was in itself akin to a choice in favour of Campbell's concepts.

Sidqi himself was eager to force a choice: devices to avoid it, such as the notions of leased bases or a regional military alliance, were dismissed by him, quite easily, as impracticable and irrelevant.[51] The representation—and rejection—of such ruses did little to enhance British credibility or Egyptian flexibility; this later shaped Campbell's and Stansgate's conviction that if a concession had to be made, it had to be made early in the negotiations rather than be triumphantly extracted by Sidqi. Sensing that British inclination, Sidqi did not bargain for the concessions he sought but rather repeatedly—and in writing—hammered home the need for them. His *aide-memoire* of 4 April was followed by a *projet de note* of the Egyptian delegation, which Sidqi first sent to London through Archibald Clark Kerr (on his way back from his service in Moscow) and officially submitted two weeks later, on 18 April, upon Stansgate's arrival.[52] Both documents rejected any notion of keeping British troops as incompatible with the sovereignty and dignity of Egypt and with the principles of the new world order: a point of departure for the negotiations which deliberately left no room for bargaining on that issue.

'If one were convinced that this was Sidky's final conclusion, or even that Sidky himself believed in his own arguments, it would be open to question whether Lord Stansgate's journey would serve any useful purpose,' wrote Scrivener on 6 April.[53] The Chiefs of Staff did not favour the East African alternative; and this confirmed him in his view that Sidqi's objections would have to be overcome—perhaps with help from Faruq, who was believed to be more responsive to British military desiderata.[54] Campbell, however, was already advocating a clear choice between the two courses—insistence on maintaining troops, or evacuation—both of which, he knew, were gambles: but gambling on keeping the troops meant the risk of tension, ill-will, violence, and perhaps an Egyptian appeal to the UN—an outburst of nationalist activity that could not be controlled; while a gamble of evacuation would still make it possible to argue for the necessary military concessions from the Egyptians. Campbell therefore did little to press London's views on Sidqi, as both settled down to await Stansgate's arrival.[55] The delegation, indeed, arrived with new instructions.

Bevin's new plan—which he outlined to Stansgate and his assistants prior to their departure, but which still had to be approved by the Chiefs of Staff—consisted of five points: gradual evacuation of all combatant troops (the Canal Zone to be evacuated last); naval, land and air defence organizations to be maintained by the Egyptians with British help; transit rights—and the relevant establishment—for British troops; regional headquarters in the Canal Zone; and the provision of arms and supplies for the Egyptian forces. It was Bevin's hope that generosity on points one and five would be met by Egyptian flexibility on the other points; and in line with Campbell's attitude, the Cabinet agreed that the concessions involved—agreement, albeit conditional, to evacuate—should be made forthwith. The Joint Planning Staff and the Chiefs of Staff introduced one major modification, a demand for the retention of British fighter squadrons in Egypt; and the instructions—known as 'Plan A'—were approved by the Defence Committee on 15 April, the day on which the Stansgate delegation arrived in Egypt, and sent to Egypt a day later.[56]

Campbell and Stansgate, however, found the plan inadequate for their purpose. It was a design for a bargain; what they were after was not a bargain but a change of atmosphere, a gesture magnanimous enough to create trust instead of suspicion, goodwill instead of hostility—the Egyptian position being attributed to suspicion and hostility, not to the concrete purposes of Egyptian politicians. The delegation thus decided not to present 'Plan A' as the official British position but to discuss it informally first with Sidqi and Faruq.[57] This 'somewhat pusillanimous attitude' alarmed the Chiefs of Staff: the risks involved in 'a gamble of Egypt's goodwill' were too great to take, ruled the JPS.[58] Scrivener, and apparently Bevin, who approved his sharply-worded telegram, agreed with the planners: what the Foreign Office wished to see was a clear indication whether or not the Egyptians appreciated what was at stake. London evidently did not believe in the prospects of transforming Egyptian attitudes through concessions: 'If Egyptian attitude proves as uncompromising as you suggest, I think we shall have to consider whether it is worth our while to negotiate in such an atmosphere.' The Egyptians, Stansgate was told, 'must come clean. I want no oriental bargaining.'[59]

This telegram arrived too late to influence Stansgate's first meeting with Sidqi (who was recovering from pneumonia) on 18 April. Even according to Stansgate's own version of the conversation, it seems clear that in it he was touched by Sidqi's references to his past support for Egyptian nationalism, and that he did not try to dispute Sidqi's basic premises about evacuation as a *sine qua non* of any settlement, and about the goodwill which might emerge if Britain proved magnanimous, as opposed to the hostility which would go on if no gesture came. Unlike the Egyptian Department, Stansgate—searching for evidence which would confirm his (and Campbell's) basic preconceptions—saw signs of goodwill in Sidqi's written presentations.[60] Sidqi thus had some cause to complain, a day later, that the attitudes reflected in 'Plan A' were intransigent in comparison with the sentiments expressed by Stansgate. Moreover he had already forced previous attempts at compromise out of the way and thus sensed how eager his interlocutors were to avoid a confrontation. He therefore insisted that the continued occupation, in any guise and form, would be violently rejected; and Stansgate and Campbell, offering little more than half-hearted responses, evidently shared his assessment on that point.[61] Sidqi was, of course, in a position to stir up some violence himself, and as such his predictions of trouble had to be taken into account; moreover, his arguments—influenced as they were by the

US Minister's musings about the strategic implications of the atomic weapon—that the Soviet threat was political and not military, deprived the British of one of the strongest arguments against evacuation.[62] Faruq—upon whose powers the British forces constituted a direct limitation—was equally adamant on evacuation, depriving the Foreign Office of another hope of compromise.[63]

Pressing the challenge home by the use of deliberately insulting language, Sidqi put before Campbell and Stansgate, on 22 April, a note he had prepared a day earlier: it totally rejected any notion of a British or an 'Allied' base in Egypt. Neither the alleged threat from the East or 'any other product of the always fertile imagination of Chancelleries' would convince Egypt to 'alienate her independence'. His Egyptian military advisers offered the 'technical' view that Egypt could defend the Canal Zone herself, with help, in times of crisis, from British forces in Palestine and Cyprus.[64] To Sidqi's own surprise, neither Campbell nor Stansgate tried to argue against his note, despite the violence of its language. 'I fear that our conversation with the Prime Minister has not advanced the matter in the direction we desire,' Stansgate reported. If Sidqi's account of it can be relied on, this was an understatement. Sidqi seems to have forced Stansgate back upon the notion of British 'experts' with the Egyptian Army, out of uniform and responsible to the Egyptians alone—in other words, upon total evacuation; and he asked for prompt action, to outmanœuvre the 'extreme' members of the Egyptian delegation.[65] It was under these circumstances—defying its instructions in pursuit of Sidqi's elusive goodwill—that the British delegation sought to confront London with the need to choose.

Stansgate's notes indicate that he was aware of the ambiguities of the Egyptian political situation and of the British forces' ability to put down any violence, if need be; but that he nevertheless felt that the British position was internationally untenable, and the sooner it was transformed, the better.[66] Urgency bred brevity: Stansgate's decisive telegram to Bevin (no. 713) deliberately glossed over the uncertainties involved. He did trace the situation in Egypt—which, he suspected, Bevin did not understand—to the agitation which Sidqi and Faruq had encouraged and to the fears and ignorance of the Egyptian delegation. Yet he ultimately saw these not as political ills (curable by a change in the political situation) but as manifestations of authentic aspirations and fears (thus curable by an act of magnanimity, namely, evacuation). He seemed as confident that evacuation would procure goodwill as he was that refusal to evacuate would lead to disorders: 'The Egyptians would meet us half-way in facilitating operation of any scheme worked out on these lines, and of course they would give us complete freedom of action in Egypt at a time of apprehended emergency and in war. ["Ha! Ha!" scribbled Scrivener bitterly some time later] ... This is surely worth more than a position gained at the point of a bayonet.' He therefore urged for an early statement that 'HMG were proposing to withdraw all British armed forces from Egyptian soil' and to negotiate for the necessary arrangements for mutual assistance.[67]

This was not the isolated judgment of an inexperienced newcomer to Egyptian affairs: it was the view of the delegation, of senior members of the embassy staff, and of several diplomats in Cairo that Britain would only gain if attention was paid, above all, to Egyptian *amour propre*.[68] Thomas Russell Pasha, head of the Cairo Police—a formidable authority—also argued along these lines, so as to avoid a possible confrontation with the extremist elements within the Egyptian Army and a collapse of the Egyptian state.[69] General Paget, the Commander-in-Chief Middle East, wrote to the Chief of Staff, Alanbrooke, on 24 April to report a conversation he had with Smuts in which they both agreed that the evacuation would be disastrous and that the 'policy of scuttle' should be halted; but this new assertion of a tough line could not undo the impact of the Commanders'-in-Chief earlier position in favour of evacuation: only two days earlier they still wrote to London and agreed, albeit reluctantly, that the course advocated by Stansgate's telegram 713 was the lesser of two evils.[70]

This specific confusion points, perhaps, at the manner in which Stansgate and Campbell influenced the considerations for or against evacuation: it was the inability of the delegation, or the embassy, to contemplate a change in the political circumstances in Egypt, their tacit assumption that *tertium non datur*, that led them to point to the two evils of violence or concessions and consistently prefer the second. In this tacit acceptance of the given situation, Campbell's sympathy towards Sidqi and Stansgate's inclination to defer to Egyptian nationalism were both of some import; but the decisions which had left them powerless in Cairo had, in fact, been taken well before their arrival there. Once Lampson's concept of intervention was discredited, the British in Egypt could not freely participate in the power game into which they were drawn; they could only resist its pressures, perhaps violently, or be ejected, more or less gracelessly from their position. Scrivener, rejecting Lampson's strategies, had hoped to put an end to the irrationalities of Egyptian politics by allowing Faruq a free run—but failed; he now found it increasingly difficult to resist the pressure to try out a new way. On 23 April—despite the doubts of his superior, Howe—he conceded that a 'purely political decision' was now called for—in other words, that the Egyptian Department no longer felt competent to oppose the delegation's views. Orme Sargent, the new Permanent Under-Secretary, did feel competent to do so—and continued to feel so throughout the period of the negotiations.[71] But his objections, while they stood, did not prevail.

General Jacob, a member of Stansgate's delegation and an experienced negotiator at the first stages of the establishment of UNO, came back to London on 23 April; the US legation deduced, and Sidqi must have known, that his purpose was to present evacuation as the only solution to the deadlock.[72] Jacob was, indeed, the key speaker in the crucial Defence Committee discussion held on 24 April 1946; and his assessment was the decisive element in convincing the Chiefs of Staff, and the Committee, that the choice between violent disorders or evacuation was indeed inevitable, since 'all articulate levels of Egyptian opinion' demanded it (ignoring the association of most such articulate opinion with concrete political purposes, purposes which shows of British goodwill could not satisfy). Moreover, Jacob assured Bevin that wartime facilities in Egypt could be secured, and that a five-year period for evacuation might prove acceptable to the Egyptians. It was only on the basis of these optimistic assertions—made by a man of no intimate knowledge of Egyptian politics (beyond the notion that 'pride and ignorance' motivated Egyptian politicians)— that Attlee concluded the discussions by deciding to recommend to the Cabinet 'Course B'—an early announcement on evacuation.[73] The Cabinet decision, taken on the same day, was based on even less accurate information: while Bevin chose the five-year figure for reasons of political re-appraisal, Attlee presented the evacuation in any shorter time as physically impossible, and the decision to evacuate was endorsed by the Cabinet on the assumption that Egyptian acceptance of the five-year period can be and would be secured.[74]

Neither the Defence Committee nor the Cabinet accepted the extreme form of the delegation's doctrine—limiting British requirements altogether to 'what the Egyptians will accept'. The choice, in the fullness of its implications, of abandoning all claim to determine the future of the position in Egypt was thus never entirely made. This left the sceptics in the Foreign Office room for delaying action, and it left the delegation in a position to claim that the concessions they had suggested failed to achieve their purpose because they were made only half-heartedly and conditionally. Typical of the ambiguities, which arose out of the manner in which this crucial decision was taken, was the complex discussion on the wording and timing of the British announcement. The Egyptian Department wished to include in the instructions to Cairo a clarification, based on Sargent's observations, that the commitment to defend Egypt will hold only if the facilities for doing so were provided. Jacob's advice, however, was to separate the announcement on evacuation and the clarification on defence, so as not to 'plunge the Egyptians into a further fever of suspicion', and it was decided to send two separate telegrams to Cairo. Even so, the very hint that the continued alliance must depend on the availability of defence facilities seemed to Stansgate to damage the impact of evacuation as an act of magnanimity and to create the impression (which he hoped to avoid) of retreat under pressure, and perhaps a tactical and insincere retreat.[75] Stansgate does not seem to have realized that no Egyptian was likely, ever, to attribute anything to British 'magnanimity': in a struggle for power such abstractions are meaningless, and a retreat by any other name is still a retreat.

The Egyptian Department, for their part, were reluctant to try and give an apparently false appearance to a decision which had been forced upon them: 'if we are not being "kicked out" we are none the less evacuating against our better judgment'. Bevin was equally unhappy with Stansgate's line:

> I have assumed in all this, as a result of what I have been told, that I am dealing with great friends who believe that our interests are bound up together and that both the governments here and in Egypt are determined to act honestly and honourably.[76]

A note of sarcasm towards Stansgate's tactics and the illusions they were based on thus crept into Bevin's attitude; as the pattern of concessions repeated itself during the negotiations, this note became more pronounced ('When you go to Sidky and put to him my revised Article 2 [on the purposes of the alliance] ... as persuasively as you have put the Egyptian case to me, he will allow himself to be convinced', wrote Bevin to Stansgate on 9 August).[77] And ultimately Bevin took direct control of the talks and tried for a direct and hard bargain with Sidqi rather than a well-intentioned quest for Egyptian goodwill. (The bargain was struck in London in October 1946; but it did not survive Sidqi's return into Egyptian politics.) All this was yet to come, however; at the end of April it was still London's decision to allow Stansgate's strategy an opportunity to evolve.

Thus not only the reservations about the alliance met with Stansgate's and Campbell's reluctance to antagonize the Egyptians; so did the Cabinet's expressed wish to secure Egyptian acceptance of the five-year period. The British delegation seemed to the US Minister to share his feeling that it would come as a 'bitter blow' to the Egyptians, who had been speculating—probably with Tuck's tacit encouragement—that six months to a year would suffice.[78] Sidqi—by now fully aware of his interlocutors' purposes and responses to pressure—convinced the British delegation on 4 May that any public reference to five years would raise a public outcry which would undo the effects of the concession of evacuation. The delegation therefore went back to a wording similar to that suggested in telegram 713 of 22 April:

It is the considered policy of H.M.G. in the U.K. to consolidate their alliance with Egypt as one between two equal nations having interests in common. In pursuance of this policy negotiations have begun in an atmosphere of cordiality and goodwill. The Government of the U.K. have proposed the withdrawal of all British Naval, Military and Air Forces from Egyptian territory, and to settle in negotiations stages and the date of completion of this withdrawal and arrangements to be made by the Egyptian Government to make possible mutual assistance in time of war or imminent threat of war in accordance with the alliance.

The argument that this would leave the Egyptians' hands free, wrote Stansgate on 4 May, was irrelevant: 'We cannot, in any case, go back on our offer of withdrawal, and we shall have to do our best to negotiate on details.' The delegation was thus firmly embarked upon the slippery slope; they pressed for a statement within a day.[79]

Attlee was reluctant to be pushed into a hasty declaration which would in effect contradict the purpose of the Cabinet's instructions; but the delegation were adamant that a declaration of intent was necessary if Faruq and Sidqi were to succeed in calming down the Egyptian public, and that any reference to the five years would wreck these efforts (which at this stage they still thought were sincere— despite the fact that up to that point it was precisely the prospects of violence, not of calm, which had best served Sidqi's interests). 'The fat would be probably in the fire and we would have to brazen it out, though knowing well that in the last resort we are not prepared to force our will on the country.'[80] Campbell thus stated, again, the principle of accepting whatever deal the Egyptians would consent to, for lack of a better alternative; he was evidently hoping to see this understood and approved in London. Bevin (from Paris) agreed, without specific comments, to have the issue brought before the Cabinet, and it was on the basis of very scanty discussion of the real issues that the Cabinet took up a line which could be read as accepting the delegation's premises: 'It would be impracticable for us to seek to maintain our existing position in Egypt by the use of force. . . . We can only secure military facilities there by agreement with the Egyptian Government.' The delegation's text was approved.[81]

Attlee thus brought before Parliament, on 7 May 1946, a statement which he himself had just been reluctant to make on a policy which had been endorsed with grave misgivings. He could not entirely hide this from the House, no matter how magnanimous he had wished to seem. Churchill rose to decry the offer of evacuation as 'a very grave statement, one of the most momentous I have heard in this House . . . sixty years of diplomacy and administration ["That is long enough", cried a radical Labour MP] ... cast away with great shame and folly'.[82] Whereas Eden attacked the unwisdom of abandoning the 1936 Treaty, other Conservative members pointed to Attlee's unease and to his inaccurate claims to have the backing of the Dominions and of the Chiefs of Staff. While Labour members (including Kenneth Lindsay and Richard Crossman) advocated accommodating Egyptian nationalism, Conservatives (including Quintin Hogg and Brigadier Low) accused the Cabinet of appeasing 'over-emotional, nationalistically-minded students'—an accusation to which Morrison inadvertently lent some weight when he admitted that the Cabinet had only 'reluctantly' agreed to evacuation.[83]

Churchill's adjournment motion was rejected by 307 to 158. But the debate deepened, rather than resolved, the ambiguities of the British position. To have hoped, as the delegation did, to present the evacuation concession as a spontaneous and magnanimous act was to reckon without British opinion—and without what the Egyptians already knew about the development of the British position. Sidqi, in his memoirs, attributed the British decision—a victory for Egypt—to the nation's unified will (in fact, however, up until 1945 only the Watanists stood for 'evacuation before negotiations'); his enthusiastic biographer attributed it to Sidqi's own determination, courage and cunning.[84] Neither account gave any scope to the manifestations of magnanimity which Stansgate had hoped to stress. This proved to be of decisive importance in the negotiations which followed: again and again British proposals were rejected as arousing Egyptian suspicions or as wounding Egyptian pride. The core of the problem, which the British concessions were supposed to resolve, was evidently still there and did not prove amenable to rational suasion.

The problem, indeed, was a problem of power, not of policy. Stansgate, quite simply, felt that the British had no cards to play: 'What means have we of bringing pressure to bear on the Egyptians? ... If a national coalition is formed [there was a rumour at the time that a former Wafdist President of the Senate, Zaki al-Urabi, might be asked to form a coalition Cabinet], what means have we for compelling them to accept our terms?'[85] In the debate of 7 May, Churchill suggested one possible answer: 'We have been hampered,' he said, 'by our respect for the authority of the Egyptian potentates and assemblies and by not wanting to interfere too much in the affairs of the country. But it is shocking how little progress there had been among the great masses of Egyptian Fellaheen.'[86] Implied in this observation was a train of thought not unlike that of Lampson's more audacious suggestions: that a generation of dealing with the nationalist political classes in Egypt had benefited neither Britain nor the great majority of Egyptians. Churchill left the conclusions unsaid; but the problem of intervention—of the ability to exercise power in Egypt—was evident in the alternative answers already provided. Scrivener had hoped to avoid the exercise of power by dealing with a strong throne; Stansgate had hoped to do so by making British goodwill manifest for all. Both failed; but the failure did not make for a radical alternative. Both contributed, in disappointments rather than in hopes, to the duality and ambiguity of the British purpose in Egypt.

In mid-June, the negotiations having come to a halt, Campbell turned to the contemplation of these 'inherent contradictions'. Policies of non-intervention and of evacuation had been announced; but in 'the time-lag between the adoption of a policy and its full application' the troops were still there—and with them the remembered practice, the constant temptation, and often the need, of intervention. More-over, 'there is on the Egyptian side a corresponding time-lag between the achievement of independence and the loss of the "occupied" mentality, which expects [and, he might have added, which sees the political benefits of] "intervention" action in certain circumstances and regards anything less as a sign of weakness.' This kept alive the 'spell of morbid sickness', the obsession with 'the Egyptian question' at the expense of the acutely-needed attention to Egypt's awesome social and economic problems. But for the British there was no alter-native: to confront the entire Egyptian system directly was an un-happy prospect; to leave them 'to flout us with impunity' would have entailed the loss of the entire Middle Eastern position.[87] Neither the negotiations of 1946 nor the Security Council debate of 1947, nor again Egypt's military adventure in 1949, could provide a way out of the Anglo-Egyptian deadlock.

Notes

1. Shone's telegram 325, 27 September 1943, and F.O. minutes, P.R.O., F.O. 371/35528/J4152.
2. See Bahi Al-Din Barakat's articles in *al-Ithnain*, 11 September, and *al-Musawwar*, 17 November 1944.
3. Minutes of the DC(44) 4th meeting, 19 April 1944, P.R.O., AIR 23/6201.
4. Lampson's telegrams 731, 13 April 1944 (P.R.O., F.O. 371/41327/J1318), and 732 (most secret and most personal, to Chur-chill), same date (P.R.O., F.O. 954/50).
5. On the 'juxtaposition' of Ahmad Mahir *vs.* Palace, see Lamp-son's telegram 2365, 15 November 1944 (P.R.O., F.O. 371/41335/J4079): on the subsidy, see Embassy minutes, 12–14 Feb-ruary 1944 (P.R.O., 141/937/1/39); on his gambling, see Gerald

Delaney's letter to Scrivener, 10 February 1945 (F.O. 371/45917/J627).

6. Lampson's telegram 12, 13 January 1945 (P.R.O., F.O. 371/45916/J301).

7. Copies or summaries of Egyptian internal documents outlining diplomatic strategy are in P.R.O., F.O. 371/46028/J1634 and F.O. 371/45921/J1811 and J1885.

8. Some of the Military Sub-Committee correspondence with the Reconstruction Department (Admiral Bellairs' correspondence with Gladwyn Jebb) during 1943 is in P.R.O., F.O. 371/35407/U3313 and U4225 and P.R.O., W.O. 32/10254; Cornwallis' letter to Peterson, 19 March 1944 (F.O. 371/40740/U5908).

9. Peterson's letter to Lampson, 28 April 1944 (F.O. 371/40740/U748).

10. Peake's paper, 'The Long Term Problems of the Suez Canal'. February 1945, S.C. (m) (45)2, and the Committee's conclusions, S.C. (m) (45) 1st [and last] meeting, 13 March 1945 (P.R.O., C.A.B. 95/18).

11. Bevin's report on the Middle East Conference, C.P. (45) 174, 17 September 1845 (P.R.O., F.O. 371/45253/E7151).

12. Lampson's minute, 18 April 1945 (P.R.O., F.O. 371/45921/J1811).

14. Lampson's telegram 1401, 23 June 1945 (F.O. minutes) and Churchill's note to Cadogan, 26 June (P.R.O., F.O. 371/45921/J2054); Sargent's memorandum to Churchill, 30 June (F.O. 954/5D).

15. Scrivener's minute, 20 June 1945 (P.R.O., F.O. 371/45921/J1875).

16. Lampson's telegram 1870 (to Cadogan), 18 August 1945 (P.R.O., F.O. 371/45924/J2748).

17. Campbell's memorandum, 12 August 1945, on his talk with Amr, 8 August, and Scrivener's brief for Bevin, 10 August (P.R.O., F.O. 371/45923/J2677 and J2626).

18. Howe's memorandum to Cadogan, 29 September 1945, on his talk with Amr (P.R.O., F.O. 371/45926/J3372).

19. Scrivener's draft memorandum, prepared for Howe, 18 October 1945 (P.R.O., F.O. 371/45927/J3526).

20. US Military Attaché report R-555-45, 1 November 1945 (USNA-RG226/XL-24600).

21. See, for example, Lampson's draft telegram 2498, 28 November 1945, and Embassy minutes (P.R.O., F.O. 141/1005/1/242).

22. Amr's official note, 20 December 1945 (P.R.O., F.O. 371/45929/J4236).

23. See papers on the assassination and the trial in P.R.O., F.O.

371/53341, and compare Ahmed Murtada al Maraghli, *Gharaib Min Ahd Faruq wa-bidayat al-Thawrah ah-Misriyyah* (Beirut, 1976).

24. Lampson's telegrams 36, 9 January 1945, and 61 (personal to Howe), 17 January (P.R.O., F.O. 731/53282/J132 and J193).

25. F.O. telegram 131 to Cairo, 25 January 1846 (P.R.O., F.O. 371/53282/J289).

26. Correspondence on that incident is in P.R.O., F.O. 371/53283/J407, J431, J457 and J550; see also Muhammad al-Tabi'i, *Misr ma qabl al-Thawrah, min asrar al-Sasah wal-siyasah* (Cairo, 1978), p. 332.

27. Text of rescript quoted in Sinniyah Qara'ah, *Namir al-Siyasah al-Misriyyah* (Cairo, 1950), pp. 429–30; Winant's telegram 2134, 20 February 1946 (USNA-RG59/883.00/2-2046).

28. Scrivener's minute, 5 March 1946 (P.R.O., F.O. 371/53286/J966); Smart's note, 7 March (P.R.O., F.O. 371/53288/J1256); Tuck's telegram 289, 13 February 1946 (USNA-RG59/883.00/2-1346).

29. Security intelligence, middle East, [S.I.M.E.] Reports on Egypt for January and February 1946 (sent by A. J. Kellar, MI5, to Scrivener) (P.R.O., F.O. 371/53286/J941 and and F.O. 371/53289/J1416).

30. On the circumstances of the Ikhwan's deal with Sidqi, see Mahmud Abd al-Halim, *Al-Ikhwan al-Muslimun, Ahdath Sana'at al-Ta'qrikh* (Alexandria, 1979), pp. 363–6.

31. Farquhar (British Minister in Cairo) despatch 1205 (personalities list), 29 August 1945, copy in House of Lords Record Office [HLRO], Stansgate Papers, 188/11(2).

32. Chiefs of Staff conclusions, C.O.S. (46), 30th meeting, 22 February 1946 (P.R.O., C.A.B. 79/45); Defence Committee conclusions, D.O. (46), 6th meeting, same date (P.R.O., C.A.B. 131/1); Bevin's minute to Attlee, same date (P.R.O., F.O. 371/53285/J889.

33. Sidqi's note to Bowker, 22 February 1946, and minutes (P.R.O., F.O. 371/53286/J982); S.I.M.E., report on February (F.O. 371/53289/J1416); US Strategic Services Unit, Cairo Report G-9383, 11 March 1946 (USNA (Military Branch), RG226/XL-47579); Abd al-Halim, *Al-Ikhwan al-Muslimun . . .*, pp. 367–73.

34. Doolittle's telegram 29, 5 March 1946, and despatch 207, 6 March (USNA-RG59/883.00/3-546 and 3-646).

35. Bevin's telegram 488 to Cairo, 16 March 1946 (first drafted 3 March) (P.R.O., F.O. 371/53287/J1088); Tuck's airgram 116, 26 March 1946 (reporting Sidqi's complaint) (USNA-RG59/883.00/3-2646).

36. Sidqi's letter to Bowker, 23 March 1946 (P.R.O., F.O. 371/ 53292/J1752).
37. Scrivener's minute, 23 February 1946 (P.R.O., F.O. 371/53285/ J766).
38. Bowker's telegram 101—Lampson's *swan-song*—6 March 1946, and minutes (P.R.O., F.O. 371/53288/J1135).
39. Lampson's telegram 438, 8 March 1946, and minutes (P.R.O., F.O. 371/53287/J1059); Lambert's minute of a discussion with Bevin, 11 March (F.O. 371/53288/J1151).
40. Cabinet conclusions, C.M. 25(46), 18 March 1946, minute 4 (P.R.O., C.A.B. 128/5).
41. Sidqi, *Mudhakkirati* (Cairo, 1950), pp. 61–2; Campbell's telegrams 575 and 576, 30 March 1946, and minutes (P.R.O., F.O. 371/53289/J1363, J1402 and J1403).
42. Berque, *Egypt: Imperialism and Revolution* (London, 1972), p. 579; Tuck's telegram 542, 29 March 1946 (USNA-RG59/741.83/3–2946).
43. Campbell's telegram 625, 6 April 1946 (P.R.O., F.O. 371/53290/ J1534).
44. Campbell's saving telegram 123, 25 March 1946 (P.R.O., F.O. 371/53289/J1393).
45. Commanders-in-Chief Middle East, telegram CCL/79, 22 March 1946 (P.R.O., C.A.B. 79/46).
46. Keown-Boyd's letter to Smart, 20 March 1946, and Campbell's record of his personal talk with Sidqi at Keown-Boyd's house, 25 March (P.R.O., F.O. 141/1081/30/20).
47. Campbell's telegram 548, 25 March 1946 (P.R.O., F.O. 371/ 53289/J1301).
48. Scrivener's minutes, 26 and 27 March 1946 (P.R.O., F.O. 371/ 53289/J1309 and J1327).
49. Scrivener's minute to Howe, 2 March 1946, and minutes (P.R.O., F.O. 371/53286/J942) and Howe's note to Bevin, 17 March (F.O. 371/53289/J1306).
50. Bevin's telegrams 559, 28 March 1946 (P.R.O., F.O. 371/53289/ J1327) and 599, 1 April (F.O. 371/53290/J1446); Royal Institute of International Affairs, *Great Britain and Egypt 1914–1951* (London, 1952), p. 87.
51. Campbell's telegram 598, 2 April 1946 (P.R.O., F.O. 371/ 53290/J1444); compare with Sidqi's record (in French), same date (F.O. 371/53291/J1599), and his *Mudhakkirati*, pp. 62–3.
52. Campbell's telegram 609, 610 and 630, 5 and 7 April 1946, and Sidqi'a (draft) *Projet de note* as sent with Clark Kerr, 4 April (P.R.O., F.O. 371/53290/J1507, J1511 and J1531); copy of the

final project, Tuck's despatch 1410, 25 April (USNA-RG59/
741.83/4–2546).

53. Scrivener's minute, 6 April 1946 (P.R.O., F.O. 371/53290/
J1511).

54. Defence Committee paper, D.O. (46)48(o), 2 April 1946
(P.R.O., C.A.B. 131/2); Howe's note to Bevin, 4 April (F.O.
371/53289/J1305), and Paget's personal telegram 946/C.I.C. to
CIGS (Alanbrook), 10 April (F.O. 371/53290/J1508).

55. Campbell's telegrams 636, 638, 658 and 660, 9 and 12 April
1946 (P.R.O., F.O. 371/53291/J1580, J1583, J1630 and J1628
(respectively)).

56. Scrivener's note to the COS, 10 April 1946 (P.R.O., F.O. 371/
53291/J1661); C.M. 33(46), 11 April 1946, minute 4 (C.A.B.
128/5); J.P. (46)73 (final, and revised final), 11 and 15 April
1946 (C.A.B. 84/80); COS (46) 59th and 60th meetings, 12 and
15 April (C.A.B. 79/47); D.O. (46) 12th meeting, 15 April
(C.A.B. 131/1); F.O. telegrams 718 and 719 to Cairo, 16 April
1946 (P.R.O., F.O. 371/53291/J1659 and J1669).

57. Stansgate's telegram to Bevin (Campbell's 679), 17 April 1946
(P.R.O., F.O. 371/53291/J1669).

58. COS (46) 61st meeting, 18 April 1946 (P.R.O., C.A.B. 79/47),
and J.P. (46)84 (final), same date (C.A.B. 84/81).

59. Bevin's telegram 744 to Stansgate, 18 April 1946 (P.R.O., F.O.
371/53291/J1669).

60. Stansgate's record of the meeting with Sidqi, 18 April 1946,
HLRO, Stansgate Papers, 188/14; and contrast Lambert's minute, 10 April (P.R.O., F.O. 371/53290/J1531).

61. Sidqi, *Mudhakkirati*, pp. 67–71; Stansgate's record of the meeting
of 19 April 1946, HLRO, Stansgate [ST] Papers, 188/10, and
his telegram to Bevin (Campbell's 703), 20 April (P.R.O., F.O.
371/53292/J1723).

62. See Campbell's telegram 719, 23 April 1946 (P.R.O., F.O. 371/
53292/J1788), in conjunction with Tuck's airgram 117, 28
March 1946 (USNA-RG59/741.83/3–2846).

63. Campbell's telegrams 714, 717 and 718, 22 and 23 April 1946
(P.R.O., F.O. 371/53292/J1734, J1769 and J1771); Stansgate's
records of talks with Faruq, 19 April, HLRO, ST/188/10, and
21 April, ST/188/14.

64. Sidqi's note (including the military advisers' views), 21 April
1946, Cabinet Paper C.O. (46)170, 24 April 1946 (P.R.O.,
C.A.B. 129/9).

65. Sidqi, *Mudhakkirati*, pp. 71–2; Stansgate's telegram to Bevin
(Campbell's 714), 22 April 1946 (P.R.O., F.O. 371/53292/
J1734.

66. Stansgate's 'appreciation' notes, 20 and 22 April 1946, HLRO, ST/188/8.
67. Stansgate's telegram to Bevin (Campbell's 713), 22 April 1946 (P.R.O., F.O. 371/53292/J1735).
68. Bowker's letter to Scrivener, 6 April 1946 (P.R.O., F.O. 371/53291/J1675); Campbell's saving telegrams 153, 154 and 155, 21 April (F.O. 371/53292/J1786, J1790 and J1785 (respectively)).
69. Campbell's despatch 505, 15 April 1946 (P.R.O., F.O. 371/53292/J1764); Stansgate's record of a talk with Russell, 20 April, HLRO, ST/188/10.
70. Paget's unnumbered personal telegram to Alanbrooke, 24 April 1946, and Alanbrooke's minute to Bevin, BM/24/642, same date; and compare C.-in-C. telegram 06041/81/CCL, 22 April 1946 (F.O. 371/53292/J1789 and J1723).
71. Scrivener's, Howe's and Sargent's minutes, 23 and 24 April 1946 (P.R.O., F.O. 371/53292/J1723).
72. Ireland's memorandum of conversation with Speaight, 26 April 1946 (USNA-RG59/741.83/4–2946).
73. D.O. (46) 14th meeting, 24 April 1946, minute 2 (P.R.O., C.A.B. 131/1).
74. C.M. 37(46), 24 April 1946, minute 1 (P.R.O., C.A.B. 128/5).
75. F.O. draft telegram 782, 25 April 1946, Scrivener's minute to Dixon, same date, and F.O. telegram 794, 27 April (P.R.O., F.O. 371/53292/J1735); Stansgate's note, 26 April, HLRO, ST/188/8, and his telegram 754, 28 April 1946 (P.R.O., F.O. 371/53293/J1854).
76. F.O. telegram 813, Scrivener's and Bevin's draft, 29 April 1946 (P.R.O., F.O. 371/53293/J1854).
77. Bevin's telegram 39 to Stansgate in Alexandria (Scrivener's draft), 9 August 1946 (P.R.O., F.O. 371/53309/J3520).
78. Tuck's telegram 746, 30 April 1946 (USNA-RG59/741.83/4–3046).
79. Stansgate's telegram to Bevin (Campbell's 795), 4 May 1946 (P.R.O., F.O. 371/53293/J1957).
80. Campbell's telegram 805, 5 May 1946 (P.R.O., F.O. 371/53294/J1960).
81. Bevin's telegram 95 to Attlee (from Paris), 5 May 1946 (P.R.O., F.O. 371/53294/J1993); C.M. 42(46), 6 May, minute 1 (P.R.O., C.A.B. 128/5).
82. 422 H.C.Deb.5.s., cols. 781–4, 7 May 1946.
83. Ibid., cols. 849–903, 7 May 1946.
84. Sidqi, *Mudhakkirati*, p. 73; Qara'ah, *Namir al-Siyasah* ..., pp. 479–99.

85. Stansgate's untitled note, 2 May 1946, HLRO, ST/188/8.
86. 422 H.C.Deb., 7 May 1946, col. 894 (in the 24 May debate it was, paradoxically, a Labour MP who pointed out that it was the Egyptian government who wanted the British out, 'Fellaheen or no Fellaheen').
87. Campbell's letter to Howe, 15 June 1946 (P.R.O., F.O. 371/ 53303/J2742).

Egypt, the Arab States and the Suez Expedition, 1956

ELIE KEDOURIE

From a very early date Egypt became a well-defined and distinctive political entity. In antiquity, it remained for many centuries one of the great powers of the Mediterranean and of the Near East—which is to say one of the great powers of the world. After the Muslim conquest, the distinctive character of Egypt by no means disappeared. And, under the Fatimids, the Ayyubids and the Mamelukes, it once more became a centre of empire. The Ottoman conquest of 1517, again, did not prevent Egypt from retaining, to all intents and purposes, a large degree of autonomy which, in the first half of the nineteenth century, was considerably enlarged and consolidated. This was the achievement of an Ottoman officer Muhammad Ali, who became viceroy of Egypt.

There are two aspects of Muhammad Ali's rule which are relevant to our subject. In the first place, he had the ambition of making Egypt into a regional great power. Control over the resources and population of a large country, ruthlessness and the ability and willingness to make use of European advice and techniques, enabled him to become a formidable military power. He conquered the Sudan, he sent military expeditions to Arabia and the Morea, and finally levied war on the Sultan, his suzerain, coming very near to destroying the Ottoman dynasty, and occupied the Levant for a decade. But his vaulting ambition crashed to the ground by the intervention of European great powers, chiefly of Great Britain, and, at the time of his death in 1849, of all his conquests only the Sudan remained in his possession.

Muhammad Ali established a dynasty which, in some fashion or another, ruled over Egypt until 1952. His example and his record bequeathed to his successors the ambition to use the resources of Egypt in order to gain regional primacy. And this ambition was transmitted to the regime which supplanted Muhammad Ali's dynasty in 1952. Muhammad Ali's history, then, shows that, in modern times, Egypt had the potential to become a regional power. Its rulers have been continuously aware of this, and they have intermittently tried, in one way or another, to realize this potential.

The other aspect of Muhammad Ali's rule which is relevant to our subject is his modernization policy. Both industrially and militarily the policy was clearly a failure, but his educational innovations brought into being a numerous—and ever-increasing—class of educated people who, in due course, served to make Egypt—a country which is predominantly Muslim in its religion and wholly Arabic in its speech—into the intellectual centre of an Arab world—itself overwhelmingly Muslim—which, after the First World War and even more after the Second, was becoming increasingly aware of its Arab character, and whose political leaders aspired to make common Arab speech, and a shared Arab–Muslim culture, the foundation of Arab political unity. In the pan-Arab politics which became a feature of the Middle East after 1945 this particular legacy from Muhammad Ali's era served appreciably to increase Egypt's prestige and its weight in regional politics.

In spite of the ruin of Muhammad Ali's policies, his heirs intermittently attempted to revive his ambitions. But they were restrained and hobbled by the European balance of power, by their own increasing indebtedness (particularly under the Khedive Ismail), and by the British occupation, which made Egypt from 1882 until 1936 a subsidiary and wholly dependent part of the British imperial system. Even so, Muhammad Ali's descendants attempted, on at least two occasions, to gain for themselves and for Egypt that larger and more commanding role which their ancestor had in the end failed to assert. Thus the Khedive Abbas Hilmi (r. 1892–1914) embarked on various grandiose, but shadowy and ineffectual, projects to become, if not himself the Caliph, then the patron of an Arab Caliphate based on Mecca, which would supplant the Ottoman Caliphate. These projects came to nothing because Cromer would not allow such adventures, and because Abbas Hilmi's tactics—inconsequential conspiracies and desultory subversion—could never seriously threaten Ottoman rule, or diminish the enormous prestige which Sultan Abd al-Hamid enjoyed as an Islamic ruler, all over the Arabic-speaking world.

A second attempt at a grandiose regional policy was made by King Fu'ad (r. 1917–36) after the abolition of the Ottoman Caliphate by Mustafa Kemal Atatürk in 1924. Fu'ad now aspired to become the Caliph, and to make Cairo the centre of the Muslim world. After the British Declaration of 28 February 1922 which terminated the protectorate and recognized (subject to certain reservations) Egypt as an independent, sovereign state, Fu'ad was not so impeded in his plans as his predecessors had been. He made tremendous efforts to promote his candidacy and, when he failed in this, to prevent other possible

124

candidates from being successful. Fu'ad failed in his schemes, because by the time the Ottoman Caliphate had been abolished, the idea of the Caliphate had become somewhat unreal. If Fu'ad had succeeded in being proclaimed Caliph, he would have been no more than a kind of Muslim Pope. The Caliphate as Papacy was a paradoxical and self-defeating notion, and it was furthermore doubtful whether many Muslims would have even looked up to Fu'ad as a spiritual authority. The Muslim world had become greatly fragmented, and secular notions of government, in Egypt and elsewhere, had made great progress among the intellectual and official classes. But the ghost of the Caliphate and the ambitions which this ghost incited took a long time to fade away. Fu'ad's son and successor Faruq (r. 1936–52) was still in the late 1930s making determined efforts to get himself recognized as Caliph, receiving the allegiance of the whole Muslim world.

By that time, the international position of Egypt had been transformed. The Anglo-Egyptian Treaty of 1936 had given Egypt much greater freedom of action in international and—what particularly concerns us here—in regional politics. And it was precisely events taking place during 1936–8 in a neighbouring country which gave a new impulsion to Egyptian regional ambitions and determined the shape of these ambitions for nearly four decades. The Arab rebellion which began in Palestine in 1936 forced Great Britain, the mandatory power, to re-examine its policies regarding the promotion and development of the Jewish National Home. A Royal Commission (the Peel Commission) examined the problem and proposed, in 1937, partition as the best solution for the conflict which opposed Arabs and Zionists in the territory. The Foreign Office, however, particularly its Eastern Department, and specifically the head of this Department, George Rendel, took a very different view of the Palestine problem and its solution from that propounded by the Peel Commission—a view which was supported by the Colonial office (which was responsible for the administration of the mandate) and initially approved by the Cabinet. In Rendel's view—which became the Foreign Office view—the Palestine issue was not a local, but a pan-Arab question, and any attempt to deal with this issue which failed to satisfy the Arab states was radically defective. It was, in Rendel's view, imperative to placate and pacify Saudi Arabia, which was championing the rights of the Palestine Arabs. But once Saudi representations over Palestine were entertained, there was no way of refusing similar representations which Iraq, out of rivalry with Saudi Arabia, felt impelled to make. Nor was it really possible, once Saudi and Iraq intervention over Palestine was admitted, to reject Egyptian approaches over the same subject, which now also speedily followed. These peripetia were neither foreseen, nor their consequences appreciated either by the

125

Elie Kedourie

Foreign Office which made its own Rendel's views, or by the Cabinet which in turn adopted them, in spite of the Colonial Secretary's opposition. Rendel's fatal triumph was consecrated at the so-called Palestine Round Table Conference of 1939, where Palestine's neighbours, Egypt included, were officially admitted by the British Government to have a legitimate say in the conduct of Palestine policy. British initiative in, and control over, Palestine affairs was irremediably damaged, and Palestine became the cockpit in which the pan-Arab ambitions of the Arab countries were joined in contest and combat.

Egypt's intervention in Palestine affairs heralded a change in the orientation and character of Egyptian foreign policy. Egyptian ambitions now went not so much in an Islamic as in an Arab direction. This was a far-reaching change. Egypt was of course Arabic-speaking, but this fact had not been hitherto considered to be politically significant. The Arab revolt against the Ottomans initiated in 1916 by Husayn, the Sharif of Mecca, had attracted much hostility in Egypt, on the score that it tended to weaken the Ottoman Empire which was the only Islamic great power in the world, and was hence a blow to Muslim solidarity. The pan-Arab leaders themselves were, and long remained, indifferent to Egypt, their ambitions centring on the Fertile Crescent and the Arabian Peninsula. The events of 1938-9 decisively changed this state of affairs—a change which was confirmed by the establishment in 1945 of the League of Arab States, in which Egypt was unmistakably acknowledged to have the primacy!

After 1945, Faruq's ambition to become the dominant power in the Middle East became one of the two mainsprings of Egyptian foreign policy. The other was the pursuit of 'the unity of the Nile Valley', i.e. Egyptian control of the Sudan—the only territory among those taken by Muhammad Ali where Egypt still had position and a *locus standi*, as one of the two co-domini who administered the Sudan after the destruction of the Mahdist state. As is well-known, in the event Egypt lost the Sudan, which became an independent republic in 1956. 'Unity of the Nile Valley' was in reality the only manageable and realistic regional objective for Egyptian foreign policy, since the Sudan was a hinterland which could become a real resource for Egypt. Failure over the Sudan was thus a great setback for Egypt.

There remained the other—infinitely more ambitious—objective of dominating the Arab Middle East. Egypt now had an Arab policy which was central to its management of foreign affairs. It followed therefore that the other states of the Arab League had now to have an Egyptian policy—a preoccupation from which they had hitherto been free. Egyptian involvement in the Arab-Israeli war of 1948 was the direct consequence of the new orientation of Egyptian foreign policy. As is well-known, it was late in the day—at the end of April 1948—

126

that Faruq himself personally decided to send the Egyptian army to fight the Zionists in Palestine from which the British mandatory would shortly leave. This decision seems to have been a response to that taken by King Abdullah of Transjordan—who had the backing of Iraq—himself to intervene militarily in Palestine. The Palestine war was then the sign and consequence of divisions and rivalries between the Egyptian and the Hashimite camps within the Arab League and in pan-Arab politics.

The Palestine war ended disastrously for Egypt and for the other Arab States. The military *coup d'état* of 23 July 1952 which ended the reign of the Muhammad Ali dynasty was the aftermath of the failure in Palestine and of the discredit it brought on the monarchical regime.

The new ruler of Egypt, Colonel Nasser, inherited the problems of the monarchy, but also its vast ambitions. The ambition to annex the Sudan, as has been seen, ended in failure. But the freeing of Egyptian territory from British military and naval forces, which the monarchical regime was unable to bring about, became a feather in Nasser's cap. When the Anglo-Egyptian Treaty of 1954 was signed, few people thought that its span of life would be so short. Great Britain considered itself then—and was considered by others—as a Middle Eastern great power. There were still substantial British interests outside Egypt. In Aden and the protectorates in Muscat and Oman, in the Persian Gulf, British power was visible and paramount. Jordan and Iraq were bound by alliances which made provision for the maintenance of British bases. There was also a valuable British investment in the oil industry which had to be protected. A main instrument for the defence of British interests following the decision to evacuate the Suez Canal base was the Baghdad Pact of which Great Britain was the only full non-regional member, and Iraq the only Arab member. This, of course, automatically enhanced Iraq's prestige and its ability to pose as a serious rival to Egypt in the search for primacy in pan-Arab politics. This fact automatically led to Nasser's being bitterly antagonistic to the Pact. The British Government then, in conceding the evacuation of the Suez Canal base, and thus enhancing Nasser's power and prestige, and in also joining the Baghdad Pact, was following an incoherent policy. Was this incoherence seen, taken into account and judged to be an acceptable risk? The public rhetoric of the time, and the apologias which various political figures have subsequently produced, give no indication of such a caluculation having been made.

The conflict which followed Nasser's nationalization of the Suez Canal Company inevitably had an Arab dimension. Pan-Arab rhetoric had become the obligatory language of politics in the Arab world. Arab political leaders could not but speak in support of Nasser, whatever their real feelings, and however much they feared and hated him.

The only Arab state, however, to go beyond rhetoric and to take action in support of Nasser was Syria, which blew up the oil pipeline which went through its territory from Iraq to the Lebanese coast. This action was directed as much against Iraq, the expansionism of which Syria feared, as against the two Western powers which had invaded Port-Said. Thus, Nasser's triumph at Suez was procured not by Arab help or solidarity, but was rather encompassed by the USA. But this triumph had far-reaching consequences in the Arab world. Nasser's prestige was prodigiously enhanced, and he came to think it possible for Egypt to dominate the whole of the Arab world. He became, to adopt Stalin's expression, dizzy with success. And for a time after Suez events seemed to justify the highest hopes for Nasser and Egypt. In February 1958, Syria petitioned for the formation of an United Arab Republic in which Egypt became the senior partner. A civil war which broke out in the Lebanon shortly afterwards bade fair to make this country into a satellite controlled by the new authorities in Damascus. The Lebanese disorders led Iraq to send troops to the Syrian border in order to intimidate Damascus. During their march through Baghdad on their way to the border, the troops seized the opoortunity of toppling the monarchical regime in Iraq and proclaiming a republic. The leaders of the *coup d'état* professed themselves to be Nasser's fervent admirers and followers; and they indeed shortly afterwards denounced the Baghdad Pact which Nasser hated so much. But soon enough, these promising developments came to nought. The US intervened to put a stop to the Lebanese civil war, the new regime in Baghdad soon became alienated from Nasser, and the United Arab Republic fell apart and was dissolved in July 1961.

Egyptian activism found, however, new scope in the Yemen, where the monarchical regime was destroyed in 1962 and a civil war broke out. In this civil war Nasser intervened with an Egyptian expeditionary force. The hope was that an Egyptian-controlled Yemen would enable Nasser to extend his domination over the Arabian Peninsula and thus to control the revenues accruing from oil which were by now enormous. With these revenues at his disposal Nasser would be able to solve the economic problem in Egypt, and Egyptian power would become irresistible everywhere in the Middle East. But it did not prove possible for Egypt to win the war in Yemen, and the dream faded with Nasser's defeat in the Six-Day War.

The period which runs from 1956 to 1967 shows the same overweening ambition, the same over-extension of power and resources which is the hallmark of Muhammad Ali's fateful legacy. The Six-Day War proved to be the nemesis of this policy. The war was the direct consequence of Nasser's stance as the champion of the pan-Arab cause. He was needled and egged on to a provocative policy towards

Israel by taunts that as a champion he was inadequate and by the enormous expectations which Egyptian activism had conjured up all over the Arab world. The debacle of 1967 was the ironical outcome of the propaganda triumph of 1956. Whether this debacle, which broke Nasser, has finally exorcised Muhammad Ali's ghost only time will tell.

Note

This paper is based on work done over a number of years in modern Egyptian and Arab history. The various points discussed in this paper are amplified and documented in the three following books:

The Chatham House Version ad other Middle-Eastern Studies (1970) (see particularly, chapter 7, 'Egypt and the Caliphate 1915–1952', and chapter 8, 'Pan-Arabism and British Policy'.)

Arabic Political Memoirs and other Studies (1974) (see particularly chapter 7, 'The Politics of Political Literature: Kawakibi, Azoury and Jung', chapter 10, 'The Apprentice Sorcerers', chapter 12 'Anti-Marxism in Egypt', and chapter 13 'The Arab–Israeli Conflict').

Islam in the Modern World and other Studies (1980) (see particularly chapter 6, 'Arab Unity Then and Now', chapter 8, 'Great Britain and Palestine: The Turning Point', and chapter 9, 'Sucz Revisited').

'Collusion' and the Suez Crisis of 1956

GEOFFREY WARNER

Two of the most frequent objections levelled at contemporary historians when they attempt to illuminate the recent past are that they do not possess sufficient perspective and that, in many cases, the archives are not yet open for research. The first implies that some necessary interval has to elapse between an event and the historian's attempt to discuss it, but proponents of this view rarely enlighten us as to the length of the interval in question. Are we now able, for example, to see the First World War in proper perspective? Or the French Revolution? To ask these questions is to expose the falsity of the problem, for our perspective is of course continually changing. The second objection presupposes that we do not have enough information to reconstruct what happened with a reasonable degree of accuracy, but that if we wait until that day—thirty, fifty or one hundred years after the event—when the historian is allowed into the archives, all will be revealed. Neither of these presuppositions is in my view correct.

As far as the first is concerned, the reader is simply invited to contrast what is already available in the form of first-hand testimony on the subject of this article—the Suez crisis of 1956—with the sources available for the study of, say, the British Isles in the fifth century AD. Historians of that period would give a great deal to have the equivalent of even the most partial of the Suez memoirs, but its absence quite rightly does not prevent them from producing a great deal of valuable history.

The second presupposition—that the truth is only to be found in the archives—displays an excessive faith in the integrity and procedures of the politicians and officials responsible for producing the documents which eventually find their way there. Confining ourselves to British policy, we would do well to bear in mind Lord Tedder's strictures upon the integrity of official records. These 'are not perhaps the ideal, and certainly not the whole, source on which I have to rely', he wrote in the preface to his war memoirs. 'I expect that most of us have seen, sometimes with amusement and sometimes with anger, reports and orders obviously worded with an eye to the future his-

torian, or, as we used to call them, "for the record". The wording of
signals and orders "for the record" is a very fine art and well calculated
to fox the historian.'[1] There are doubtless many documents on the
Suez crisis which were written 'for the record'; indeed, we shall have
occasion to refer to one in due course.

When we turn to procedures, we find that these sometimes conceal
as much as they reveal. One might suppose, for example, that since
the Cabinet is reputedly the principal locus of decision within the
British system of government, its records are particularly informative.
In reality, however, Cabinet minutes are among the blandest official
records in existence. As Patrick Gordon Walker, himself a former
Cabinet minister, has written, they 'give no indication of the order in
which the points were made: they are always marshalled pro and con.
There is no way of telling who spoke or even how many Ministers
spoke. Not all the points made in argument are recorded. No indication is given of the tone or temper of the debate.'[2] Two of Lord Gordon
Walker's Cabinet colleagues, moreover, are on record to the effect
that the minutes can sometimes be quite misleading even in what they
do say.[3]

In the case of the Suez crisis, there are some even more intractable
problems. Evidence exists, as we shall see, that normal bureaucratic
routines were not always observed: officials were purposely excluded
from important meetings and not told what had taken place; records
were deliberately not kept of certain vital discussions, and so on. There
are even suggestions that documents have been wilfully destroyed.
The Israeli Prime Minister in 1956, David Ben-Gurion, told the
American journalist, Cyrus Sulzberger, almost twelve years later that
'Eden sent over to Paris after the affair in order to have all the original
documents destroyed. But he found that I had copies. And I may note
that it was only then that he became friendly to Israel.'[4] There would,
of course, have been nothing to prevent the destruction of documents
in British hands and, indeed, the Whitehall correspondent of *The Times*,
Peter Hennessy, has written that 'For years there have been persistent
rumours among those in the know that what little genuinely sensitive
material was committed to paper during the build-up to the invasion
of Egypt was destroyed at the time or shortly after. The little that has
survived is said to be kept in the closely guarded registry of the Secret
Intelligence Service, or MI6 . . .'[5] As Hennessy remarked, the archives
of that particular organization are unlikely ever to be opened.

While the opening of the normal run of British government records
for 1956, which will take place on 1 January 1987, will therefore yield
some new information, it is doubtful whether it will compel us drasti-
cally to revise what we already know about Suez from existing first-
hand accounts. Some of these accounts are a lot more precise than

others and all are self-serving to a greater or lesser degree, but there are enough of them to enable the historian, by a process of comparison and confrontation, to establish a reasonably full reconstruction of what happened and why.[6]

It might be helpful if a little more was said about some of the more important of these accounts. On the British side, the earliest memoirs—those of the Prime Minister, Sir Anthony Eden,[7] and the Lord Chancellor, Viscount Kilmuir[8]—deliberately glossed over or ignored some of the vital issues. It was Anthony Nutting, who resigned his post as Minister of State at the Foreign Office over Suez, who in a book published in 1967 first provided an authoritative British account of much that had hitherto only been suspected.[9] Even then, as senior a member of the Eden Cabinet as Harold Macmillan could totally ignore Nutting's revelations in the volume of his memoirs which dealt with the Suez crisis and which appeared in 1971.[10] We had to wait until 1978 for one of the chief architects of Britain's policy during the Suez crisis, the Foreign Secretary, Selwyn Lloyd, to produce anything like a comprehensive account of what happened.[11] He did so only just in time, moreover, for he died shortly after completing the manuscript and never saw it through the press.

On the French side, the most useful account is that of General Paul Ely, the Chief of Staff of the French armed forces, which appeared in 1969.[12] The memoirs of the French Foreign Minister, Christian Pineau, which were published in 1976,[13] are a curious phenomenon. Their author had been one of the most forthcoming of informants in private interviews with the many journalists and contemporary historians writing secondary accounts of Suez, but when it came to putting pen to paper himself, he became so coy that parts of his book are more like the children's fairy stories he is well known in France for writing than a serious contribution to our understanding of events. Finally, there are the memoirs of Abel Thomas, the *directeur de cabinet* (or private secretary) to the French Minister of Defence, Maurice Bourgès-Maunoury, which came out in 1978.[14]

General Moshe Dayan, the Chief of Staff of the Israeli armed forces, published the first authoritative Israeli account of Suez in an expurgated version in 1965.[15] A much fuller account is contained in his memoirs, which appeared in 1976.[16] In the meantime, the Director-General of the Israeli Defence Ministry, Shimon Peres, had shown his diaries to a journalist, Yosef Evron, who printed extracts from them in a book published in 1968.[17] Peres himself produced his own much less precise account in 1970.[18] Finally, the copious diaries and papers of David Ben-Gurion were made available to another journalist, Michael Bar-Zohar, who cites them in his recently published multi-volume biography of the Israeli Prime Minister.[19]

The question of Israeli participation

The aspect of the Suez crisis which has attracted most attention over the years is of course the question of 'collusion'; or, in other words, whether the British, the French, and the Israelis were acting in concert when they invaded Egypt in 1956. When this possibility was raised in the House of Commons at the time,[20] it was vigorously denied by British government spokesmen. 'It is quite wrong to state that Israel was incited to this action by Her Majesty's Government,' Selwyn Lloyd declared on 31 October. 'There was no prior agreement between us about it.'[21] Sir Anthony Eden went even further on 20 December: 'I want to say this on the question of foreknowledge, and to say it quite bluntly to the House,' he stated, 'that there was not foreknowledge that Israel would attack Egypt—there was not.'[22] No foreknowledge; no prior agreement, and no incitement: that was the British government's position in 1956 and for many years afterwards. The remainder of this chapter attempts to assess the truth of these claims in the light of the accounts mentioned above.

To some extent, it would have been hardly surprising if the British, French and Israelis had colluded in 1956, for even before the nationalization of the Suez Canal in July all three had reasons for striking a blow at Colonel Nasser's regime in Egypt. The British believed it was deliberately seeking to undermine their position throughout the Middle East and Africa; the French were certain that it was aiding and abetting the rebels in Algeria; and the Israelis knew it was organizing terrorist raids into their territory as well as preventing their shipping from using either the Suez Canal or the Gulf of Aqaba. At the same time, however, if France and Israel had been moving closer together, there was still an enormous legacy of mutual suspicion between Israel and Britain which went back to the days of the Palestine Mandate and which found its current justification in the alliances which Britain had concluded with Arab countries like Jordan and Iraq, both sworn enemies of the Jewish state. The existence of these alliances did not encourage the Israelis to negotiate with Britain. By the same token, it made the British highly sensitive about any dealings with Israel.

Anglo-French military planning for a possible joint operation against Egypt in retaliation for the nationalization of the Suez Canal began early in August 1956. The French told the Israelis that 'the British insisted that Israel shall not participate in the operation; and at this stage will not even be informed'.[23] This implies that the question of Israeli participation was raised right at the beginning, but there is no direct evidence from a French or British source that this was the case. The request that the Israelis should not be informed is confirmed by Abel Thomas, but he does not mention the question of participation. Since we know that the French themselves preferred not to involve the Israelis until the last moment, it may well be that their communication was no more than a convenient fabrication which, given the nature of relations between Britain and Israel, was unlikely to be challenged by the latter.[24]

We do know, however, that some members of the British Cabinet were contemplating some form of Israeli intervention by the first half of September. On 3 September, Selwyn Lloyd told the Canadian Foreign Minister, Lester Pearson, that 'he rather wondered whether, if things dragged on, Israel might not take advantage of the situation by some aggressive move against Egypt' and 'seemed to think that this might help Britain out of some of her more immediate difficulties. . . .' Not long afterwards, an unnamed Cabinet minister asked Colonel Robert Henriques, a leading British Jew who was about to visit Israel, to tell Ben-Gurion that 'at all costs, Israel must avoid war with Jordan. But if, when Britain went into Suez, Israel were to attack simultaneously, it would be very convenient for all concerned.' Pearson, however, claimed that he succeeded in convincing Lloyd that both the short-term and long-term consequences of Israeli intervention would be 'deplorable and dangerous', while Henriques did not believe that his interlocutor was expressing the Cabinet's official view, but only that of a body of opinion within it.[25]

By the middle of September, the French had serious doubts as to whether the British would ever resort to force, for the latter seemed more interested in pursuing various diplomatic initiatives—such as the proposed Suez Canal Users' Association (SCUA)—which the French regarded as futile. On 23 September, the French Defence Minister, Maurice Bourgès-Maunoury, told Shimon Peres that, two days earlier, just as he was leaving London at the conclusion of the international conference to discuss SCUA, Pineau had seen Eden and told him, in a state of high dudgeon and disappointment, 'It looks as if we [i.e. the French] have no choice but to work hand-in-hand with the Israelis.' 'Provided they don't hurt the Jordanians,' the British Prime Minister is said to have replied.[26] But Bourgès-Maunoury was trying to persuade Peres of the possibility of a joint Franco-Israeli military operation against Egypt if the British dropped out. It was in his interest, therefore, to allay the Israeli fear that Britain might try to prevent it. Thus, he may simply have been telling Peres what he wanted him to believe.[27]

It is possible that the question of Israeli intervention was raised and discussed in more detail at the Anglo-French ministerial conversations in Paris on 26 and 27 September 1956. These conversations were shrouded in more than the customary secrecy. The Paris correspondent of *The Times* reported that for most of the three hours of discussions on the evening of the 26th, the four ministers—Eden, Lloyd, Pineau and the French Prime Minister, Guy Mollet—were alone, and he commented: 'These talks evidently mark a return to the secret diplomacy whch has been so absent from international statesmanship in recent times.'[28] Given that the French knew that a high-level Israeli delegation was coming to France a couple of days later, it would have been natural for them to have raised the possibility of Israeli intervention, if only to discover the British reaction. They certainly intimated to the Israelis that they had done so. On the other hand, there is no direct evidence that they did. Indeed, one British source which can scarcely be accused of trying to conceal the truth about 'collusion'— Anthony Nutting's book—states specifically that the matter was not raised.[29] Nutting, however, did not accompany his superiors to Paris, so we still cannot be certain.

Although the ostensible purpose of the Franco-Israeli conversations in Paris on 30 September and 1 October was to explore the possibility of a purely Franco-Israeli operation against Egypt, the impression which emerges from the accounts we have of the talks is that the French were really trying to engineer Israeli participation in a form which could trigger off that of the British. This was perhaps not surprising, for General Ely had informed Bourgès-Maunoury when the conversations began that a Franco-Israeli operation without British participation was so fraught with risk that he could not recommend it, even from a purely military point of view.[30] At any rate, Pineau reminded the Israelis that 'under the Anglo-Egyptian Treaty of 195[4], in time of war Britain had the right to seize the [Suez] Canal by force, so that war between Israel and Egypt could provide Britain with the juridical pretext to put her army back in the Canal Zone'. The French Foreign Minister wanted Israel to start military operations 'on her own before the British and French. If Israel were prepared to do this, he was confident that it would strengthen the chances of a British decision to participate.'[31]

The French proposal

It is tempting to conclude that these points were made as a result of the earlier conversations with the British but, as we have seen, there is no firm evidence that this was the case. Such ideas, moreover, could just as easily have come from the French. General Ely, for example, tells us that he felt that the Suez crisis had been mismanaged at the diplomatic level and believed that there was only one way in which any form of military intervention could be justified to the world at large: namely, if either Egypt or Israel attacked the other and Britain and France occupied the Canal Zone in order to separate the combatants.[32] As we shall see, this was the very scenario eventually adopted.

It was put to the British at a secret meeting at Chequers, the British Prime Minister's official country residence, on 14 October 1956, by General Maurice Challe, the Chief of Staff of the French air force, and M. Albert Gazier, who was acting as French Foreign Minister during Pineau's absence at the UN Security Council in New York. The British participants were Eden, Nutting and one of the Prime Minister's private secretaries. According to Nutting, whose account is likely to be as authoritative as any in the apparent absence of any official record,

> Challe ... proceeded to outline what he termed a possible plan of action for Britain and France to gain physical control of the Suez Canal. The plan, as he put it to us, was that Israel should be invited to attack Egypt across the Sinai Peninsula and that France and Britain, having given the Israeli forces enough time to seize all or most of Sinai, should then order 'both sides' to withdraw their forces from the Suez Canal, in order to permit an Anglo-French force to intervene and occupy the Canal on the pretext of saving it from damage by fighting. Thus the two powers would be able to claim to be 'separating the combatants' and 'extinguishing a dangerous fire', while actually seizing control of the entire waterway and of its terminal ports, Port Said and Suez.[33]

Nutting adds that the timing of this proposed operation was not discussed, although the French made it clear that they wanted to act as soon as possible. He also states that they did not say whether the Israelis had agreed to play the role allotted to them, although he got the impression that preliminary soundings had been taken and that the French had received sufficient encouragement to broach the matter with the British.[34]

Eden's reaction to Challe's proposal certainly suggests that this was the first occasion upon which anything so precise had been put to him. Nutting describes a great state of excitement on the Prime Minister's part, while Challe told Ely on his return to Paris that Eden genuinely seemed not to have thought of this possibility before. 'If M. Gazier had not been there and had the same impression,' he said, 'I should have wondered whether Mr. Eden wasn't making fun of me.'[35]

A small group of British ministers met on the morning of 16 October to discuss the French proposal. Since there has been a great deal of controversy about who was privy to the decisions taken during the Suez crisis, and since Selwyn Lloyd fails for once to provide his customary list of participants, we are fortunate to have a contemporary press report of who was present: namely, Eden, Kilmuir,

Macmillan, the Commonwealth Secretary, Lord Home and Nutting. Selwyn Lloyd who, like Pineau, had been at the Security Council in New York, flew to London for the meeting and arrived halfway through. Field Marshal Sir Gerald Templer, the Chief of the Imperial General Staff, was also called in.[36] Unlike some of their colleagues, perhaps, these men cannot claim to have been kept in the dark about what was going on.

At the meeting, Nutting argued strongly against participation in what he called 'this sordid manoeuvre'. It would, he claimed, cause a rift with the United States, split the Commonwealth, jeopardize British oil supplies and unite the Arab world against Britain. Lloyd evidently agreed, telling Nutting on his arrival, 'You are right.... We must have nothing to do with the French plan.' Nevertheless, it was decided that the Prime Minister and Foreign Secretary should both go to Paris that same afternoon for further talks with the French.[37]

On Eden's and Mollet's insistence, all officials were excluded from the Anglo-French conversations on 16 October and, according to Nutting, no record was kept.[38] Explaining that the Israelis were on the point of attacking Egypt, the French asked the British what their reaction would be. Eden replied that the British government had repeatedly made it clear that if Israel attacked Jordan, it would have to honour its treaty obligations, but that 'an Israeli attack on Egypt was a different matter'. The two sides agreed, subject to approval by their respective cabinets, 'that if this happened Britain and France would intervene, putting into operation the plans already prepared, the object being to safeguard the Canal and stop the spread of hostilities'.[39]

This summary is taken from Selwyn Lloyd's account. What he does not say is what he told Nutting on his return to London: namely, 'that further consultations would take place in Paris between French and Israeli representatives. He hoped that we would not have to be directly associated with these talks, at any rate at the political level; but he could not rule this out, as there were a number of crucial political as well as military problems involving us which would have to be settled in a very short space of time.'[40] The omission is, of course, of vital importance, for it enables Lloyd to claim that he was unaware of the nature and extent of the contacts between the French and the Israelis and that the British had no proposals of their own to put forward, simply reacting to suggestions put to them.

When the full British Cabinet met on 18 October, the likelihood of an Israeli attack upon Egypt was described as 'probable'. If Lloyd's summary of the minutes is full, and if the minutes themselves are accurate, there was no mention of the Chequers meeting, or of the fact that the French and Israelis, with British approval and possibly participation, would shortly be negotiating the details of the attack in question. To this extent, therefore, it can perhaps be maintained that, with the exception of those few ministers already in the know and those subsequently added to their number, the Cabinet was misled about what was taking place. At any rate, it agreed that if Israel did indeed attack Egypt, Britain and France would intervene to protect the Canal.[41]

The French had in the meantime communicated the British position to the Israelis in the form of a written declaration signed by Eden. This made it clear that the British would only participate in a military operation with Israel if—as Challe had suggested at the Chequers meeting—they and the French could issue an ultimatum to both Israel and Egypt to withdraw their forces from the area of the Canal, thus providing a justification for their intervention.[42] Lloyd claims that this declaration was 'embroidered on the way beyond all recognition', presumably by the French.[43] He does not, however, explain how a written and signed declaration can be so 'embroidered' in transmission.

According to General Dayan, Ben-Gurion was far from enamoured of the British proposition. 'He insisted that we should not be the ones to launch the campaign and fill the role of aggressor, while the British and French appeared as angels of peace to bring tranquillity to the area. He was not prepared to accept a division of functions whereby, as he put it, Israel volunteered to mount the rostrum of shame so that Britain and France could leave their hands in the waters of purity.'[44] Nevertheless, he agreed to lead a delegation to France to see whether a satisfactory agreement could be negotiated with the French, and eventually with the British as well. These negotiations took place, in the greatest secrecy, at a private house in the Paris suburb of Sèvres between 22 and 24 October 1956.

On 21 October, Selwyn Lloyd was summoned to Chequers for a meeting with Eden, Macmillan, the new Minister of Defence, Anthony Head, and the Lord Privy Seal, R. A. Butler. Two senior civil servants, Norman Brook, the Secretary to the Cabinet, and Richard Powell, the Permanent Secretary at the Ministry of Defence, were also present, as was General Sir Charles Keightley, the Commander-in-Chief of the British land forces in the Middle East and the Supreme Commander of the Anglo-French expeditionary force which was preparing the invasion of Egypt. The meeting was told that the Israeli leaders were due to arrive in Paris on the follqwing day and that the French thought it important that Britain should be represented at the discussions with them. It was agreed that Lloyd should go incognito, and he excused himself from his previous engagements by pretending to have a cold.[45] The importance of this meeting is twofold: it shows that there had been further contacts with the French about Israeli intervention since the Paris conversations of 16–17 October and the British Cabinet meeting of 18 October, and that other senior ministers and officials in addition to those present at the meeting on 16 October must have known what was happening.

The Sèvres meetings

Accompanied by one of his private secretaries, Donald Logan, Selwyn Lloyd arrived at Sèvres on the afternoon of 22 October, after the French and Israelis had begun their talks. The French briefed him on the Israeli position and he then met their delegation. According to his account, 'Ben-Gurion wanted an agreement between Britain, France and Israel that we should all three attack Egypt. In particular, he wanted an undertaking from us that we would eliminate the Egyptian Air Force before Israeli ground forces moved forward. He said that otherwise Israeli towns like Tel Aviv would be wiped out. British prior air action was a sine qua non.' The British Foreign Secretary pointed out that military action of the kind proposed would almost certainly be brought to a halt by United Nations action, if not in the Security Council, where Britain and France had a veto, then in the General Assembly. A tripartite agreement was 'impossible', moreover, because Britain 'had thousands of subjects in Arab countries with valuable property, and oil installations of great strategic importance'. If there were a joint attack, these people might be slaughtered and the installations destroyed.[46] What the British wanted—although Lloyd does not say so in his memoirs—was a sufficiently long interval to elapse between the Israeli attack and the Anglo-French intervention in order to preserve the illusion that the latter was a response to the former and not part and parcel of the same operation.

The Israelis put forward a compromise proposal which slightly narrowed the gap between the two sides, but when Lloyd left for London at about midnight, he allegedly told Pineau that he did not think that his colleagues would accept it. The French Foreign Minister told Ben-Gurion that he did not trust Lloyd and would go to London himself in order to brief Eden. The Israeli Prime Minister was pessimistic: 'I fear that Pineau's trip will be in vain,' he noted in his diary, 'since Lloyd will secure the decision that he desires as opposed to the view of the French and ourselves.'[47]

After reporting to his senior colleagues, Lloyd attended a full Cabinet meeting on 23 October. He records that he told ministers that he 'was doubtful whether Israel would launch an attack against Egypt in the immediate future'. Did he, one wonders, explain why? Did he say that he had just returned from negotiating with the French and the Israelis at Sèvres? We do not know. The Cabinet was told, however, that Pineau was coming to London that evening, and Eden said that he and Lloyd would report on their talks with the French Foreign Minister the following day.[48]

Pineau's meetings in London, which are once more said to have taken place in the absence of officials and without a record being kept,[49] resulted, according to Lloyd, in 'greater precision about the actions which we would take if Israel attacked Egypt', together with a decision that a further tripartite meeting at Sèvres was worthwhile.[50] In other words, the French Foreign Minister's gamble had paid off. He told the Israelis on his return that he 'had found [Eden's] approach far warmer than that of Lloyd',[51] a comment which the latter cites with no attempt at denial.[52] Indeed, the Foreign Secretary told Nutting that Eden had been 'greatly put out about the meeting with Ben-Gurion', but had sent Pineau back to Paris, 'with an assurance that Israel need have no fear of being left in the lurch and that, if she led the way with an attack in Sinai, Britain would lend her fullest support'.[53] The only condition, as Eden explained on the following day to the delegation he was sending to Sèvres, was that there must be 'a clear military threat to the Canal'.[54] How much the Cabinet was told of all this at its meeting on 24 October is unclear. Lloyd merely states that Eden 'concluded by saying that ... further talks with the French were necessary'. He evidently said nothing about the Israelis.[55]

Lloyd states that the reason he was unable to return to Sèvres himself was that he had to answer questions in the House of Commons.[56] In the light of what had happened on the occasion of his first visit, however, one cannot help wondering whether he wanted to go again, or even whether the Prime Minister wanted to send him. Be that as it may, his place was taken by two officials: Donald Logan and Sir Patrick Dean, a Deputy Under-Secretary at the Foreign Office. At the end of their discussions with the French and the Israelis on the evening of 24 October, a document was signed embodying the conclusions which had been reached. Lloyd maintains that this was a quite unexpected development, the document in question being produced out of the blue, and that Dean only agreed to sign it as a record of the discussion.[57] Israeli and French sources tell a rather different story. According to Ben-Gurion's diary, he suggested that a protocol be prepared of the joint plan 'which will be signed by the three parties and which will be ratified by the three governments', and the British delegates participated in the drafting.[58]

Pineau's and Thomas's memoirs give a full account of this document. Indeed, the latter provided what is purported to be the actual French text, although it is evidently incomplete, and comprised seven articles. Article 1 announced the Israeli intention of launching an important military action on 29 October 1956, with a view to reaching the Canal Zone on the following day. This, of course, was in response to the British insistence upon 'a clear military threat to the Canal'. It was to be achieved by means of a parachute drop near the Mitla Pass, which was about 40 miles to the east of the southern entrance to the Canal. Article 2 registered the intention of the British and French governments to issue simultaneous ultimatums to Egypt and Israel, calling upon them to cease fire, to withdraw their forces to a distance of 10 miles from the Canal and, in the case of Egypt, to submit to a temporary Anglo-French occupation of the Canal Zone in order to safeguard navigation through the waterway. Article 3 stated that if Egypt rejected this ultimatum, the British and French would begin military operations against its territory in the early hours of 31 October. No sanctions were to be implemented against Israel, for it would accept the Anglo-French demands. In any case, its principal military objective was not the Suez Canal at all, but the Gulf of Aqaba, and Article 4 gave the Israelis permission to occupy its western shore, together with two important islands just off the coast. Article 5 pledged Israel not to attack Jordan during the period of hostilities with Egypt. By the same token, Britain agreed not to go to Jordan's aid if it attacked Israel during the same period.[59] Article 6 stipulated that the agreement reached at Sèvres should remain secret, and Article 7 provided for its ratification by the three governments.[60] This was the document which Lloyd assures us was no more than a record of the discussion.

It was ratified at a Cabinet meeting on 25 October, although to judge from Selwyn Lloyd's account it is doubtful whether ministers were actually shown the text or even informed of its existence. According to him,

> Eden said that on 18th October he had told the Cabinet that he thought Israel would attack Egypt; on 23rd October he had said he thought it less likely. Now he believed that the Israelis were advancing their military preparations with a view to attacking Egypt, and the date might be 29th October. The French felt strongly that if that happened we should both intervene, as we had agreed between us on 18th October.... Eden therefore suggested that, if Israel did attack, we and the French should issue an ultimatum to both sides. If Nasser complied, his prestige would be fatally undermined. If he did not, there would be ample justification for Anglo-French action to safeguard the Canal. It was better that we should seem to hold the balance between Egypt and Israel rather than be accepting Israeli co-operation in an attack by us on Egypt.

Selwyn Lloyd supported the Prime Minister and the Cabinet agreed.[61]

Official notification of the ratification of the Sèvres agreement was sent by Eden in the form of a signed letter to Mollet. As if to preserve the fiction that there had been no contact with Israel, no communication was sent to Ben-Gurion and Israel was not even mentioned in that sent to Mollet. The French Prime Minister, however, thoughtfully provided a copy for his Israeli opposite number, and it is from the latter's archives, as released to Michael Bar-Zohar, that we know the contents. 'Her Majesty's Government has noted the information about the progress of the talks which were held in Sèvres between 22 and 24 October,' it read. 'It affirms that in the situation which was envisaged then, it will take the planned action. This is in accordance with the declaration attached to my announcement of 21 October. Signed, Anthony Eden.'[62]

Two of the three claims which the British made at the time—that there was no foreknowledge of the Israeli attack upon Egypt and no prior agreement about it—are thus seen to be manifestly untrue. The third claim—that Israel was not incited to attack—is more difficult to assess. When Pineau visited London on 23 October, he was given a letter by Lloyd which stated: 'It must be clear ... that the United Kingdom has not asked the Israeli government to undertake any action whatever. We have merely been asked what our reactions would be if certain things happened.'[63] This, however, seems as clear an example as any of the kind of document 'for the record' referred to at the beginning of this chapter; for if we can agree with Lloyd that the Israelis needed little prompting to attack Egypt, they did, as we have seen, need a great deal of prompting to attack it in the precise way that they did.

Does all this amount to 'collusion'? Not according to Selwyn Lloyd, who tries to argue that 'the test of "collusion" is the motive. Was the action fraudulent or disreputable?'[64] But is this the test? One of the government's back-benchers, Sir Robert Boothby, was surely more accurate when he wrote to *The Times* on 24 December 1956—albeit in complete ignorance of nearly everything set out in this chapter—in order to defend it against the charge:

Collusion is defined in the dictionary as a secret agreement or understanding for the purposes of trickery or fraud. If the British and French governments had decided, last October, to attack Egypt, for the purposes of getting rid of Nasser and occupying the Suez Canal, and to use Israel as an instrument of their policy by giving her the green light for an invasion of the Sinai Peninsula in order to justify their own intervention in the eyes of the world, they would have been guilty of collusion in the accepted sense of the word.

One could hardly improve upon this as a concise statement of what the British and French governments actually did in October 1956.

Notes

An earlier version of this essay was delivered as an inaugural lecture at the University of Leicester on 24 October 1978 and published in *International Affairs*, Vol. 55, No. 2 (April 1979), pp. 226–39.

1. A. W. T. Tedder, *With Prejudice* (London, Cassell, 1966), p. ii.
2. Patrick Gordon Walker, *The Cabinet*, 2nd edn (London, Fontana, 1972), p. 51.
3. Richard Crossman, *The Diaries of a Cabinet Minister*, Vol. 1, *Minister of Housing 1964–66* (London, Hamish Hamilton and Cape, 1975), pp. 103–4; Richard Marsh, *Off the Rails* (London, Weidenfeld and Nicolson, 1978), p. 92.
4. Cyrus L. Sulzberger, *An Age of Mediocrity: Memoirs and Diaries 1963–72* (New York, Macmillan, 1973), p. 449.
5. *The Times*, 20 June 1978.
6. There are, of course, some excellent secondary accounts of the Suez crisis which make good use of a research method open only to contemporary historians as opposed to those working on remoter periods: the personal interview. These accounts have deliberately not been used in this article, however, as it is rarely possible for the reader to check the sources personally.
7. Anthony Eden, *Full Circle*, Memoirs, Vol. 3 (London, Cassell, 1960).
8. Viscount Kilmuir, *Political Adventure: The Memoirs of the Earl of Kilmuir* (London, Weidenfeld and Nicolson, 1964).
9. Anthony Nutting, *No End of a Lesson: The Story of Suez* (London, Constable, 1967).
10. Harold Macmillan, *Riding the Storm 1956–59*, Memoirs, Vol. 4 (London, Macmillan, 1971) Macmillan was Chancellor of the Exchequer in 1956.
11. Selwyn Lloyd, *Suez 1956: A Personal Account* (London, Cape, 1978).
12. General Paul Ely, *Memoires*, Vol. II, *Suez ... le 13 mai* (Paris, Plon, 1969).
13. Christian Pineau, *1956 Suez* (Paris, Laffont, 1976).
14. Abel Thomas, *Comment Israel fut sauvé* (Paris, Albin Michel, 1978).
15. Moshe Dayan, *Diary of the Sinai Campaign 1956* (London, Sphere Books, 1967). The original Hebrew version appeared in 1965. For the expurgated nature of the account, see p. 9 of the English edition cited.

16. Moshe Dayan, *Story of My Life* (London, Sphere Books, 1977). The original Hebrew version appeared in 1976; first English edn, London, Weidenfeld and Nicolson, 1976.

17. Yosef Evron, *Beyom Sagrir: Suez Me'ahorei Haklayim* [*At a Stormy Time: Suez Behind the Scenes*] (Tel Aviv, Otpaz, 1968).

18. Shimon Peres, *David's Sling: The Arming of Israel* (London, Weidenfeld and Nicolson, 1970).

19. Michael Bar-Zohar, *Ben Gurion*, Vol. III, Hebrew edn (Tel Aviv, Am Oved, 1977). An abridged English translation of all three volumes of Bar-Zohar's book was published by Weidenfeld and Nicolson at the end of 1978. I have, however, retained my earlier references to the Israeli edition. In this connection, I should like to express my gratitude to Avi Shlaim of the Department of Politics at the University of Reading for making this and other Hebrew language sources available to me.

20. It should be noted that contemporary accusations of 'collusion' were prompted primarily by information from the United States and not, as might be expected, from Egypt. See *Evening News*, 31 Oct. 1956; *The Times*, 1 and 20 Nov. 1956.

21. HC Deb., 5th series, Vol. 558, col. 1569.

22. Ibid., Vol. 562, col. 1518.

23. Ben-Gurion diary, 3 August 1956, cited in Bar-Zohar, op. cit., p. 1212.

24. Ely, op. cit., p. 91; Thomas op. cit., pp. 114–15.

25. Lester Pearson, *Memoirs*, Vol. II, *The International Years: 1948–1957* (London, Gollancz, 1974), pp. 231–2; Robert Henriques, 'The Ultimatum: A Dissenting View', *The Spectator*, 6 Nov. 1959, p. 623; and letter, ibid., 4 Dec. 1959, p. 823. Compare Selwyn Lloyd's account of his conversation with Pearson in *Suez 1956*, op. cit., pp. 123–4.

26. Peres' diary, cited in Evron, op. cit., p. 74.

27. It is perhaps worth adding in this connection that neither I nor the skilled staff of the Chatham House press library have been able to trace a contemporary press report of a private meeting between Eden and Pineau when such an exchange could have taken place, although this is of course not proof that there was no meeting.

28. *The Times*, 27 Sept. 1956.

29. Nutting, op. cit., p. 68.

30. Ely, op. cit., pp. 121–2.

31. Dayan, *Story of My Life*, op. cit., pp. 206–8. See also Thomas, op. cit., pp. 146–56 for a French account.

32. Ely, op. cit., p. 111.

33. Nutting, op. cit., p. 92, states that in response to a nervous look

from Gazier, Eden instructed his private secretary to stop taking notes just before General Challe began speaking.

34. Ibid., p. 93. General Challe confirms the essence of this conversation in his memoirs, *Notre Révolte* (Paris, Presses de la Cité, 1968), pp. 27-8.
35. Ely, op. cit., pp. 137-8.
36. *Daily Telegraph*, 17 Oct. 1956. For Lloyd's late arrival, see *The Times*, 17 Oct. 1956.
37. Nutting, op. cit., pp. 96-8; Lloyd, op. cit., p. 166. It is interesting to note that Lloyd confirms his opposition to the French plan.
38. Nutting, op. cit., p. 98.
39. Lloyd, op. cit., pp. 173-4.
40. Nutting, op. cit., p. 98.
41. Lloyd, op.cit., pp. 175-7.
42. Dayan, op. cit., p. 224.
43. Lloyd, op. cit., p. 175.
44. Dayan, op. cit., p. 224.
45. Lloyd, op. cit., p. 180.
46. Ibid., pp. 181-4.
47. Ben-Gurion diary, 22 Oct. 1956, cited in Bar-Zohar, op. cit., p. 1240. According to Abel Thomas, Lloyd expressed his scepticism about the plan for tripartite intervention to the French General Martin (Thomas, op. cit., p. 180).
48. Lloyd, op. cit., pp. 185-6.
49. Nutting, op. cit., p. 104.
50. Lloyd, op. cit., p. 186.
51. Dayan, op. cit., p. 345.
52. Lloyd, op. cit., p. 188.
53. Nutting, op. cit., p. 104.
54. Lloyd, op. cit., p. 187.
55. Ibid., pp. 187-8.
56. Ibid., p. 186.
57. Ibid., p. 188.
58. Ben-Gurion diary, 25 Oct. 1956, and other material cited in Bar-Zohar, op. cit., p. 1248. See also Thomas, op. cit., pp. 193-4
59. This provision had recently acquired crucial importance, for the Israelis had launched a reprisal raid against Jordan on 10 October in response to terrorist attacks and the Jordanians had appealed to the British for help. It took skilled diplomacy to reduce the level of tension.
60. Pineau, op. cit., pp. 149-53; Thomas, op. cit., pp. 194-5. Thomas does not include the last two articles.
61. Lloyd, op. cit., pp. 188-90.

62. Eden letter, cited in Bar-Zohar, op. cit., p. 1254. The reference to 'the declaration attached to my announcement of October 21' is obscure, for no text of this declaration or announcement can be found in the available sources. It is unlikely that it refers to the declaration transmitted to the Israelis after the Paris conversations on 16 and 17 October (see above) for the date is too late. It may have been a statement drawn up at the Chequers meeting of senior ministers and officials on 21 October (see above) and sent, or brought by Lloyd, to Sèvres. Its existence, however, serves to undermine still further Lloyd's attempt to deny any British agreement with Israel. According to Thomas (op. cit., p. 196), Eden's letter was brought to Paris on the afternoon of 25 October by Logan and Dean.

63. Pineau, op. cit., p. 137; Lloyd, op. cit., p. 186.

64. Lloyd, op. cit., p. 248.

The Significance of the Suez Canal for Western Strategy since 1956

EDWARD M. SPIERS

The Suez Canal, on account of its location and its traditional promi-
nence in British imperial thought, has evoked extravagant and gran-
diloquent writing. On the eve of the Suez crisis, *The Economist* described the Canal as 'the Achilles Heel of Britain and of Europe'. In
subsequent years, it was still regarded as possessing 'great strategic
importance' and as 'the main artery connecting Western Europe to
Asia and East Africa'.[1] For a more precise examination of the Canal's
geo-strategic significance, this chapter will examine the commercial
and military uses to which the Canal has been put over the past
twenty-five years, the ease with which these activities have been
prevented, and the cost and availability of alternative routes. These
criteria are essentially subjective; each major user will evaluate the
Canal differently in view of its own geographical location and its
political, military and economic interests.[2] Any changes in the Canal's
significance, therefore, will be assessed by reference to its commercial
usage, particularly in respect of oil, and its strategic utility over the
past generation.

The economic impact of the first closure of the Suez Canal was
comparatively slight. Western Europe's shipments of oil were met by
re-routing the world tanker fleet and the despatch of additional supplies from the USA and Venezuela. The crisis proved to be short-
lived; within six months the Canal was re-opened and soon working
efficiently under Egyptian control.[3] Yet the crisis had demonstrated
the vulnerability of the Suez route, through which some two-thirds of
Western Europe's oil supply passed.[4] To reduce this vulnerability,
European governments had to accumulate larger reserves of oil, to
diversify their sources of supply and, above all, to develop more flexible
means of transport, so avoiding dependence upon the Canal.[5]

In 1956, some 95 per cent of tankers could use the Canal either fully
or partially laden. Even the seven 45,000 tonners found it more
profitable to transit the Canal at 80 per cent capacity and then to 'top
up' in the ports of the Levant, rather than to travel fully laden round

the Cape.[6] To use the Cape route profitably required the construction of much larger vessels, the harbinger of which was the *Universe Leader* (84,730 tons deadweight), launched from the Japanese shipyards in August 1956. Planned and constructed before the crisis erupted, this vessel confirmed the massive economies of scale which could be exploited in supertanker construction. Using mass-production techniques, the supertankers were cheaper per ton to construct than smaller vessels. Their operating costs were also relatively lower; a long vessel, if properly designed, moves through the water more easily than a shorter one, and so its engine size does not increase proportionately, but only marginally, with the size of tanker. Finally, as the larger vessel does not require any new job specialities, it does not require a larger crew.[7] Given such economies in the building, running and manning of supertankers, the trend towards their development was always likely, even if accelerated by the Suez crisis. In the decade following the crisis, world tanker capacity more than doubled to 95 million tons. Although the Suez Canal was deepened to 38 feet in the late 1950s to take 60,000 tonners fully laden, the proportion of ships in excess of 65,000 tons rose to 24.1 per cent of the world fleet by 1966.[8]

On 6 June 1967, in the midst of the Six-Day War, the Canal was officially closed and blocked for the second time in ten years. Superficially, Western Europe faced an even more severe crisis than in 1956. Not only was the Suez Canal blocked and the pipeline from Iraq severed, but the Arab oil producers joined in a selective embargo of exports to Britain and the USA and, less unitedly, in an embargo against West Germany. The Trans-Arabian pipeline ceased to move oil through the Mediterranean, strikes by oil workers interrupted supplies from Kuwait and Libya and, in July, a civil war prevented the export of oil from Nigeria. Western Europe, finally, was far more dependent upon oil than it had been in 1956. What more than compensated for these difficulties was the fact that Suez was no longer a vital artery for the movement of oil bound for Western Europe. Britain and France had diversified their sources of supply, relying increasingly upon oil from the newly developed African fields and upon use of the Cape route. They only imported 25 per cent and 39 per cent of their oil requirements through the Canal.[9] The oil shortage, moreover, was quickly overcome. The embargo was never fully effective as Iran doubled its oil production and the strikes in Kuwait and Libya were soon settled. Adequate oil supplies were matched by a considerable surplus in world tanker capacity. Although freight charges rocketed, imposing a particularly heavy burden on Britain's balance of payments, about 200 tankers, totalling three million tons, were brought back to oil carrying and they assured Western Europe's oil supplies.[10] The oil crisis, unlike the Canal's closure, proved to be short-lived.

The Suez Canal was blocked for eight years, testifying to the abject state of relations between Egypt and Israel. Its protracted closure emphasized the instability of the region and bolstered the economic arguments for by-passing the waterway. Already, in September 1966, Japan had launched the first 200,000 ton tanker, the *Idemitsu Maru*, and another seventy such vessels were on order by June 1967. By the following October, the number on order had doubled to 140. The economic savings were massive. A 200,000 tonner, carrying oil from the Gulf to British ports, could shave 45 pence per ton off the price of carrying the same tonnage of oil in smaller vessels via the Canal.[11] The proportion of vessels in excess of 65,000 tons, that is above the Canal's limits, grew from 24.1 per cent in 1966 to 79.8 per cent in 1976 and to 83.1 per cent in 1980. By 1980, indeed, ships in excess of 205,000 tons comprised 56.8 per cent of the world's fleet.[12]

As Maurice Cooper, the president of Seabrokers Incorporated, predicted: 'Every day that goes by makes the Suez a second class waterway.'[13] When the Canal re-opened in June 1975, the dry cargo traffic returned but not the lucrative oil trade. Whereas oil transits represented about 66 per cent of the Canal's total in 1966, providing some three-quarters of its revenue, they comprised only 30 per cent in 1976. Despite plans to deepen and widen the channel, so enabling the passage of 150,000 tonners from 1981, Suez is unlikely to recover its former volume of tanker traffic.[14] Other routes are more cost-effective in peace and less easily blocked in war. Should another oil crisis erupt in the Middle East, the fate of the Suez Canal would be of much less concern than passage through the Strait of Hormuz, which currently carries some 50–60 per cent of the oil for Western Europe, 70 per cent for Japan, and 10 per cent for the USA.

Militarily, in the mid-1950s, the Suez Canal was still viewed as a principal link between Britain and her possessions in East Africa, Asia and the Far East. Although independence for India, Burma and Ceylon had reduced Britain's imperial responsibilities, she still retained colonies or bases in East Africa, the Gulf and South-East Asia. In the 1950s, Britain had also assumed broader regional security obligations. She had assisted in the creation of the South-East Asia Treaty Organization (SEATO), pledging to act in concert to resist aggression in the Far East, and undertook similar responsibilities in the Middle East by entering CENTO (Central Treaty Organization) with Turkey, Iraq, Iran and Pakistan, supported by the USA. For successive governments, access through the Canal would enable Britain to honour these obligations, protect her oil supplies, cope with colonial disturbances, and block possible Soviet encroachments in Africa. To support troops either stationed or airlifted east of Suez, their heavy equipment—stores, supplies, ammunition, armour and artillery—could be sent most quickly via the Canal. But most importantly the Canal underpinned, or leant credibility to, British influence and authority in the Middle and Far East. When Nasser nationalized the Canal, he directly challenged that influence. Failure to respond, argued Sir Anthony Eden, 'spelt certain disaster for the West's authority'. He firmly believed that 'the Suez Canal remained of supreme importance ...'.[15]

An analysis of this assumption does not require another account of the crisis,[16] only consideration of whether the outcome—i.e. Nasser's retention of the Canal—undermined Britain's position east of Suez. The debacle was a profound psychological shock and, under Harold Macmillan's government, there were important changes in the style and emphasis of British diplomacy. The liquidation of the Empire, already underway, was accelerated. Relations with the USA, if not France, were improved and, in a sweeping defence review, nuclear weapons received an enhanced priority, so justifying a reduction of conventional forces and the phasing out of National Service. Yet the east of Suez role, far from being diminished, was steadily upgraded in the late 1950s and early 1960s. While army manpower was reduced on the Rhine and in the Mediterranean, the cuts were much less severe in the Gulf and the Far East. Additional forces were moved into Africa and Britain's mobile capability was considerably strengthened.[17]

In explaining this enhanced priority for a global role, successive governments declared that Britain could still honour her treaty commitments overseas, undertake peacekeeping operations, and preserve her economic interests east of Suez. They also had more immediate and instinctive concerns. In the first place, British troops were already involved in operations in Malaya and Kenya. These insurgencies were seen as campaigns to be fought and won, and not as opportunities for a re-appraisal of the British involvement. Secondly, all three armed services were imbued with an imperial ethos; they highly valued their overseas responsibilities and, at various times, each used an overseas role to justify requests for new weaponry and increased appropriations. Thirdly, governments felt responsible for the manner in which Britain divested herself of her imperial possessions. They believed that an orderly process of withdrawal was preferable to the Belgian policy of colonial scuttle. Finally, there was still a belief that Britain, though no longer a world power, could fulfil a peace-keeping role in Africa and Asia.[18] Strongly supported in this aspiration by the Kennedy and Johnson administrations,[19] Britain undertook to maintain a degree of stability around the rim of the Indian Ocean. As Harold Wilson asked the Parliamentary Labour Party in June 1966, 'if we abdicate responsibility who will exercise that role?[20]

Britain sought to fulfil this responsibility by constructing a central reserve, later known as the strategic reserve, from which mobile forces could be airlifted to potential crisis zones. The capacity of RAF Transport Command was greatly expanded; it was more than trebled in the period from 1957 to 1962.[21] What complicated this policy was not Egypt's control of the Suez Canal but the emergence of an air barrier in the Middle East, when Israel and the Sudan denied Britain over-flying rights during the Jordan emergency of 1958. British forces had to detour over central Africa, so reducing the speed of their movements and the amount of airlift which could be used. Accordingly, elements of the strategic reserve were stationed in Kenya and Singapore, while heavy equipment and supplies were pre-positioned at selected points in the region. A balanced fleet was based at Singapore, an Amphibious Warfare Squadron at Aden, and the Middle East and East Africa commands were completely re-organized.[22]

Despite this re-organization, the east of Suez role proved increasingly onerous. Given Britain's recurring economic difficulties in the 1960s, and her reduced conventional forces (army manpower was halved in the period from 1956 to 1966), the gap widened between her capabilities and commitments. There were political costs, too. While a British presence was welcomed in some quarters, reflected in the repeated calls for British military assistance, it was resented by several nationalist movements and some African and Asian states, so compounding the difficulties about over-flying rights, training facilities and base tenure. Within Britain, critics of this policy urged the government to distinguish between its obligations—not all of which required military support—to recognize that market forces and not military bases would sustain the flow of oil, and to realize that a military presence could act as an irritant to nationalism, possibly endangering rather than protecting British interests.[23] Such criticism, however, carried little weight so long as the policy seemed to be effective and economically tolerable. Despite protracted difficulties in Aden, government spokesmen could claim successes in Jordan and Kuwait, in Kenya, Uganda and Tanganyika, and in Malaya and Borneo. Only economic constraints, and not doubts about the role, precipitated an abrupt reversal of policy. In the wake of the devaluation crisis of November 1967, the government devised a package of economies which it announced in the following January. They included cancellation of the F-111, a long-range strike aircraft earmarked for Far Eastern duties, and withdrawal from east of Suez by 1971, so heralding an end of two centuries of British involvement.[24]

Within a month of Wilson's announcement, Admiral Sergei Gorshkov, Commander-in-Chief of the Soviet Navy, visited India, presumably to arrange refuelling and repairing facilities for Soviet warships in Indian ports. In the following March, the first Russian flotilla

151

(composed of a cruiser, missile-carrying destroyer, a nuclear-powered submarine, and a naval oil tanker) appeared in the Indian Ocean and called on various Indian ports.[25] Another two squadrons appeared in the latter half of 1968, beginning a regular pattern of Soviet naval deployments. By 1971, there were between ten and twenty Soviet naval vessels in the Indian Ocean. The force was expanded during crises, like the Indo-Pakistani War of 1971 and the Yom Kippur War of 1973 and, by the late 1970s, a squadron of approximately twenty units was maintained in the Indian Ocean.[26]

To explain this novel deployment, Gorshkov stated that Soviet warships were stationed in the Indian Ocean 'for a limited purpose—to ensure the safe descent of Soviet space craft'.[27] Western naval observers were understandably sceptical. They were concerned not so much about the power of the Soviet naval presence (France often had as many, if not more, warships in the Indian Ocean during the 1970s) but what that new presence symbolized, namely 'the drive of a rising power to world status' and its impact upon a vitally important region, from which the old imperial powers were gradually withdrawing.[28]

Speculation has mounted about the possible Soviet objectives in moving into the Indian Ocean. Soviet diplomacy may be served by showing the flag in port visits, proferring support for client states, and generally displacing a former Western presence. Outflanking China may also be a valuable objective, as the Trans-Siberian railroad would be vulnerable to interdiction in a Far Eastern war. Of even more importance would be the countering of any potential deployment of the US seaborne nuclear deterrent in the Indian Ocean. The pushing of the Soviet defensive perimeter outwards and away from the southern borders has been a priority ever since the development of the Polaris A3 and Poseidon missiles, both of which could hit Soviet targets from the Arabian Sea. As the longer range of Trident C4 has increased the attractions of the Indian Ocean as a launching site, the Soviet navy has had to intensify its anti-submarine warfare activities in the area.[29] Finally, the squadron could consider more offensive missions, including intervention in local wars (as in Ethiopia) and, conceivably, in a global confrontation, to attack the oil routes from the Persian Gulf to Western Europe and Japan. But the Indian Ocean squadron possesses very limited capabilities to undertake offensive missions. It lacks an adequate aircraft carrier and the aircraft with which to project power ashore. The sheer distance from the Soviet Union, coupled with the shortage of adequate shore facilities or floating docks, have compounded the maintenance problems of the fleet. And the small size and configuration of the force—a cruiser, several destroyers, three or four hunter-killer submarines, one or two submarines and an assortment of auxiliaries—hardly suggests an immediate operational readiness for global conflict.[30]

Several commentators feared that the Soviets would overcome these difficulties once the Canal was re-opened. Hitherto the Soviet navy has had to maintain four separate fleets (the Northern Fleet, Baltic Fleet, Black Sea Fleet (with its forward deployment in the Mediterranean) and the Pacific Fleet). In a war, the Black Sea Fleet and the Pacific Fleet would be fully engaged against more powerful adversaries and hardly in a position to assist the stranded Indian Ocean squadron. Re-opening the Canal raised the possibility of linking-up the Black Sea and the Pacific Fleets. Some commentators, including James Schlesinger, then US Secretary of Defence, feared that the Soviet Union could exploit the waterway to improve its support for units in the Indian Ocean; one writer even claimed that the Mediterranean would 'become a mere anti-room for the real theatre of operations ... East of Suez'.[31]

These predictions overlooked the consequences of the massive rift in Soviet–Egyptian relations. From 1967 to 1972, the Soviet Union had established a substantial base in Egypt, including access to ports, especially Alexandria, and the virtually exclusive use of seven airfields for the protection of her Mediterranean squadron.[32] This relationship foundered in July 1972 when Anwar Sadat expelled most of the Soviet military personnel from Egypt. He resented the arrogance of Soviet behaviour in Egypt, the quality and terms of their arms supplies, and suspected the Soviets of plotting on behalf of his internal enemies as well as of supporting Gaddafi. He now needed Arab money and support to launch a war against Israel, followed by American pressure upon Israel to compel a withdrawl from Sinai.[33] Despite the resumption of Soviet arms supplies in 1973, and assistance in clearing the blocked Canal, the Soviets had lost their former position of influence. When the Suez Canal was re-opened, the link-up between the Black Sea Fleet and the Pacific Fleet never occurred. It would only have been feasible had Soviet land-based forces been able to protect the vulnerable waterway and ensure the safe passage of Soviet ships.[34] Lacking this security, the Soviet squadron in the Indian Ocean has remained comparatively small.

Nevertheless, the Soviet naval contingent still remains a potentially imposing presence within the confines of the region. Fearing the consequences of an imbalance of power, Edward Heath's government re-deployed a modest air and naval capability east of Suez in the early 1970s. It also urged India to augment its maritime strength and persuaded the USA to collaborate in expanding the communications facilities on the island of Diego Garcia. India, who had signed a treaty of friendship with the Soviet Union in 1971, was less alarmed by the Soviet presence than the USA. Henry Kissinger, then President Nixon's National Security Advisor, recalls that Heath 'called our attention to the strategic significance of Africa and the Indian Ocean at a time when these were not yet high priorities on our agenda'.[35]

Although less dependent on Middle Eastern oil than her European allies, the USA had interests in the region. The Ocean remains a potentially attractive area for deploying the US seaborne deterrent, although somewhat distant from her submarine bases. The security of maritime traffic and the support of several regional allies were also concerns, as was the desire to contain the scope of local conflicts lest they draw in outside powers and threaten Western economic interests. But during the Vietnam War, the Nixon administration could not permanently assign any military forces to the region. As Kissinger remarks, 'Congress would have not supported it.' 'Fortunately,' he adds, 'Iran was willing to play this role. The vacuum left by British withdrawal, now menaced by Soviet intrusion and radical momentum, would be filled by a local power friendly to us. Iraq would be discouraged from adventures against the Emirates in the lower Gulf, and against Jordan and Saudi Arabia. A strong Iran could help damp India's temptations to conclude its conquest of Pakistan. And all of this was achievable without any American resources, since the Shah was willing to pay for the equipment out of his oil revenues.'[36] Although Saudi Arabia emerged as a major financial power in the wake of the 1973 oil crisis, and reference was made to a 'twin pillar policy', based on the Saudis and the Shah, Washington continued to rely primarily upon the latter.[37]

Over the next five years, the USA proffered military assistance to the Shah, its ally of twenty years standing, on an unprecedented scale. The Shah purchased some $18 billion worth of advanced weapon systems, sent a small expeditionary army against the Dhofar rebels in Oman, and reassured the West about the continued supply of oil through the Strait of Hormuz.[38] The Carter administration, impressed by the Shah's personality and his image as a modernizing pro-Western ruler, swallowed its doubts about the human rights record of his regime. It sustained the supply of arms and technical advice while largely concentrating upon more pressing diplomatic issues (the strategic arms talks with Russia, the Middle East peace process and the improvement of relations with NATO allies in the wake of the neutron bomb fiasco). When the revolution erupted in Iran, Carter proffered the Shah verbal encouragement but openly declared that the USA would not interfere 'in the internal affairs of Iran'.[39] After some thirty years of pervasive interference, this was a clear sign of American retreat.[40] Carter still remained confident that the Shah would survive;

on New Year's Eve, he toasted Iran as an 'island of stability', only sixteen days before the Shah's flight into exile.[41]

The fall of the Shah exposed the limits of American power and undermined the credibility of her commitments. On the one hand, America's close identification with the Shah's regime had done little to enhance its popularity. The wave of anti-American demonstrations reflected protests about the political and military support of the Shah and, on a deeper spiritual and cultural level, about the effects of indiscriminate modernization—a powerful warning for other Moslem nations.[42] On the other hand, America's failure to support the Shah in his moment of peril compounded doubts about the value of American commitments in the wake of the Vietnam war and the abrogated obligations to Taiwan. Such concerns prompted a flurry of American missions to reassure pro-Western regimes in the Gulf, particularly Saudi Arabia from whom America was receiving some 10 per cent of her oil requirements.

The limitations of this approach were quickly apparent. Saudi Arabia welcomed the prospect of further arms sales from the USA (in the seven years since 1973 the Saudis have spent $34 billion on foreign arms sales).[43] She also appreciated implicit American military support, but could neither countenance American bases on Saudi soil nor approve the Camp David process nor meet all Western requests for increased oil production at stable prices. The Saudi royal family remains acutely, and understandably, conscious of its own security, its identification with other Arabs, the solidarity of OPEC, and its role as guardians of the Islamic holy places and protectors of the faith. Having survived several attempted coups in recent years, including the assault on the Grand Mosque of Mecca in November 1979, the Saudi royal family cannot afford to be too closely associated with American interests.[44]

Stunned by the fall of the Shah, thwarted by the Saudis over the Camp David accord, embarrassed by the seizure of hostages in Tehran and faced with a difficult election year, the Carter administration reacted sharply to the Soviet invasion of Afghanistan. The President described the invasion as 'the greatest threat to peace since World War II' and as 'a sharp escalation in the aggressive history of the Soviet Union'.[45] Whether the invasion merited such comment is at least arguable. Ever since the Afghan coup of April 1978, the Soviet Union has invested heavily in support of the subsequent regime. To let it now founder, and allow Afghanistan to slip from the socialist camp, would mean accepting the encirclement of the Soviet Union by hostile powers from Norway to Japan and would let the Brezhnev doctrine, first formulated to justify the invasion of Czechoslovakia, be undermined. Soviet leaders may also have been concerned about the revival of Islamic fundamentalism in Iran, its possible reverberations within its own Moslem population, and the domino effect of Soviet passivity over Afghanistan. The invasion, in short, may have reflected a concern about the security of the Soviets' southern perimeter—a sign of perceived vulnerability—rather than a signal of predatory intent.[46] If such ideas occurred to the White House staff, they paid them scant respect. Zbigniew Brzezinski, the National Security Advisor, viewed the initiative as merely part of a 'longer term ... Soviet drive towards the Indian Ocean and the Persian Gulf'.[47] Sharing these views, especially the potential threat to the 'movement of Middle East Oil', Carter announced a new containment doctrine in his State of Union message of 23 January 1980. He declared that

> an attempt by outside force to gain control of the Persian Gulf region will be regarded as an assault on the vital interests of the United States. It will be repelled by the use of any means necessary, including military force.[48]

Carter announced that the USA would buttress her regional commitments by deploying carrier task forces in the Gulf and by accelerating the development of her Rapid Deployment Force (RDF). In the planning of this intervention force, the Americans have virtually discounted the Suez Canal. The sea route from Pearl Harbour to the Persian Gulf is only 1,100 miles longer than from the east coast of America via the Canal. Reinforcement from the Mediterranean was not a priority, indeed the aircraft carriers of the Sixth Fleet were too large to pass through the Canal before its recent expansion.[49] Although carrier task forces have been deployed in the Gulf, the Americans recognize that any threat to the shipping lanes need not come from the sea: land-based air attack could pose a powerful deterrent to the passage of ships through the Strait of Hormuz. If the oilfields themselves were threatened, then the rapid movement of ground forces into the vicinity would become essential. So any credible intervention force requires a mix of ground, air and naval units and it does not depend upon access through the Canal.

The RDF, however, faces a daunting proposition if it is to fulfil the expectations of the Carter and Reagan administrations. The original concept—a joint service force drawn in an emergency from existing air, ground and naval units and projected over incredibly vast distances—encountered a fair measure of incredulity. James Schlesinger examined the confused command apparatus, an airlift capability which will not be available until at least 1985, and the lack of heavy armour, to conclude that the RDF might not be rapid, nor easily deployed, nor even much of a force.[50] Even if the command structure is rationalized and Congress is persuaded to fund the extremely expensive Sea-Lift Readiness programme and the new CX aircraft (a long-haul plane, capable of operating within combat theatres and of landing on small austere airfields)—the RDF still faces profound difficulties. Advance bases are vital if the airlifted marines and air-borne forces are to link up safely with their heavy equipment and supplies, stored upon ships which are pre-positioned in the area. But the USA has found it extremely difficult to supplement its base on Diego Garcia which is 2,500 miles from the Strait of Hormuz. The port facilities of Mombasa, Berbera and Mogadishu, though useful, are also somewhat distant, while Ras Banas, an Egyptian air base, would merely be available as a temporary staging point. Of the Gulf countries, only Oman has offered facilities (on the island of Al Masirah and the Thamarit airfield) but these are woefully inadequate. The basing problem would seem to be twofold. First a general unwilling-ness throughout the Gulf, with the exception of Oman, to accept that armed intervention from outside constitutes a prime source of vulner-ability. Indeed, there is a contrary fear that granting bases could make the host regimes more vulnerable by arousing opposition from within the states concerned. Secondly, there is a residual dislike of America's pro-Israeli policy. While the USA has sought a collective opposition against the Soviet Union, many Gulf governments utterly reject any re-ordering of Middle Eastern priorities which sets the Soviet threat— real or imagined—above the settlement of the Arab-Israeli dispute. They would claim that only a settlement of the Palestinian question could lead to a diminution of Soviet influence in the area.[51]

In these circumstances, the potential scope of the RDF seems fairly limited. On account of the region's volatile politics, it could only act by invitation. It symbolizes America's interest in the region and pro-vides an aura of military power to support her diplomacy. It could proffer discreet and limited assistance in local or civil wars, but whether it could support a tottering regime or operate oilfields in defiance of local opposition is very unlikely, not only in military terms but also in case such action revived memories of US imperialism, damaged East-West relations and complicated the Middle East peace process. Finally, the RDF's ability to deter Soviet military action seems extremely doubtful. Currently it would take a fortnight to despatch an airborne division—about 16,000 troops—to the Gulf and thirty days to move another division by sea. But the Soviets already retain eight divisions, some 70,000-80,000 men, on the Iranian bor-der; their planes are a mere one hour's flight from the Strait of Hormuz. The Pentagon candidly admits that the Soviets could move all twenty-three mechanized divisions—some 200,000 men—in the Caucasus, Transcaucasus and Turkmenistan military districts, backed by a formidable array of airpower, into north-west Iran within a month.[52] Facing such odds, the RDF could only act as a 'trip-wire', invoking the spectre of nuclear escalation. At most, the RDF could complicate Soviet calculations and, to that extent, possibly assist in dissuading open adventurism.

Overall, the Suez Canal has now little geo-strategic significance for Western strategy. It is no longer a main commercial artery and is unlikely to recover its former volume of world oil traffic. Militarily, it was never absolutely vital, but what importance it once had has much diminished. Britain managed to project power east of Suez without relying upon the Canal. Russia, who might have used it more extensively, has not done so. Having lost her Egyptian base, she could not protect the waterway and, in any case, does not yet regard the Indian Ocean as a principal theatre of naval operations. The USA has never depended upon the Canal and has been able to ignore it in the planning for the RDF. Indeed, the chequered history of great power involvement east of Suez cannot be ascribed to the Canal *per se*, but to the difficulties of devising a coherent policy towards an area, so volatile politically and so important economically. Neither super power may be able to exert much influence over events in the Gulf, still less to expect to control them. Client states seem likely to act increasingly in their own self-interest, exerting pressure or leverage upon the super powers.[53] Nevertheless, the West has interests in the Indian Ocean and, in trying to protect these interests, the USA has sought to bolster her allies in the Gulf, particularly Saudi Arabia, to display a more prominent naval presence in the area, assisted by Britain and France, and to develop an intervention capability. Whether these measures will constitute an effective policy remains an open question.

Notes

1. 'Europe's Achilles Heel', *The Economist*, 4 August 1956, p. 381; A. Hottinger, 'The Opening of the Suez Canal', *The Round Table*, Vol. 64 (1974), p. 394; Arab Republic of Egypt, *The Suez Canal after six years June 5 1975, June 5 1981* (Al-Ahram Press, 1981), pp. 6–7.

2. M. McGwire, 'The Geopolitical importance of strategic waterways in the Asian–Pacific Region', *Orbis*, Vol. 19, No. 3 (Fall 1975), p. 1061.

3. H. J. Schonfield, *The Suez Canal in Peace and War 1869–1969* (Valentine Mitchell, London, 1969), p. 164.

4. S. Lloyd, *Suez 1956: a personal account* (Hodder & Stoughton, London, 1970), p. 83.

5. B. Shwadran, *The Middle East, Oil and the Great Powers* (Israel University Press, Jerusalem, 1973), p. 539 and W. Laqueur, *The*

Struggle for the Middle East (Routledge & Kegan Paul, London, 1969), pp. 126–7.
6. The Canal could take 38,000 ton ships fully loaded. D. H. Grover, 'Whither the Supertanker?', *The Oil Forum*, XI (June 1957). But slightly larger tankers still transited the Canal partially loaded, 'Supertankers round the Cape?', *The Economist*, 11 August 1956, p. 512. For data on the world tanker fleet, see *BP Statistical Review of the World Oil Industry* (1966), p. 23.
7. D. H. Grover, op. cit., p. 204 and C. Tugendhat, *Oil: The Biggest Business* (Eyre & Spottiswoode, London, 1969), p. 187.
8. B. J. Abrahamsson and J. L. Steckler, 'Strategic Aspects of Sea Borne Oil', *International Sage Professional Papers in International Studies Series*, Vol. 2 (1973), pp. 23–4 and *BP Statistical Review of the World Oil Industry* (1966), p. 23.
9. H. J. Schonfield, op. cit., p. 172.
10. C. Tugendhat, op. cit., p. 186 and J. E. T. Hartshorn, 'Oil and the Middle East War', *The World Today* (April 1968), pp. 152–3.
11. C. Tugendhat, op. cit., p. 187 and D. C. Watt, 'Why there is no commercial future for the Suez Canal', *The New Middle East* (January 1969), pp. 19–20.
12. *BP Statistical Review of the World Oil Industry* (1976), p. 31 and (1980), p. 27.
13. G. H. Wierzynski, 'Tankers move the oil that moves the world', *Fortune*, Vol. 76 (September 1967), p. 85.
14. Seatrade Study, *Suez: One Year On* (June 1976), pp. 5 and 13 and Arab Republic of Egypt, *The Suez Canal* (n.d.), pp. 9, 28–9.
15. Sir A. Eden, *Memoirs: The Full Circle* (Cassell, London, 1960), pp. 260 and 518. See also D. C. Watt, op. cit., p. 22 and N. Brown, *Strategic Mobility* (Chatto and Windus, London, 1963), pp. 28–9.
16. S. Lloyd, op. cit., Sir A. Eden, op. cit., and A. Nutting, *No End of a Lesson* (Constable, London, 1967).
17. *Defence: Outline of Future Policy*, Cmnd. 124 (1956–7), XXIII, pp. 3–5 and P. Darby, *British Defence Policy East of Suez 1947–1968* (Oxford University Press, London, 1973), p. 163.
18. Ibid., pp. 150–6.
19. R. H. S. Crossman, *The Diaries of a Cabinet Minister*, 3 vols. (H. Hamilton and J. Cape, London, 1975–7), Vol. 1, p. 74. See also P. Darby, op. cit., p. 222.
20. *The Times*, 16 June 1966, p. 11.
21. P. Darby, op. cit., p. 184 and N. Brown, op. cit., p. 156.
22. P. Darby, op. cit., pp. 174–5.
23. N. Brown, *Arms without Empire* (Penguin, London, 1967), pp. 27–

75 and C. Mayhew, *Britain's Role Tomorrow* (Hutchinson, London, 1967), pp. 52–83.

24. R. H. S. Crossman, op. cit., Vol. 2, pp. 620–2.
25. B. Vivekanandan, 'Britain and the Indian Ocean', *Indian Ocean Power Rivalry*, ed. T. T. Poulose (Young Asia Publications, New Delhi, 1974), p. 25.
26. A. E. Graham, 'Soviet Strategy and Policy in the Indian Ocean', *Naval Power in Soviet Policy*, ed. P. J. Murphy (Studies in Communist Affairs, Vol. 2, 1978), p. 277.
27. B. Vivekanandan, op. cit., p. 27.
28. P. Towle, *Naval Power in the Indian Ocean: Threats, Bluffs and Fantasies* (The Strategic and Defence Study Centre, Canberra, 1979), p. 33.
29. A. Sella, *Soviet Political and Military Conduct in the Middle East* (Macmillan, London, 1981), pp. 49, 53–5, 58–9; J. Erickson, 'The Soviet Strategic Emplacement in Asia', *Asian Affairs*, Vol. XII, Part 1 (February 1981), p. 14; A. E. Graham, op. cit., pp. 276, 281–2, 287–9.
30. A. Sella, op. cit., pp. 51–2 and 65–6 and P. Towle, op. cit., p. 29.
31. A. Hottinger, op. cit., pp. 395 and 398. See also Major K. K. Dogra, 'Re-opening of the Suez Canal', *Journal of the United Services Institution of India* (April/June 1975), p. 163 and US Congress, Senate Committee on Armed Services, *Disapprove Construction Projects on the island of Diego Garcia*, 94th Congress, First Session (10 June 1975), p. 8.
32. R. G. Weinland, 'Egypt and Support for the Soviet Mediterranean Squadron', in P. J. Murphy, op. cit., pp. 264–7; G. Golan, 'Soviet Power and Policies in the Third World: The Middle East' in 'Prospects of Soviet Power in the 1980s Part II', *Adelphi Papers*, No. 152, p. 47; *Soviet Naval Diplomacy*, ed. by B. Dismukes and J. M. McConnell (Pergamon Press, New York, 1979), pp. 374–7.
33. W. E. Griffith, 'Soviet Influence in the Middle East', *Survival*, Vol. XVIII (January/February 1976), p. 3 and A. El-Sadat, *In Search of Identity* (Collins, London, 1978), pp. 204–31.
34. A. Sella, op. cit., pp. 69, 126–7 and P. Towle, op. cit., pp. 33–4.
35. H. Kissinger, *The White House Years* (Weidenfeld and Nicolson, London, 1979), p. 935.
36. Ibid., p. 1264.
37. V. Yorke, *The Gulf in the 1980s* (Royal Institute of International Affairs, London, 1980), p. 12.
38. S. Chubin, 'Iran's Defense and Foreign Policy', *Iran in the 1980s*, ed. by A. Amirie and H. A. Twitchell (Stanford Research Institute, Palo Alto, 1978), pp. 309–34 and *World Armaments and*

Disarmament SIPRI Yearbook 1979 (Taylor and Francis, London, 1979), p. 183.

39. President Carter, press conference, 30 November 1978, *International Communication Agency*, p. 7.
40. S. Chubin, 'Repercussions of the Crisis in Iran', *Survival*, Vol. XXI, No. 3 (May/June 1979), p. 101.
41. President Carter, press conference, 13 December 1978, *International Communication Agency*, p. 9 and L. Whetten, 'The lessons of Iran', *World Today*, Vol. 35 (October 1979), p. 397.
42. S. Chubin, 'Repercussions of the Crisis in Iran', p. 103.
43. 'The U.S. Military in Saudi Arabia: Investing in Stability or Disaster', *The Defense Monitor*, Vol. X, No. 4 (1981), pp. 3–8.
44. B. R. Kuniholm, 'What the Saudis really want: a primer for the Reagan administration', *Orbis*, Vol. 25, No. 1 (Spring 1981), pp. 107–21.
45. President Carter, briefing to Congressmen, 8 January 1980, *International Communication Agency*, p. 3.
46. J. Erickson, op. cit., p. 16.
47. Z. Brzezinski, interview, 14 April 1980, *International Communication Agency*, p. 7.
48. President Carter, 'State of the Union Address to the second session of the 96th Congress', 23 January 1980, *International Communication Agency*, pp. 3–4.
49. P. Mangold, *Superpower Intervention in the Middle East* (Croom Helm, London, 1978), p. 17.
50. J. R. Schlesinger, 'Rapid (?) Deployment (?) Force (?)', *Washington Post* (24 September 1980), p. 27.
51. B. R. Kuniholm, op. cit., pp. 110–13.
52. *The New York Times*, 2 February 1980, p. 4. See also E. Asa Bates, 'The Rapid Deployment Force Fact or Fiction', *Journal of the Royal United Services Institute for Defence Studies*, Vol. 126, No. 2 (June 1981), p. 26 and W. Tapley Bennett, address to the Hanns-Seidel-Stiftung conference, Munich, 4 November 1981, *International Communication Agency*, p. 4.
53. J. Alford, 'Strategic Developments in the Indian Ocean Area', *Asian Affairs*, Vol. XII, Part II (June 1981), p. 145.

Index

As the transliteration of Arabic names into English is inconsistent, the index adopts widely used versions. Changes in British ranks and titles are noted when they took place during and after the period of the chapter. Britain, Egypt, imperialism and nationalism occur too frequently to be listed.

163

Index

British Tanker Co., 84
Brook, Sir Norman (after 1963 First
 Baron Normanbrook), 138
Brzezinski, Zbigniew, 156
Bulgaria, 36
Bulwer, Sir Henry (after 1871 First
 Baron Dalling and Bulwer), ix
Burke, Edmund, 3
Burma, xi, 77, 82, 149
Burmah Oil Co., 82
Butler, R. A. (after 1965 Lord
 Butler), 138

Cadman, Sir John, 90
Cairo, 12, 26, 32, 39, 62, 69, 70, 124
Caisse de la Dette Publique, 15, 59
Caliphate, 11, 45, 47, 53 n.75, 124,
 125
Cambon, Mme, 32
Cambon, Paul, 32, 44, 45
Camp David Agreement, 155
Campbell, Sir Ronald, 105-11, 113,
 114, 116
Campbell-Bannerman, Henry (after
 1895 Sir), 20
Cape Route, xi, 20, 28, 30, 77, 79,
 85-87, 91, 147, 148
Capitulations, Capitulatory Powers,
 3, 15, 58, 60, 61, 72
Carter, James E., 154, 156
Carter Administration, 154-56
Cecil, Lady Gwendolen, 20
Central Powers of Europe before
 1914, 13
Central Treaty Organization
 (CENTO), 149
Ceylon, xi, 77, 82, 149
Challe, General Maurice, 136, 138
Chamber of Notables, Egyptian, 7
Chamberlain, Austen (after 1925
 Sir), 64, 65
Chapman, Major-General Edward
 (later General Sir), 27, 31
Chequers
 Anglo-French talks at (October
  1956), 136
 British conference at (October
  1956), 138-39

Chiefs of Staff, British, 69, 70, 108-
 9, 112, 115
Childers, H. C. E., 7-8
China, 65, 77, 80, 83, 152
Chirol, Valentine (after 1912 Sir),
 57
Christendom, Christianity, 2, 4, 14,
 20
Christians, native, in Egypt, 16, 18-
 19
Churchill, Lord Randolph, 46
Churchill, Winston (after 1956 Sir),
 20, 59, 64, 97-98, 100, 114-15
Clark Kerr, Archibald (after 1935
 Sir and after 1946 First Baron
 Inverchapel), 62, 108
Clayton, Brigadier-General Gilbert
 (after 1919 Sir), 57
Coal, British, and the Canal, 79-80,
 86
Commons, British House of, ix, xi, 1,
 17
Communists, Egyptian, 104
Conservatives, British (see also
 Tories, Toryism), 28, 42, 115
Constantinople (see also Turkey;
 Ottoman Empire), 26-29, 31-
 35, 37, 39, 41-47
Constantinople Convention. See
 Suez Canal Convention
Constitutions, Egyptian
 1883, 6-7
 1923, 61-62, 69, 96, 97, 101
Cooper, Maurice, 149
Copts, 16
Cornwallis, Sir Kinahan, 99
Coup d'État of 23 July 1952 in Egypt,
 127
Courcel, Baron Alphonse de, 35, 44,
 47, 52 n.64, 54 n.90
Coverley-Price, Foreign Office
 official, 100
Crimean War, 11, 35, 42, 43
Cromer, First Baron and Earl
 (before 1892 Sir Evelyn
 Baring), 3, 4, 7, 8, 10-20, 35,
 47, 56

165